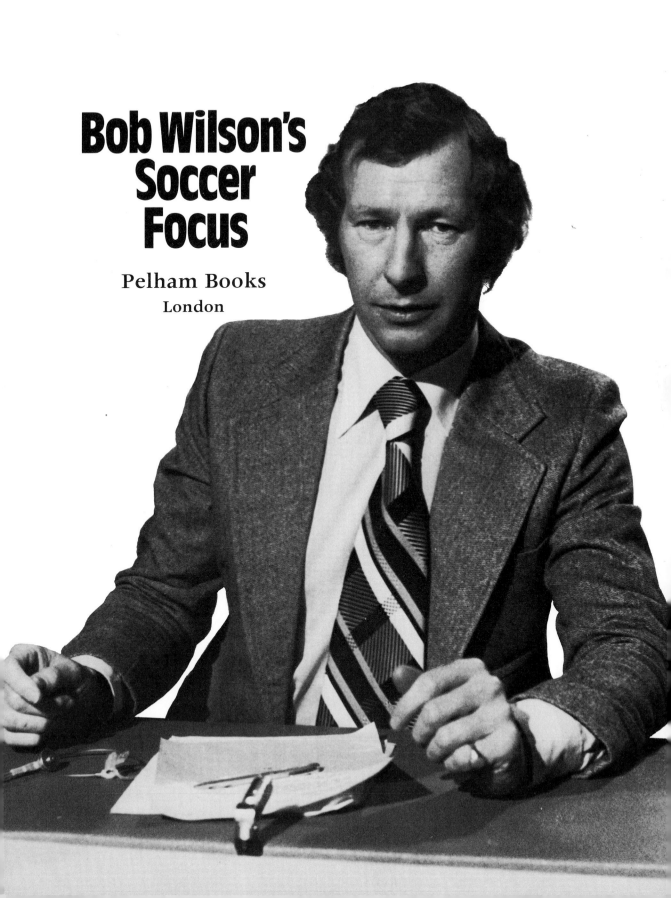

Bob Wilson's Soccer Focus

Pelham Books
London

By the same author
THE ART OF GOALKEEPING

First published in Great Britain by
PELHAM BOOKS LTD
44 Bedford Square
London WC1B 3DU
1980

ISBN 0 7207 1283 1

Filmset and printed in Great Britain by
BAS Printers Limited, Over Wallop, Hampshire
and bound by Dorstel Press Limited, Harlow

Acknowledgements

Grateful acknowledgement is due to the following for permission to reproduce their photographs in this book: Central Press Photos Ltd, Colorsport, Popperfoto, the Press Association Ltd, Sporting Pictures (UK) Ltd, Syndication International and Bob Thomas. The photograph on the title page is BBC copyright.

Contents

	Acknowledgements	2
1	Soccer is Blowing for Extra Time	5
2	Tomorrow's Game	15
3	The Evolution of the World Cup	21
4	Spain Prepares for the 1982 World Cup	32
5	Kevin Keegan—the Man	35
6	Soccer in Europe	45
7	Memorable Matches	54
8	Players I Will Never Forget	73
9	Great Postwar Managers	82
10	World Soccer Stars	90
11	Black is Beautiful	101
12	Great Clubs of My Time	113
13	The Rise of Eastern Europe	137
14	South American Soccer	143
15	Soccer in the USA	152
16	Tactical Formations	160
17	Yes, Television is Good for Football	168
18	Do You Know?	173
	APPENDIX I Soccer Statistics	176
	APPENDIX II Laws of the Game	179
	Index	190

ABBREVIATIONS IN THE TEXT
FIFA: Fédération Internationale de Football Associations
NASL: North American Soccer League
UEFA: Union of European Football Associations

Chapter 1

Soccer is Blowing for Extra Time

One of the most demanding penalties, if you will forgive the pun, of having been involved in soccer for a quarter of a century, is facing the attempt to answer the question: What do you think of soccer today?

I started as the most enthusiastic player in the world, as a schoolboy, and I graduated to trials with Manchester United. I signed amateur forms for Wolves and spent nearly three years with the famous Midlands club before turning professional with Arsenal, an institution. So, I'm a football man. I have a love affair with the game that can never die. I can't imagine ever being involved with anything else. But the future of the greatest game of all is something we can never take for granted.

The level of competition in the Football League, whose championship is still the hardest title of all to win, is dropping; the administrative and organizational side of the game needs a complete rethink; and the commercial possibilities need to be totally exploited.

Take the playing standards, first. The Football League leaves the national competition of any other country in the world far behind. But when I played my first games in the League in 1963–64 there were no easy matches. Now there are. In the early sixties, the differences between the twenty-two First Division clubs were minimal. Now there is a gap. The general standard has fallen. We have not yet reached the situation in Scotland where the chances of any other club depriving Rangers or Celtic of the major honours is remote. Nor anything similar to the almost complete domination of Real Madrid and Barcelona in Spain, and Feyenoord and Ajax in Holland. But a number of clubs are breaking away in the English First Division and might leave the others standing.

There are those who currently have the best teams. Liverpool, almost permanently. Nottingham Forest, who have done so brilliantly in the past few seasons. Southampton and Ipswich, who have proved that success is not the prerogative of big city clubs in London, the Midlands, Manchester, Merseyside and the north-east. But at the end of the day it is an inescapable fact that, unless legislation decrees otherwise, the dice are loaded in favour of the clubs who can draw on the biggest population.

English football is sailing perilously close to a harbour that will accommodate only the biggest ships. Eventually some ten or so big city clubs will moor in the top berths of the First Division table and stay there. They will be able to acquire the best players, and the other clubs will be useful as opponents. The number of

OPPOSITE A clash between Southampton (stripes) and Ipswich, two teams who have challenged the dominance of the big-city clubs. (*Photo: Bob Thomas.*)

their fans will decrease and so will their takings at the turnstiles. The vicious circle starts.

A free-for-all is no good. Even the super clubs need opponents, good opponents. One-sided matches do not attract the crowds, and with them the money. Attendances in Scotland, Spain and Holland substantiate that.

There are all manner of reasons why our playing standards have fallen to the degree that the game is in danger of a big club monopoly, and the usual excuses tend to centre on finance in some shape or form. I think it is basically more simple than that. There are not as many extraordinary players as there used to be. Good players of the past had holes in their shoes. Great players? Well, not all of them had shoes.

There are social reasons. Not so many lads want to take up the game professionally. Though the income at the top is exceptional, so are the few players who get there. In a society that is conditioned to take fewer risks than previous generations, security is often a more attractive option than a career that can be glorious but brief, sometimes pathetically so if injury ends it prematurely.

It was thought, in the early sixties, when the maximum wage restriction was lifted, that youngsters with special gifts would be able to stay in football rather than be attracted away by higher wages that could be earned elsewhere. This hasn't happened because inflation has ensured that soccer salaries have not outstripped those of the average working man.

I have an old newspaper, printed in Birmingham early in 1939. The price of a modern semi-detached house with two and a half bedrooms is quoted at £375. The maximum wage then, and by no means all players were on it, was £8 per week. That meant that the price of a new house was forty-seven weeks' wages. Let us assume that the average player today earns around £150 a week. The modern semi-detached, new, will cost about £30,000. That means that the house costs the player 200 weeks' wages, not forty-seven. So, if the average footballer can do better than £150 a week, he doesn't become the average professional player.

That is the main reason why standards have dropped. That is why the Third and Fourth Divisions of the Football League must go part-time eventually. That is why the lower divisions of the League must be regionalized again, as they were before 1958 when they were Third Division (North) and Third Division (South). It makes no sense to have clubs travelling from Devon to the north-east to play in front of crowds of no more than two or three thousand.

I did not agree with Ted Croker, the secretary of the Football Association, when he advocated putting all the biggest eggs in the smallest basket and abolishing promotion and relegation. There must always be an incentive. It is difficult to see how, without financial transfusions, Plymouth Argyle could pay their way unless they had First Division gates. Therefore they must never be denied their chance of battling their way through to the elite. Back in 1956, both Ipswich and Southampton were in the Third Division. Look where they finished last season. Take Portsmouth and Huddersfield, both of whom spent

OPPOSITE ABOVE Battle of the giants. Liverpool, in dark shirts, against Arsenal. (*Photo: Press Association.*)

OPPOSITE BELOW Nottingham Forest (dark shirts) defend a Crystal Palace attack. (*Photo: Syndication International.*)

last season in the Fourth Division. Do we give them no chance of ever recapturing the League title? Huddersfield has won it three times and Portsmouth twice.

More money must be generated into the game, and the first direction in which clubs must look is inwards, at their grounds. It is ridiculous that balance sheets show that less than ten per cent of the League's clubs are in the black. Grounds are not used more than three times in a fortnight, and I'm not surprised. Perhaps those of us in football who have become spoiled by the free passes should put our money where we say our heart is, at the turnstiles, and join those on the terraces.

There is so much more that could be done for them, to bring their facilities into the twenty-first century before it is upon us. Yes, we're back to money again. But name me the businessman who uses his premises no more often than a professional football club and the chances are that we'll be talking about a bankrupt.

British football has to go continental. We are becoming commercially minded but not sufficiently fast enough. There are multimillion-pound organizations whose happiest claim to public relations fame would be a tie-up with a football club, hopefully a successful one.

Some clubs played last season with sponsors' names across their shirts. But not on television. I think we worry too much about this situation and the belief that other advertisers get uptight if they have paid for the boards around the pitch and the shirt sponsors are getting away scot free. Were it not for the rule that stipulates that players in televised matches must not wear shirts

Kevin Reeves of England joins the million-pounds club. He signs for Manchester City from Norwich, flanked by officials of the Manchester club, secretary Bernard Halford, (left) and general manager Tony Book (right) with coach Malcolm Allison behind. (*Photo: Press Association.*)

carrying large advertising emblems, every club would be parading sponsors' names. The situation would become the norm, rather than the abnorm. If the television companies still objected, I don't think sponsors would mind paying an additional fee.

But the crisis is coming, and I don't think football can bury its head in the sand. Let us consider the part-time player again. Britain's best competitions outside the Football League are the Alliance Premier League, the Northern Alliance and the Southern League. There are good players in these competitions who will not sign for League clubs. I am not surprised. Most of them hold down useful jobs which they combine with their part-time professional status as footballers. The two incomes have been known to be a source of envy between Third and Fourth Division players and their non-League counterparts.

There is a school of thought that top-class footballers need a lot of training. It isn't the quantity but the quality that counts. Malmö, the Swedish team who reached the final of the European Cup when Nottingham Forest won the trophy in 1979, were reckoned to be part-timers. True, they trained only five or six times a week and in the cool Swedish evenings at that. But were they any less fit than Forest who normally have a rest day after every game?

I think a lot of Third and Fourth Division players would be happy to switch to part-time, given the Malmö training methods. It makes a deal of sense, but so do the pleas for rest days that come from our leading players. Successful British footballers spend so much time playing and travelling that they hardly seem to find the time for wives and families, let alone training.

I remember hearing Bill Nicholson, whose Spurs side was running into the later rounds of one of the Europe competitions, complaining that several problems, both collective and individual, needed sorting out on the training pitch. And then saying, more vehemently, that the routine of play, travel, rest, travel, play etc. had rendered the gymnasium at White Hart Lane temporarily surplus to requirements.

I can sympathize. When Arsenal won the League championship and FA Cup double in 1970–71, I played in upwards of seventy matches. Take it from me, with those games and the hard slog of pre-season training, there wasn't much else we wanted apart from temporarily stopping the whirlaway routine and getting off for a couple of saner moments. We just didn't wind down after that season. Eventually, we had to be brought to earth by the calendar ordering us back for pre-season training.

Soccer must soon start picking up the best of United States style presentation. Dancing girls I like. Cheer leaders I like. I can put up with balloons, and I have been known to accept the occasional bag of goodies. But razzmatazz? No, it isn't. Soccer in the States is for the family, and the so-called razzmatazz is no more than the extra on a marvellous entertainment. The Americans are comparatively new to football. But they've cottoned on quickly. Once the serious play starts, they put the extras out of their mind and concentrate on the game. They watch as intently as any fans in the world, except those of Liverpool when they are two-up at Goodison Park.

Climate prevents British clubs developing a carbon copy of facilities at some sun-soaked United States complexes but I played some games, in the summer of 1979, on Second Division grounds in Denmark where the facilities and amenities were embarrassingly high, by British standards.

European football has done and is doing the game in Britain a tremendous amount of good, again with the aid of television. It is astonishing now to recall the opposition there was in the mid-fifties to the start of the European club competitions. Once the British soccer fan was able to see the standard of the game as it was played in Munich and Madrid, he wanted the same in Manchester and Middlesbrough. I am a firm believer in the interchange of soccer ideas. The game is the most universal language in the world.

I remember going to Brazil some years back for an international indoor tournament. There was Bobby Moore, the England captain, Derek Dougan from Northern Ireland, the famous Brazilians, Gerson and Carlos Alberto, and players from the leading European countries. We had to make it work, and we did. Portuguese, Spanish, English, German, Italian, it didn't matter. The ball did the talking.

We all have something to offer each other. The success of Kevin Keegan and Tony Woodcock in the German Bundesliga helps to make my point. Bill Shankly and Bob Paisley, his managers at Liverpool, insist that Keegan was a great player when he left Anfield for Hamburg. I don't disagree. But would he have twice become European Footballer of the Year if Hamburg hadn't added other dimensions to his game? I think not.

The careers of Keegan and Woodcock, culminating in the huge sums of money they have earned, emphasize how thin the soccer margins are between total success and having to accept something substantially less. Keegan was once rejected by Coventry City because he was too small. Liverpool watched him several times when he was playing for lowly Scunthorpe before they decided to sign him.

Woodcock came so close to losing his way during his teenage days at Nottingham Forest, who were then a Second Division club. The impact he made on their first team was so slight that he was sent on loan to Doncaster Rovers and then to Lincoln, clubs who exist in football's Poverty Row. Woodcock was thinking seriously of a permanent transfer to Lincoln when he was recalled by Forest. A few years later, I saw him in Cologne, recognized and acknowledged wherever he went, the English star everybody wanted to know with a life-style he owed to his own tenacity and courage. He could have settled for Doncaster or Lincoln, but he didn't, and when the time came for him to leave Forest, who were then European champions, he weighed the circumstances very calmly. I believe that the final inducement to make the move was not the money but the fact that it would help him become a better player.

There is a certain amount of difficulty when Woodcock rejoins the England squad. Both he and Laurie Cunningham, who went from West Bromwich Albion to Real Madrid, find that adjustments are necessary. With Keegan it is different. He can be left to play his own exceptional role and it is the other

OPPOSITE ABOVE Liverpool fans are unique. Here they are massed in Rome when their team beat Borussia Moenchengladbach to win the European Cup. (*Photo: Central Press.*)

OPPOSITE BELOW England striker Tony Woodcock scores his first goal for his new club, Cologne, against his old club, Nottingham Forest. (*Photo: Bob Thomas.*)

players who adapt. But the revival in the fortunes of the England team during the time Kevin played in Germany is hardly coincidental, and some of his thinking rubs off on his colleagues, especially Trevor Brooking.

One of the delights of watching the England team in the late seventies was to see the almost telepathic understanding between Keegan and Brooking. They would exchange passes from some twenty yards before Keegan would run at the opposing defence. Then, with perfect control and accuracy, Brooking would find him in space with the goal chance on. Keegan has told me that Brooking is the almost perfect partner for him, and it is a tribute to Brooking's belief in himself and his attitude to the game that he has improved his value to the England side even during West Ham's years in the Second Division.

A mild infusion of talent from another country does no harm to domestic football, provided it is not allowed to get out of hand. Ossie Ardiles, the midfield star who played for Argentina in the 1978 World Cup final, has done splendidly at Tottenham, especially for Glenn Hoddle, who burst so dramatically into the England team in the winter of 1979. I am certainly not suggesting that Hoddle would have been just another player had Ardiles not joined Tottenham, but the improvement in Hoddle after a season with the Argentinian was most marked.

Yugoslavian Ivan Golac won a Football League Cup medal in his first season as Southampton's right-back, and the midfield skills of the Dutchmen, Arnold Muhren and Frans Thijssen, made Ipswich one of Britain's most attractive sides in the 1979–80 season that started so badly for the East Anglian club. Football is a game you never stop learning. Even at the age of thirty-two, when my playing career was nearing its end, I was still adapting my method of saving penalties.

Football has changed a lot in my time. It is different today. But being a professional footballer is the best job in the world, for the one in a hundred youngsters who makes it to the top. When you get there, you've earned it, but getting paid to do something you enjoy isn't work. The glow that comes from being superbly fit is a feeling that only the professional athlete can fully appreciate. And there is all that travel, seeing the world at no personal expense. Would I do it all again? You've got to be joking. *Of course I would*!

Would You Believe It?

When Newcastle United met Portsmouth in a First Division match on 5 December 1931 not only was the match devoid of goals—neither side gained a corner kick either.

In the modern first-class game a number of players wear contact lenses. But, in the 1922 FA Cup final between Huddersfield Town and Preston North End at Stamford Bridge, Preston goalkeeper J. F. Mitchell (an England amateur international) appeared in spectacles. Huddersfield won 1–0 with a penalty by Billy Smith.

OPPOSITE Tottenham Hotspur stars Osvaldo Ardiles (left) and Glenn Hoddle. (*Photo: Colorsport.*)

Tomorrow's Game

Sir Stanley Rous, in more than half a century of active involvement in the game, has seen it all. He was, first, a top referee, then Secretary of the Football Association and finally President of FIFA, the controlling body for world football. Now, in this special feature, he shows that he is still looking forward.

Football has undergone a revolution in thinking and development during the past decade or so. Many of the changes have been for the better, but if the game is to continue to prosper we must avoid change for change's sake.

I believe we should resist suggestions to change the laws. There are only seventeen laws expressed in simple, straightforward, easily understood language. As these laws must have a universal interpretation, I think they should remain in the revised form adopted in 1936. Recent experiments to change the laws have not been convincing and, therefore, have not been adopted by the International Board which controls them. The short corner was tried, but it led to confusion. It would be possible to introduce a 'sin bin' in warmer climates where players can be sent to calm down after outbursts of petulance, but you could scarcely have it in a British winter.

A wrong use of coloured cards is being made by referees. I introduced these cards at the Mexico World Cup in 1970, when I realized that, in one game, the two teams, the referee and his linesmen did not understand each other's language. The cards were to overcome that language barrier. Now referees sometimes use these cards for dramatic effect and it can embarrass a player. I know of an overseas match when the referee, seemingly, could not make the defenders understand that they must be ten yards away from the ball at a free kick. In desperation, he tore up the yellow card into eleven pieces and gave a piece to each player in the offending team. Hungary will not have coloured cards for domestic football and I believe we should discontinue their use in our home competitions.

I look to the time when FIFA, UEFA and the national associations will adopt consistent forms of punishment for offences occurring in matches under their control. We would then see an end to such startling variations in punishment as a one-match suspension for a foul tackle in one country and an eight weeks' suspension in another. I hope, too, that the over-jubilation at scoring a goal—the un-British gestures of hugging, kissing, jumping on the scorer and even hair pulling—will be replaced by a handclap or some equally modest reaction. I am sure that if, say, the players of one leading club were to set an example and their attitude was highlighted by TV commentators, other clubs would follow suit and eventually it would be standard practice at all levels of the game.

Hooliganism *within* football grounds seems, thanks be, to have decreased

OPPOSITE ABOVE The first FA Cup final at Wembley, 1923: crowd control was a problem even then.
(*Photo: Press Association.*)

OPPOSITE BELOW Yellow card for Leeds and England defender Trevor Cherry. The referee is Eric Read and the Southampton players Steve Williams (no. 4) and Mike Channon. (*Photo: Colorsport.*)

marginally, but violence and vandalism *outside* the grounds are on the increase. The evil of crowd disturbances has spread to the continent. UEFA will not sanction matches between teams from different countries in stadia where there are not adequate fences. However, it would be a sad day if we needed moats to separate spectators from the field of play. Denis Howell MP, the former Minister for Sport, thinks that Alsatian dogs are the best safeguard against crowd invasion of pitches. I saw it work in Belgium. There were four policemen with dogs outside the playing area and no one encroached on the pitch. But I understand our police don't want dogs to be used here and their view must be heeded.

The ultimate remedy for hooliganism could be for supporters to join their local supporters' clubs and for these clubs to be linked to the parent club through social activity. I believe football clubs should do much more to make their fans feel welcome. Supporters will not break up the stadium if they are made to feel part of the organization. Indeed, more moves towards family-style football could rid Britain of this nasty element of hooliganism.

We can learn a great deal from abroad on this. I visited a South American country where one football club had 52,000 members, with different coloured cards to show the appropriate grade of membership. In Detroit, USA, there is a magnificent stadium with an air-supported roof. Families go along all day. They practise one or other club activity until ten minutes before the soccer match when a hooter blows and the spectators take their places. After the match, instead of stampeding out they stay on for some other social activity. The facilities, bars and restaurants are good. They have a crêche for infants.

The status of managers, coaches and trainers must be improved. It grieves me that some top-class players, who are also excellent men, turn out to be disasters as managers. Every manager should go on courses to learn man-management and psychology. Expert instructors could present new ideas. Too many coaches and trainers know and teach only what they learnt as players in one club or league. Too few of our managers avail themselves of the opportunities to watch European international matches. Bobby Robson of Ipswich and Dave Sexton of Manchester United are among the enlightened exceptions.

If some managers had more open minds, their tactics might be 'attack and risk' not 'defend and caution'. They should remember that players on the pitch are human beings and should be encouraged to think, not act like robots. A player should be allowed to express his talents. Yet not so long ago I heard of an international with a Third Division side who, according to his manager, was *too good* a player for the club. He was told to suppress his genius—his skills were too much for the other players to follow! Yet football is crying out for genius of the calibre of Tom Finney (he was my favourite), Stanley Matthews, Pele, Beckenbauer and Cruyff.

I remember how the crowds loved the tussles between Eddie Hapgood and Stanley Matthews. Matthews, the young Stoke winger, was determined to show that he could beat the Arsenal and England captain, who was among the best defenders in the prewar game. Hapgood was equally determined to

OPPOSITE Pele's last game for New York Cosmos—an emotional farewell. (*Photos: main picture, Colorsport; inset, Syndication International.*)

get the better of Matthews. Yet I never heard of their fouling each other.

Winter conditions frequently make grounds difficult or nearly impossible to play on. Fixtures are often postponed and outstanding fixtures accumulate. A proportion of spectators are reluctant to go out in bitter weather and gates fall. All this makes me hope that we will soon decide to have a break in the season in December and January. Former objections to extending the season to the summer months are no longer valid. There would be no need to clash with summer cricket and other sports as the football could be staged under floodlights in the evenings. And I foresee artificial pitches being brought into greater use, although the expense of providing them will inhibit this in the immediate future. They do help enormously to develop techniques and tactics.

I hope that henceforth national associations will not discard their man in charge when the team loses. I wish they would accept their defeats more realistically, more philosophically. I am sure continuity is far preferable. The Bulgarian side knew that their coach would be sacked if they lost to Switzerland. They did, and he was.

The World Cup and the continental competitions will continue to bring exchanges of referees. In the near future I expect exchanges of referees in the national leagues, for example an English referee officiating in a French League match. Such a scheme would raise the general standard and remove inconsistencies. With the support of the national and the referees' associations, they will seek to stop dissent at refereeing decisions. I do not agree with referees being engaged as full-time professionals. Making them so would remove their impartiality and, if they had no other occupation but football, it could blunt their ability to judge instantly and correctly.

In South America, the stadium has become a status symbol. Brazil has one which holds 200,000. I don't believe we need bigger stadia than we have here already. Wembley is big enough—perhaps too big. In fact, in the future there will be no need for huge stadia: a capacity of 60,000 as a maximum would suffice. The number of spectators is likely to decline because of TV coverage and increased travelling costs. Seats for everyone, as they have at Aberdeen, should be the standard to aim for. Planners should ensure adequate car parking at the grounds.

Unless TV coverage is more strictly controlled, football will be seen more and more on the screen and in the studio and less at the ground. More pre-match advertising should be provided by TV to excite interest in the matches and to make people want to go to the match. Fewer live matches and more reports would help. Higher fees will be demanded by national associations for 'star' international matches. Money and big business are not the primary ends of football, but efficient financial advisers, treasurers and accountants are necessary in football before decisions are made and before ruinous spending is undertaken. Sponsorship and fund-raising may not provide a lifeline for ever.

Merchandizing, marketing and advertising gimmicks will, I think, increase as industrialists use football as a means of promoting their products, but clubs must beware. If you take money you risk being under an obligation. There is a

OPPOSITE Two photographs of a great team in action: Liverpool (above) *v.* West Bromwich Albion and (below) *v.* Norwich. (*Both photos: Colorsport.*)

danger of football becoming a slave to the sponsors and to TV. Clubs should negotiate with wisdom and perspicacity. The money raised should be used to improve the comfort in their stadia for the benefit of their fans.

There are a few instances where I hope the clock can be turned back. I wouldn't wish to see the old heavy boots with reinforced toecaps. These, like leather footballs, could become dead weights on muddy winter pitches, but the footwear has become too lightweight and it affords little protection for the ankles.

I cannot foresee a return to the glamorous days of amateur football, important and exciting though the contributions of such clubs as Pegasus and Bishop Auckland were. But I regret the passing of the shoulder charge which, if fairly made, was perfectly in keeping with the laws and was a good element in the game. The European Cup competitions are, I think, here to stay and our British clubs can gain much and learn much from taking part and succeeding in them; they rank only second to the national leagues, which are the essence of football. I am not, however, in favour of a European League, which would either put a tremendous burden of additional matches on the top teams of a country or require the top teams of a country to withdraw temporarily from the national league.

My appointments with FIFA have brought contacts in football throughout the world and the improvement in all aspects of football has been most marked. Australia is a case in point where the level of play is agreeably good. The most rapid advance I judge to be in the USA. Large injections of finance and the importation of star players and coaches there have made big football a reality in just a few years. They understand that the grass roots are most important and over a million youngsters are playing and learning football there. This puts a great responsibility on top players for good conduct and skilful performance.

Air travel will be used more frequently by clubs and national associations, and a breakdown of barriers and the widening of horizons will result from this.

Football will continue as a peaceful world power, an influence for good, and will occupy a special place in society. The troubles in the world are not caused by games players. Sport, like music, must be a world language and must know no frontiers. Administrators must seek to keep it so. Football will remain a grand game and parents and teachers will be able to tell their boys: 'You should play it.'

OPPOSITE ABOVE Advertising comes to football. Liverpool manager Bob Paisley, and the shirts that bring in the money.

OPPOSITE BELOW Strategically placed advertisements are picked up by the television cameras at big games. Mick Thomas of Wales scores against England at Wrexham.
(*Both photos: Syndication International.*)

Would You Believe It?

The numbering of players was first seen in the FA Cup final in 1933, which resulted Everton 3, Manchester City 0. They were numbered 1–22.

Back in the 1880s, the fee to England players for appearing in an international match was ten shillings—50p in present-day currency.

Chapter 3

The Evolution of the World Cup

It all began in 1930, with no more than thirteen countries taking part. When the finals of the next tournament are played in Spain in 1982 television will bring the action to more than half the world. That is the story of the World Cup, which has grown in half a century to overshadow even the Olympic Games as the biggest sporting event of them all.

There have been ten World Cup competitions since Uruguay first cradled FIFA's infant, and only six nations have been able to proclaim themselves World champions. The honour has gone to Brazil three times, to Uruguay, Italy and West Germany twice each, and England and Argentina once each.

FIFA, the Federation of International Football Associations, conceived the idea of a World Cup in 1920. It took ten years and the inspiration of FIFA's French president, Jules Rimet, to translate thoughts to reality. And the first trophy, later to be given to Brazil to mark their achievement in becoming the first country to win the World Cup three times, was named the Jules Rimet Cup.

But why start in Uruguay, one of the tiniest of countries and half the world away from Europe and the most powerful soccer nations of that time? There were two reasons. Uruguay had won the Olympic tournaments of 1924 and 1928, and they volunteered to host the competition as a means of celebrating their centenary as a nation.

So Uruguay built a new stadium, and the world was invited. But the world didn't come. Transcontinental aircraft with big passenger pay-loads were flying machines of the future. The Atlantic had to be crossed by boat. European nations did their sums, and most of them came to the conclusion that having to employ their players for some two months was beyond their financial capabilities. France, Belgium, Yugoslavia and Romania went, the last-named only because King Carol guaranteed the players' wages. England, Scotland, Wales and Northern Ireland stayed away for a different reason. They had all resigned from FIFA two years earlier on the issue of broken-time payments to amateur players, and were not to rejoin the FIFA fold until 1946.

Uruguay became the inaugural winners with a hundred per cent record, including a 4–2 defeat of their old Olympic adversaries, Argentina, in the final. With only thirty miles of the River Plate estuary separating the two countries, there was more than a little rivalry, with the biggest coup achieved by the FIFA official who decreed that two balls be used during the match, one of Uruguayan manufacture in one half and one of Argentinian origin in the other. Europe may

OPPOSITE The great Pele, in World Cup action against Czechoslovakia in 1970. (*Photo: Syndication International.*)

well have watched from afar. The River Plate was hardly set alight. But the Uruguayans took it seriously. The team was assembled a couple of months before the final and, when one of the goalkeepers returned to headquarters late one night, he was thrown out of the squad.

On to 1934, with Italy the venue and the Europeans beginning to appreciate the financial possibilities. But politics eventually brought the World Cup finals to Italy. Mussolini saw it as the ideal vehicle to promote his Fascist party.

First among the absentees were the holders, Uruguay. As Europe, or most of it, had declined to come to them, they saw no reason to pay the compliment of going to Europe. Argentina, wary of Italian clubs waving lira-loaded cheques in the direction of their star players, brought a side well short of full strength.

Both this and the 1938 tournament were played on the straight knock-out system, the only occasions on which that method had been used. The United States, Brazil and Argentina crossed the Atlantic for just one game. The second round was all-European and eventually Italy beat Czechoslovakia 2–1 in an extra-time final. Italian centre-half Monti was happy. Four years earlier he had won a runners-up medal with Argentina, but as he was of Italian ancestry he was one of three Argentinians called up by Mussolini's minions. It seemed that the best team won, but world assessment hardly made them the most popular winners.

Vittorio Pozzo, manager of the Italian team, was to achieve the double by retaining the trophy in France in 1938 when his tactics were vastly different. The 1934 Italians were heavily disciplined. They played without a smile, and were all strength and power. Four years later Pozzo, one of the greatest of managers, gave the footballers their heads.

There was the inevitable pre-tournament wrangle. Argentina wanted to stage the finals, but they were given to France. That was too much for the Argentinian temperament. They told FIFA's Europeans that they would not enter their tournament, joined the Uruguayans gazing out at the River Plate and left Brazil to carry the South American banner. But the World Cup was becoming worldwide. Among the finalists was a team from the Dutch East Indies which gave Hungary a 6–0 first round win.

Brazil and Poland played one of the World Cup classics in the first round before Brazil emerged victors by 6–5. Their second round tie against Czechoslovakia produced another classic, of a different kind. By the time the referee's whistle signalled the end of extra-time, two Brazilians had been sent off, so had one Czech, and two other Czechs were hospital cases with a broken arm and a broken leg. But even the World Cup has a sense of humour. For the replay, won 2–1 by Brazil, the Czechs made six team changes and the South Americans nine. Giving the world a hint of what was to come, Brazil finished in third place behind Italy and Hungary, who were beaten 4–2 in a fine final. That was the end of the World Cup for twelve years, but the beginning for Brazil.

After the Second World War, football prepared itself for the 1950 finals, awarded to Brazil who had been training footballers while most of the world had been occupied with producing soldiers, sailors and fliers.

Brazil is a big country and they thought big. They promised FIFA the biggest football stadium in the world, and they built it. Or nearly. For the giant Maracana, which houses 200,000 fans, was not quite complete when the curtains parted for the finals. No matter. Even Mardi Gras was, in football parlance, relegated.

Distance was still a problem. Austria did not go. Neither did Hungary, Czechoslovakia nor, oddly enough, Argentina. Russia was still viewing the world with suspicion and their war defeat made the Germans *persona non grata*. Piqued at the amount of internal travelling 'awarded' them between matches, France pulled out at the last gasp, and so did Turkey. The workers were still sorting out the shambles of the Maracana stadium when the tournament began, and with two pools of four countries, one of three and the other only two, that was a shambles, too.

When the dust settled on the preliminaries, if never on Maracana itself, Uruguay, Spain, Brazil and Sweden were through to the last four, played for the only time on a pool basis and not knock-out. Where was England? Still recoiling from the shock of being beaten 1–0 by a United Nations team from the United States.

Belo Horizonte, Sunday 25 June 1950, is still a date that sends shivers down the spines of English football fans. The United States included only one player with fleeting claims to fame, a wing-half named Eddie McIlvenny who had gone to the States to seek his fortune after being given a free transfer by Wrexham, then a Third Division club. England went into the game against the United States with a team led by Billy Wright, who was to win more than a century of caps, and including Alf Ramsey, who was to have a day of atonement when England won the 1966 World Cup, and Tom Finney. Indeed, the eleven were to amass 380 caps between them. England's horror show robbed the competition of the joint favourites, and when the last round of matches produced the final fixture, between Brazil and Uruguay, it was all to play for. Brazil wanted a draw for the title; Uruguay had to win.

Two hundred thousand crammed into the Maracana for the final. Brazil went ahead just before half-time through Friaca, and a nation prepared to rejoice. But Schiaffino, later to decorate the pitches of Spain and Italy with his artistry, equalized for Uruguay and a hero with the unlikely name of Ghiggia stroked the winner for Uruguay with eleven minutes to go. England managed to get in on the act: the virtual final was refereed by George Reader, a schoolmaster who became chairman of Southampton. Brazil licked their wounds. The flames on the beaches of Iponema burned brighter. And Uruguay got out in a hurry.

By the time we got to Switzerland in 1954, the world of football was taking the Jules Rimet Cup seriously. There was no repeat of Scotland's insistence in 1950 that they would compete in the finals only if they went as United Kingdom champions (and were beaten by England). Even Uruguay were at last enticed across the Atlantic. Brazil arrived with mood darkened by the overwhelming favouritism for the great Hungarian team that all Europe acclaimed as the best in the world. But the Hungarians were not to win it. They were beaten 3–2 in the final by a West German team that exacted maximum penalty for Hungary's decision to risk Ferenc Puskas, their captain and chief scorer, who had been injured in an earlier match.

England reached the quarter-finals and Scotland went out after losing both their preliminary matches. Brazil, with the unrelated Santos namesakes at full-back and Didì manipulating the midfield strings, topped their group, and Hungary did likewise, beating West Germany 8–3 on the way. The significance of that, and Puskas's injury, was to become apparent only later. At the same quarter-final stage at which Uruguay, with Santamaria (later to emerge as the defensive pillar of the Real Madrid squad that won the European Champions Cup five times in a row), disposed of England 4–2, Brazil and Hungary fought the infamous Battle of Berne.

It was a tribute to the stature of British refereeing that Arthur Ellis from Halifax was given this potentially explosive clash. Explode it did. Hungary, without Puskas, won 4–2, but before Ellis blew his last whistle he had sent off Nilton Santos and Bozsik for fighting when Brazil were trailing 3–2 after being 2–0 down, and then sent off Brazil's Tozzi for kicking an opponent. Kocsis's last-minute goal for Hungary merely added fuel to the fire. The fracas continued down the corridor, dressing-room doors were burst off their hinges, and it took the law about twenty minutes to restore some semblance of order.

Brazil had to wait four more years to assume the mantle of world champions that some of their players thought was theirs by divine right. For the Hungarians, who had shown the world a new concept of the game, the ultimate accolade seemed to be only two matches away.

Came the final against West Germany. Puskas played. He was a major in the Hungarian army. By now, it was obvious that West Germany's manager, Sepp Herberger, had conceded the 8–3 fixture by fielding a weakened team. Nevertheless, Hungary were 2–0 ahead inside ten minutes, and the Jules Rimet trophy looked as good as theirs. But Puskas could not keep it going and West Germany, even though their bar was hit, and a post too, could. For the first time, the magical Magyars encountered the one factor they could not beat—luck. They were the best team in the world, without any reservations except Brazil's. But West Germany, 3–2 winners, were the world champions.

On to 1958, to Sweden, and a tournament unique in World Cup history. For the only time, England, Scotland, Northern Ireland and Wales all played in the final stages of the World Cup, and Brazil became the first, and so far only, team to win the World Cup outside its own continent. It was also the tournament in which the young Pele, then only seventeen years of age, was unleashed on the world. England (whose team was decimated by the deaths at Munich of the Manchester United trio, Duncan Edwards, Roger Byrne and Tommy Taylor) and Scotland went out at the preliminary stage, though England took Russia to a play-off.

England manager Walter Winterbottom was criticized for not playing the young Bobby Charlton, then still recovering from the mental effects of the air disaster. How easy to be wise after the event. Northern Ireland lost to France, the ultimate third-placed side for whom Juste Fontaine scored a record thirteen goals in a World Cup finals. Wales lost only 1–0 to Brazil, an achievement acknowledged by the South Americans who invited the Welsh back to Brazil to play warm-up matches for the 1962 World Cup finals in Chile.

But, in retrospect, it was the rebuilding of the dominant Brazilian team of the next five years that was the most fascinating aspect of that World Cup. Brazil opened with Gilmar, who topped a century of international caps, in goal, Nilton Santos at left-back, Didì in midfield, Altafini at centre-forward and Zagalo, manager of the successful 1970 team in Mexico, on the left-wing. They beat Austria 3–0, but for the next game the clever Zito was drafted into mid-field; the selectors at last listened to player power and restored Garrincha, the Little Bird, to the right wing, and then pulled a master stroke of their own. They gave Pele his first game and switched Vava to centre-forward instead of Altafini. They drew 0–0 with England. At last Didì had the pieces of the jigsaw as he wanted them. Vava missed the quarter-final, but he was back for the semi-final.

The French team was defeated 5–2. For the final, Djalma Santos was restored to right-back. Sweden were overwhelmed 5–2, with Pele getting two goals.

The 1962 finals were due to return to South America. Somewhat surprisingly, Chile got them. Ravaged by earthquakes, Chile received a great deal of world sympathy. Argentina, the continent's biggest nation after Brazil, would have to wait another sixteen years.

Brazil kept the trophy, comfortably (even after Pele was injured in the second match) against ultimate finalists Czechoslovakia. Pele missed the rest of the tournament. But, just as he had made the Swedish finals a rhapsody of his own, so did 'Little Bird' Garrincha become the hawk of Chile.

England, alone of the United Kingdom countries, qualified for the Chile finals. They took a young Jimmy Greaves, an even younger Bobby Moore. They had as skipper Johnny Haynes, whose passes looked as though they were made with a 40-yard slide-rule. But what Bobby Charlton, then a left-winger, and left-back Ray Wilson learned in Chile made them key players in the triumph of Alf Ramsey's men four years later. England drew their three qualifying games and then gave Brazil a fright before losing the quarter-final 3–1. Sadly, England have not played their way into World Cup finals since. In 1966 they were there as hosts. In 1970 as holders. In 1974 in West Germany, and 1978 in Argentina, they failed to make the last 16.

Sadly, every World Cup final seems to have one unsavoury occasion. This time the disgrace signals were hoisted above a qualifying round match between Chile and Italy. Adrenalin, heated by an extremely partisan crowd, surged through the Chilean team, who won 2–0.

Two Italians, Ferrini and David, were sent off and a third, the Italo-Argentinian Maschio, had his nose broken. This time, at least, all the feuding was on the pitch.

But could anybody stop Brazil? They beat Mexico 2–0, drew 0–0 against Czechoslovakia, and topped their qualifying section by defeating Spain 2–1.

Garrincha had not yet made his move, but the Little Bird's wings were about to be spread. He scored twice in a 3–1 quarter-final win which laid Brazil's England bogey; he scored two more in the semi-final defeat of Chile, 4–2. He was also sent off that day for kicking an opponent. The good and the bad don't often go hand in hand. Czechoslovakia did well to hold Garrincha, dubbed the new Stanley Matthews, and Brazil, to 3–1 in the final.

So to England, the 1966 World Tournament, and, outside Britain, the world wondered whether Brazil could win a third successive time. Brazil manager Feola had few doubts and brought largely the players of 1958 and 1962. He was wrong. Age had started to wither most of them and the rest, especially Pele, were pounced upon by Bulgarians and Portuguese. The world champions beat Bulgaria, but lost to Hungary and Portugal and were out. Pele hoisted his battered body aboard a plane, vowing that he would never play in another World Cup.

Meanwhile, England were having difficulty in convincing the natives that they were playing in this one. They struggled to a 0–0 draw with Uruguay in their opening match; were less than impressive beating Mexico 2–0 and no nearer their best form when accounting for France by the same score. Jimmy Greaves, among the best marksmen in the world and a folk-hero in Britain, had not scored and had been injured against France.

Alf Ramsey, the England manager, refused to gamble on his fitness when England met Argentina in the quarter-finals and incurred the wrath of a nation by bringing in Hurst, who got the only goal of the match against Argentina. Rattin, the Argentinian centre-half and captain, was sent off; Ramsey made his next visit to Argentina purgatory for all by labelling them 'animals' and England were on their way.

Portugal were beaten in the semi-finals in probably the best game of the tournament and on 30 July West Germany lost the final 4–2 after extra time, with Geoff Hurst scoring a memorable hat-trick for England. The Germans had equalized in the dying minutes of normal time, which evoked one of Ramsey's most quoted utterances. He said to his mentally shattered team as they sprawled on the Wembley turf: 'You've won it once. All you have to do is win it again.'

There were three very significant circumstances of those World Cup finals. Eusebio, of Portugal, the 'Black Panther', proved himself the most lethal striker in the world with nine goals; Bobby Charlton had now discovered his true midfield role, and Franz Beckenbauer had made his arrival in the West German team. Four years later, in Mexico, they were again to clash dramatically. But while the rest of the world had reservations, England rejoiced and recalled how the North Koreans, with a football pedigree as long as an inch of string, beat Italy 1–0 and led Portugal 3–0 before Eusebio hammered in four goals.

Next to Mexico, and the problems of playing 6,000 feet above sea level in intense heat. Pele, thankfully, had changed his mind and Zagalo had taken over as manager. The Brazilians, with Tostao, Gerson, Jairzinho, Clodoaldo and Rivelino in there with Pele, were all about attack. Zagalo had the easiest job of any of the managers of the sixteen finalists.

OPPOSITE ABOVE World Cup final, 1966. England's dark-shirted defenders face a West Germany free-kick.

OPPOSITE BELOW World Cup final, 1966. England, in the dark shirts, score.

(*Both photos: Syndication International.*)

Brazil and England were drawn in the same qualifying group. When they clashed in a totally absorbing tactical match, Brazil won 1–0, but they both qualified for the quarter-finals. Maybe the Brazilians had been helped by the anti-British Mexicans in Guadalajara, who maintained an all-night crescendo of noise outside the English players' hotel. A sleepless night after playing the Brazilians was acceptable, but the night before . . .

England drew West Germany in the quarter-final. Goalkeeper Gordon Banks, whose save from Pele in the qualifying match drew the admiration of the world, was struck down on the morning of the revenge match with stomach trouble. Peter Bonetti played his only game of the tournament and was blamed for two of the German goals, but the decisive moment came when, with England leading 2–0 and the game decently into the second half, Ramsey decided, with the semi-final ahead, to spare Bobby Charlton from the rest of the duel in the searing sun. He took him off, and that freed Beckenbauer from his main responsibility of marking Charlton.

One, two, three—the goals went in and England went out and a reprise of Guadalajara, everybody's dream of a Brazil–England final, was gone. Bobby Moore, the England captain, was falsely accused of stealing a bracelet when England played in Bogota in a pre-finals warm-up. But he overcame that and became accepted as the best defender in the world, just as Banks was rated the best goalkeeper.

Gerd Müller, the West German striker who was to torture European defences for a decade, got ten goals, but Brazil went inexorably on. They beat Italy 4–1 in the final with a superb display of attacking football. It underlined the achievements of a fabulous team. They had won all six matches and scored nineteen goals in the process. True, they had given away seven but, drunk with the sheer pleasure of their attacking style, nobody, least of all the Brazilians themselves, cared. FIFA gave them the Jules Rimet Cup for keeps.

West Germany hosted the 1974 World Cup finals. The great Brazil team of 1970 had broken up. Pele's part in these finals was to be the role of commentator, but Holland, whose previous contribution to world football had hardly been emphatic, had a team of virtuosos headed by the brilliant Johan Cruyff. They were, it seemed, to be the natural successors to Brazil and the Hungary team of the 1950s.

England had been knocked out in the preliminary and only Scotland were there to wave the British flag. Led by the combative Billy Bremner and graced by the skills of Kenny Dalglish, Scotland made their own bit of soccer history. They became the only side to go out of the World Cup finals without losing a match. They beat Zaïre 2–0, and drew with both Brazil, 0–0, and Yugoslavia, 1–1. But they missed a place in the quarter-finals by goal difference.

Holland swept through to the quarter-finals imperiously; West Germany and East Germany qualified from the same group; and Poland, who had won England's preliminary group, came from nowhere to win all three group matches. With the best team in their history, Poland were eventually to beat Brazil 1–0 for third place.

FIFA had abandoned the knock-out system for the quarter-finals. The eight teams were drawn in two groups and played each other. West Germany and Holland both went through by winning all three, and the stage was set for a classic confrontation in the Munich final: the improvisation of Cruyff against the discipline of the West Germans. The match was refereed by Englishman Jack Taylor, a master butcher from Wolverhampton, who made immediate impact on the game by giving a penalty in the first minute when Cruyff was brought down. Neeskens scored from the spot and Holland should have been on their way to an expected victory.

But they weren't. Years in the top strata of world football had given Beckenbauer, who was now skipper, Müller and goalkeeper Sepp Maier patience and confidence in their own game. The equaliser, by Breitner, also came from the penalty spot.

Cruyff left the field at half-time arguing with referee Taylor. It was the first sign of a crack in the Dutch edifice. No wonder. Just before the break West Germany had snatched what proved to be the winning goal, scored by the astonishing Müller, who averaged more than a goal a game in internationals.

For the second time in three World Cup finals, the trophy had gone to the host nation. Argentina, therefore, fancied their chances when the 1978 spectacular began. But Holland were still the people's choice, even though Cruyff had announced his retirement from international football. England had failed again, finishing as runners-up to Italy in their preliminary group. Scotland had made it, and, amazingly, more than 65,000 people paid admission money to pile into Hampden Park, Glasgow, to cheer them goodbye. The high hopes were shattered in the embarrassment of a 3–1 defeat by Peru and a 1–1 draw against Iran. A 3–2 success over a Holland side, already virtually assured of their quarter-final place, helped. But not much. So Scotland returned home early, discredited on the field and disgraced by the discovery that Willie Johnston had taken an illegal stimulant. He was banned by FIFA for a year and by Scotland for ever.

There was something inevitable about Argentina's progress. They cruised through their qualifying round, losing only to Italy when it didn't matter. They won their second group without conceding a goal, and there to meet them in the final, fulfilling their destiny, were the Dutch. Brazil, who took third place by beating Italy 2–1, had lost all their traditional attacking flair.

The Argentinians were not universally popular. To make sure of reaching the final, they had to beat Peru, their fellow South Americans, at least 4–0, to prevent Brazil reaching the final on goal difference. With exquisite timing, the organizers had ensured that Brazil had kicked off their match earlier, so Argentina went into the Peru game knowing exactly what they had to do. They needed four goals. They got six. The Argentinians hadn't finished yet.

When they met Holland in the final, the Dutch took the field first and waited . . . and waited . . . and waited. Suspecting gamesmanship, they walked off, protested and had to be placated. But the incident had upset them. Their edge had gone. For the second successive World Cup they finished runners-up when

Argentina won 3–1 with the gifted Mario Kempes the hero of the hour with two goals. With the possible exception of Brazil in Mexico in 1970, has there ever been such a carnival occasion?

The most successful World Cup country? Brazil, of course. They have won 52 matches in World Cup final series. West Germany have won 47 and Italy 36. Uruguay and Argentina have each won 29, Sweden are next with 28, Hungary have won 26, Yugoslavia 25, and England and Mexico, who qualify more often than not from a weak geographical group, are on the 24 mark. Czechoslovakia have won 22 and France 20. Next stop, Spain.

Would You Believe It?

Right-half-back Bert Turner scored for both sides in the 1946 FA Cup final (the first after the war) with an own-goal for Derby County and an equalizer for his own team, Charlton Athletic. Derby won 4–1 after extra time.

A missed penalty in their last match of the 1925–26 sent Manchester City down to the Second Division. They lost 3–2 to Newcastle, but would have avoided relegation if they had scored from that spot kick.

When Chelsea played a First Division match at Blackpool in October 1932, they finished with only six men on the field. Facing a second-half blizzard, five of their team suffered exhaustion and exposure. Blackpool won 4–0.

Youngest player ever seen in the Football League was Albert Geldard, of Bradford. He was only 15 years and 158 days old when, in September 1929, he appeared in a Second Division match against Millwall.

Oldest player to make his debut in a full International for England was Arsenal centre-half Leslie Compton. He was aged thirty-eight years and two months when called up for the match against Wales at Sunderland on 15 November 1950.

There is only one known instance of a player appearing for both sides in the same Football League fixture. His name was John Oakes, a full-back with Port Vale when they went to play Charlton in the Second Division on Boxing Day 1932. The match was abandoned because of bad light, and by the time it was rearranged later in the season Oakes had been transferred from Port Vale to Charlton.

In the long history of Wembley Stadium, no first-class match there had ever been postponed until the England v Bulgaria European Championship fixture on 21 November 1979. It was fogged off and played twenty-four hours later with England winning 2–0.

OPPOSITE ABOVE Antognoni of Italy scores against England in a qualifying match. The loss of this match, in Rome, cost England a place in the 1978 World Cup finals.

OPPOSITE BELOW World Cup final, 1978. Willy van der Kerkhof, of Holland, takes the ball away from the falling Mario Kempes, of Argentina.

(*Both photos: Syndication International.*)

Chapter 4

Spain Prepares for the 1982 World Cup

On 11 July 1982 a footballer destined for immortality will be presented with the World Cup. A moment when the marrow in his bones will freeze, a moment of such numbing impact that he will be lucky if he remembers more than a detail or two. He will be only the twelfth World Cup-winning skipper; acclaimed around the globe, his name on the tips of millions of tongues. And the Spanish hosts will count the cost of international prestige cheap at the price, which at a conservative estimate will be the colossal figure of around £500 million.

Yes, that is what it is going to cost to stage the next World Cup. As a sporting show, it outstrips even the Olympic Games. And the Spaniards won't regret a single peseta. The greatest soccer show on earth has been on the Spanish stocks since they made their first tentative approaches for it back in 1964. As soon as FIFA, the governing body of world soccer, confirmed Spain as the 1982 venue, a twenty-seven-man team headed by Raimundo Saporta, for years the administrative supremo of Real Madrid, swept into action. By the time the finals begin in June 1982, Spain will be a soccer nation transformed.

It is Spain's ambition to make these the biggest and best of all the World Cup finals. Certainly, they will be the biggest. Never before have as many as twenty-four countries contested the finals. In recent years, the number has been sixteen, but one of the most influential factors in the election of Joao Havelange of Brazil as the first South American president of FIFA was a promise to increase the number of countries in the finals. It won the votes of most of the non-European countries, including the South Americans en bloc.

Argentina, the 1978 winner, and Spain, as host, qualify automatically. Then there will be thirteen more countries from Europe, three more from South America, two from Africa, two from North and Central America and two from Oceania and Asia. Those are the bones on which the flesh has taken years to grow. World Cup finals don't just happen.

Spain's soccer administrators thought big, and invited King Juan Carlos to become the honorary president of the committee organizing the event. Plans were laid for a new issue of legal coinage to commemorate the finals, and a small army of public servants, whose responsibilities ranged from health to public transport, descended on the organizers. By the time the tournament kicks off, twenty-eight days before the final, in Barcelona's Nou Camp stadium, fourteen of Spain's First Division grounds will have been face-lifted, and in one instance rebuilt.

OPPOSITE Italy and England battle it out in the European Nations Cup, 1980. (*Photo: Colorsport.*)

Real Madrid's famous Bernabeu stadium will have approximately £4 million spent on it. The capacity will be reduced from 120,000 to 87,000 seats, but there will be compensations. For the organizers there will be sky's-the-limit admission prices, and for those who can afford to pay them there will be the comfort of fibre-glass and glass appointments and a tunnel under the eight-lane Castellana Avenue linking the stadium to the Congress Palace, where the organizing committee will have their headquarters. There will be subsidies of £8½ million for static advertising rights and £11 million for radio and television rights, but that is only the icing. The substance of the World Cup cake is what it will mean for local amenities, a once-in-a-lifetime opportunity.

The money for those improvements will have to come from the local population, not from the profits, which FIFA handle. In some cases, a gigantic bill is being cheerfully accepted. Valladolid, a town to the north of Madrid, is building an entirely new stadium because in 1979 a FIFA committee rejected the present El Zorilla stadium. Valladolid's half-million population will have to dig deeply into their pockets. Current estimates put the cost at more than £8 million, but in Spain football is The Game.

Not everybody in Spain is quite as enthusiastic as the townsfolk of Valladolid. Raimundo Saporta wanted an elevated railway to link Barcelona airport with the Nou Camp stadium. But, argued Barcelona's town councillors, what use would such a railway have after the World Cup? In Saragossa, a garrison town in the north-east of Spain, they have been allocated the sum of £7 million, and see the use of it differently. They will build a railway linking the Romareda stadium to the city and will spend most of the balance on a bridge commemorating the tournament. Vigo and La Corunna, the two most northerly World Cup towns, have asked for about £3½ million between them to bring the Riazor and Balaidos stadia up to standard. At Vigo, they will spend part of the money on making a stretch of the River Lagares into a canal. They cannot risk the Riazor stadium being flooded during the World Cup.

Elche, a town in the south-east, is taking itself and the World Cup seriously. The council have decided that seven public edifices are essential for the smooth running of World Cup affairs, but what form they were eventually to take was a matter for long discussion. Holiday town Alicante, also in the south-east, has its feet in the future. Most of their £5½ million budget was earmarked for roads and parking lots, means of ease and income after the heady World Cup days. Nor was Malaga slow to appreciate the tourist potential. The southern town voted itself a World Cup expenditure of £28 million and then announced that only £1¾ million will go on the Rosaleda stadium. The rest was scheduled for roads, fly-overs and the building of a number of well-equipped sports grounds in the town's suburbs.

Ambitious projects, all of these, but among the Spanish laymen was the doubt that some of the schemes could be completed in time without modification. Local politics took a hand too. The banks of one town were found to be reluctant to subscribe to petitions of credit, until they were told by the mayor that they would not be welcome to continue operating in the province.

OPPOSITE Two FA Cup finals: above, Arsenal *v.* Manchester United, 1979; below, Arsenal *v.* West Ham, 1980. (*Photos: above, Syndication International; below, Colorsport.*)

In another, the two leading opposition parties got together and vetoed the proposed expenditure of £2½ million on improvements to the local stadium unless the governing party promised to back certain improvements to public buildings and services in the town.

But, in spite of all the hiccups, the show will be all right on the night. It is the football that counts. The twenty-four countries will be divided into six groups of four. The top two in each will comprise twelve which will be divided into four groups of three. The winners will become the semi-finalists, and meet on a knock-out basis to produce the two finalists. The winners will have played seven games—and earned the FIFA Cup.

Would You Believe It?

The first World Cup, in Uruguay in 1930, attracted only thirteen entries. More than 100 countries now enter the competition.

Portsmouth are the only club to have held the FA Cup for seven consecutive years. They won it in 1939, when beating Wolves 4–1 at Wembley, and with the Second World War breaking out five months later the Cup remained in Portsmouth's possession until the competition was resumed in the season 1945–46.

Twenty-two players started a wartime match between Chelsea and Charlton at Stamford Bridge, but only one was left at the finish. The game was abandoned through fog, and for ten minutes Charlton goalkeeper Sam Bartram didn't know the rest had left the field until a policeman loomed up out of the gloom and told him the match had ended.

Nottingham Forest's record run of fifty-one First Division home games without defeat ended when they were beaten 1–0 by bottom *club Brighton on 17 November 1979.*

An ice-cream salesman was given offside in one of Queen's Park Rangers early floodlight games at Shepherds Bush. The vendor, wearing a white jacket, was walking along the touchline selling his wares to spectators. Suddenly the ball was played in his direction and the referee, mistaking the ice-cream man for one of the white-shirted visiting team, whistled him offside.

Gate receipts at the first FA Cup final played at Wembley (Bolton 2, West Ham 0) in 1923 were £27,776 from a crowd officially recorded as 126,047.

Scottish club Stranraer, formed in 1870, made do without a manager for all but two of their first 110 years. The team was picked on Monday nights on a show of hands by the twelve directors.

Chapter 5

Kevin Keegan – the Man

Kevin Keegan is one of the wealthiest, most respected, highly publicized and commercialized players the game of football has known, yet he has managed to remain commendably well-balanced and unspoilt in spite of considerable international adulation. He is a man with values, fully appreciating and exploiting his worth as a wholehearted and intelligent player while never forgetting that there is a world outside football.

There have been other players blessed with more natural football gifts than Keegan but few who have been able to extend their talents to such extraordinary effect by sheer discipline, dedication and willpower. Physical strength and stamina are vital constituents of his play, and the development of his physique by means of weight training as a teenager played an important part in enabling him to make the remarkable transition from Pegler's Brass Works reserve and pub footballer to the captaincy of England.

Grateful for personal health and wellbeing, Keegan has made a point of finding time to take a sincere interest in some of those less fortunate than himself whenever possible, in spite of a demanding schedule of matches and commercial activity. There are several examples of his concern for the physically handicapped, especially children, which he would prefer to remain unpublicized but which show that there is more to the man than can be gauged from a showcase of medals and trophies.

As a Fourth Division player with Scunthorpe United, for instance, he spent part of a summer working as a porter at a mental hospital. Later, when fame found him at Liverpool, he paid a visit to a home for physically handicapped children and was so moved by their obvious delight that he spent many of his days off taking some of them on outings to Southport beach, even though he found their plight deeply upsetting. He has also been known on the eve of England matches to leave the team's headquarters to spend an hour or so visiting a sick person who has written to him or, as is often the case, has organized a gift for a player down on his luck. Always, Keegan treats those he visits as people rather than patients, understanding that the last emotion they wish to see from him is sympathy. He also knows from personal experience that encouragement can be as important a motivating influence as inspiration.

One of his early school reports from his headmistress, a nun, bore the prophetic message that 'Kevin's football must be encouraged', though subsequent teachers were not so convinced that this was altogether desirable.

One sports-master shattered one of the young Keegan's illusions when he informed the boy that he was too small to continue to play in goal for the school team. Another advised against his having trials with a prominent League club, being of the opinion that the boy did not have the necessary build or expertise to make the grade as a professional player.

Many talent spotters apparently shared this view. Keegan was overlooked by the selectors of the Doncaster schoolboys team, preference going to Kevin Johnson, a player who, Keegan agreed, showed abundantly greater promise as a schoolboy and for whom major success was predicted. Johnson was, in fact, signed by the then eminent Sheffield Wednesday, but was not considered to have fulfilled his potential at Hillsborough and was released, spending the rest of his career with several lower division clubs. Such is fate that when Keegan was an established Liverpool player he chanced to meet Johnson before a match at Newcastle, Johnson at this time being a player at Hartlepool.

Doncaster Rovers were also unimpressed with the ability of Keegan, a local miner's son and, after a misunderstanding over the time of a trial, he came to the conclusion that a career in professional football was not meant for him and took a job as a clerk-cum-storekeeper at the brass works. There, he preferred the more easygoing attitude of the works reserve team, whose players were determined to derive the maximum amount of pleasure from their sport, as opposed to the members of Pegler's senior team, whose endeavours were rather more earnest.

None of this may seem to represent much evidence of encouragement, but Keegan's other soccer activity, playing for a pub team in a local Sunday league, brought him to the notice of an opponent who also happened to be a part-time scout for Scunthorpe United. Keegan's performance in direct opposition to the scout, Bob Nellis, led to the offer of a trial at the Old Show Ground and, in due course, an apprenticeship.

At Scunthorpe, Keegan's duties included the menial tasks of cleaning the terraces and dressing rooms and occasionally driving the reserve team bus; the ideal type of upbringing, in fact, to prevent a player from becoming conceited. This is not to say that Keegan lacked admirers at Scunthorpe. On the contrary, the club's trainer and long-serving player, Jack Brownsword, was instrumental in persuading him to persevere with his football career during a period when Keegan became so depressed with his lack of progress that he seriously considered leaving the game. Brownsword assured him that some of the leading clubs in the First Division, like Leeds United, were continually having him watched and were on the point of making an offer for him. Eventually a word of recommendation by Brownsword to Liverpool, who were already impressed with the form of their former Scunthorpe goalkeeper, Ray Clemence, helped to take Keegan to Anfield for a fee of £35,000.

At Liverpool Keegan heard the most encouraging words of his career when, shortly after his promotion to the first team, Bill Shankly told him: 'You're the best player in the country, son.' Keegan has said that, although many people helped him, 'Shanks made me'. What Shankly did, in effect, was to liberate

OPPOSITE Kevin Keegan, playing for Hamburg. (*Photo: Bob Thomas.*)

Keegan's latent belief in himself, a conviction that whatever his shortcomings as a player might be he could compensate for any deficiency by working twice as hard as any other player.

When Liverpool made their investment in Keegan, he was generally regarded by the managers, coaches and scouts of other clubs that had evaluated him as a 'busy midfield player', and, as was remarked on more than one occasion, there was no shortage of that particular commodity.

Keegan joined Liverpool the week they played Arsenal in the 1971 FA Cup final, when a fellow by the name of Wilson was in goal for Arsenal and a Highbury prodigy, Charlie George, scored the winning goal in extra time. Shortly after Liverpool returned from London, their new, busy midfield player joined the team on an end-of-season tour of Scandinavia, and made an immediate impact on the coaching staff. Shankly had not toured with the team and was keen to see how Keegan fared in the club's pre-season matches. The hunch was that the club had unearthed a much-needed striker, and this was borne out in a club practice match which resulted in Keegan's inclusion in the first League match of the new season, at home to Nottingham Forest.

Although Keegan's success at Liverpool was instantaneous and consistent, his progression to acceptance as a fully-fledged England player was lengthy and hurtful. His early appearances were under Sir Alf Ramsey, whose World Cup winning side had dissolved, and the new cast was finding difficulty in remembering the script. It was not a convenient time for any player to represent England as they faltered towards elimination from the World Cup, in which Poland took their place in West Germany in 1974, and Keegan suffered along with most of the other newcomers.

Shankly made sure that Keegan's confidence was not shaken, and further encouragement came from Joe Mercer, who not only recalled the player to the England side when he took over as the caretaker manager of the national side following Ramsey's dismissal, but also helped to rescue Keegan from the brutal custody of the Yugoslav airport police in Belgrade after his arrest resulting from high jinks by certain players on a conveyor belt. Keegan's relationship with Don Revie was bonded following an early strain caused by Revie's omission of Keegan from a match at Wembley without explanation and the player's petulant walking out on the squad before the match.

At Liverpool it appeared that Keegan's future was assured. He married and moved to a house in North Wales, using some of his short and precious spare time in decorating and building an impressive new fireplace. In March 1976, however, his hankering for a move to the continent became public knowledge. A visit to Barcelona's magnificent stadium, the Nou Camp, where Liverpool played the first leg of their UEFA Cup semi-final, proved another turning point for him. Impressed with every aspect of the Barcelona ground, from its spacious dressing rooms and the excellent playing surface of the pitch to the club's chapel, Keegan decided that he ought to explore European football on a permanent basis and informed journalists of his intentions.

An adverse side effect of this publicity was alienation from a section of

OPPOSITE ABOVE The power of Keegan. He scores for England against Denmark. (*Photo: Press Association.*)

OPPOSITE BELOW Keegan and former Liverpool manager Bill Shankly, the man who signed him from Scunthorpe. Keegan was awarded the sword for 'distinguished service to British and International football'. (*Photo: Syndication International.*)

Liverpool supporters who saw no virtue in Keegan's plans and made their feelings known to him during matches. Yet before leaving Liverpool Keegan played a vital role in the club's remarkable season, during which they came to within one match of completing a fabulous treble of success in the Football League, the European Cup and the FA Cup. The exception proved to be the FA Cup, in which Liverpool were beaten by Manchester United in the final. Undeterred by this setback, Liverpool travelled on to Rome to meet Borussia Moenchengladbach in the European Cup final, and Keegan gave one of the most memorable performances of his career in freeing himself from the close marking of Berti Vogts to help Liverpool secure the trophy with a 3–1 victory.

In signing for Hamburg SV, a transfer which brought Liverpool a fee of £500,000, enabling them to buy Kenny Dalglish, Keegan realized there might be pitfalls ahead, but he could not have imagined the stern test of character and patience awaiting him in West Germany. Although his wife, Jean, spoke schoolgirl German, Keegan was faced with both the language barrier and an attitude of hostility from some of his new colleagues. It was difficult enough for the Keegans to leave their beautiful home in North Wales and move into a city hotel, but to be ostracized as well made what should have been a settling-in period a most uncomfortable experience.

That first season in West Germany was a severe trial. Not only did some of the other players seem reluctant to pass the ball to him, but the club were uncertain where he should play in the team. He played in five different positions in fifteen games before Hamburg decided to use him in a midfield role, operating just behind the main strikers. Club politics also played a part and before the end of the season Hamburg sacked their English-speaking coach, Rudi Gutendorf. Shortly afterwards the club's general manager, Dr Peter Krohn, who had negotiated Keegan's transfer, was forced to resign.

Keegan has since said that but for a reluctance to return home with his tail between his legs, which would have given a sense of satisfaction to some of those critics who doubted the wisdom of his move to Germany, he would have left Hamburg. Fortunately he was given much needed encouragement by the club's new general manager, Gunter Netzer, who fully understood Keegan's predicament, having experienced similar problems as a German exile playing for Real Madrid. Once Netzer had made it plain that he was backing Keegan come what may, the other Hamburg players responded and Keegan's intelligent running and indomitable spirit were put to good use. Hamburg won the Bundesliga championship and Keegan was honoured first by his fellow professionals in West Germany, who elected him their player of the year, and then by the European football reporters, who voted him the European Footballer of the Year two years in succession.

Although West German clubs play fewer matches than their counterparts in England, their training schedules are demanding of time and energy. Keegan had thought that his move abroad would automatically result in a cutting back on commercial activity. This did not prove to be the case. His name as an endorsement was considered equally profitably by continental manufacturers,

OPPOSITE ABOVE Acrobatic Keegan, playing for England against Northern Ireland. (*Photo: Syndication International*.)

OPPOSITE BELOW Farewell to Hamburg. (*Photo: Popperfoto*.)

and even during his early days with Hamburg he found himself involved in hours-long autograph sessions. He decided he would have to become more selective in accepting business contracts, especially after the arrival of his daughter, Laura Jane, but a player of Keegan's exuberant style and personality is always in demand and finds it almost impossible to regulate his time as he would wish.

Shortly before his transfer to Germany, Keegan was given a serious warning by a doctor at Northampton General Hospital. A year of almost constant travel for matches, business appointments and charity appearances had finally taken its toll. During the cycling event of a BBC Television Superstars contest, the front wheel of Keegan's bicycle touched the rear wheel of the one ridden by Gilbert Van Binst, the captain of Anderlecht, and Keegan crashed into the red shale running track, which shredded his vest and took much of the skin off his back. Although the commentators, David Vine and Ron Pickering, were insistent that he went to hospital for an injection, Keegan obdurately demanded a time-trial in an attempt to win a place in the cycling final. He succeeded in finishing second in the cycling and went on to win the steeplechase to clinch the competition. During the journey home on the M1 motorway, however, he was taken ill and after four days at the hospital the doctor told him that he had overtaxed his body. 'Your body is like a car built to do a hundred miles per hour and you've been driving it at a hundred and forty', the doctor said.

It is difficult for those not involved in top-class professional football to appreciate the special pressures entailed, and though Keegan was determined to take heed of the doctor's advice his natural inclination to sustain a happy relationship with those who watch him play has inevitably kept him busy. Ever since the time when, as a small boy in Doncaster, he stood in the rain outside the Rovers ground only to be disappointed when his favourite player refused to sign an autograph for him, he has realized the value of public relations work. He always makes a point of signing as many autographs as humanly possible wherever he goes.

Keegan's success in West Germany, both as player and an ambassador for his country, was an invaluable contribution to the image of English football abroad. What impressed the German people was that he did not simply involve himself in the day-to-day training and tactics at his club but made a genuine attempt to integrate. The fact that he was able to appear on television speaking their tongue was considered a compliment. When he left Germany he did not say goodbye. He said 'Auf Wiedersehen'.

On 11 February, 1980, when Lawrie McMenemy, manager of comparatively unfashionable First Division club Southampton, proudly announced that he had obtained the signature of Keegan with effect from 1 July, British football was both shocked and agreeably surprised.

The Press were told at a conference they thought had been called to reveal details of a new ground for Southampton. Indeed, McMenemy had that idea in mind, and what better way to attract the country's and, in fact, the world's attention, than by adding the attraction of Keegan's capture?

'Why Southampton?' almost everybody asked the European Footballer of the Year. Keegan's reply was simple. His greatest ambition, he explained, was to lead England in the World Cup finals and, with Spain looming in 1982, the best possible way to achieve this ambition would be for him to be based in England. The reasons Southampton took preference over Manchester United, Arsenal, Chelsea, and even his old club Liverpool, were yet simpler.

In McMenemy, Keegan found a man who speaks football like he lives—straight, to the point and honestly. McMenemy turned down a financially beneficial move to Leeds United a year before the Keegan situation arose because he felt he still had work to do at The Dell—Southampton's ground. But McMenemy had to fight to get his man. He had been quietly negotiating for six months before Keegan agreed to sign, facing stern opposition from Juventus, Barcelona, America, France and Saudi Arabia, not to mention other English clubs.

Southampton manager Lawrie McMenemy, the man who brought Keegan back to Britain.
(*Photo: Press Association.*)

Keegan joined Southampton for two reasons: his England place, and peace of mind in the tranquil Hampshire countryside. For he is much more than a footballer: he is a family man with a wife and baby daughter to consider. That is why he decided that an English education for his child would be best; moreover a move to Spain or Italy would have meant the ordeal for his wife of learning yet another language.

When Keegan decided to join Southampton the conversation was simple. Phoning McMenemy from Hamburg, he said: 'Yes, I will sign for you. But after seeing your result yesterday (Southampton beat Brighton 5–1), I'll be prepared to start next season sitting on the substitute's bench!' Keegan later explained: 'At twenty-nine, I've got to know I'm going to get a job satisfaction with my next club. I know I will get it with Lawrie McMenemy. I want to enjoy my football and put something back. It's not the money. I've earned enough in Germany not to worry too much about that. But once I spoke to Lawrie I needed only fifteen minutes to make up my mind.' Keegan also had time to think of old friends at Liverpool. 'They had an option to sign me back before any other English club', he said. 'But chairman John Smith, manager Bob Paisley and secretary Peter Robinson took only an hour to decide that a move to Southampton was in the best interests of everybody. In fact, the chairman said I could not sign for a better man than Lawrie McMenemy.'

Would You Believe It?

The unique instance of father and son playing in the same League side was provided by Alex and David Herd in May 1951. Father Alex, aged thirty-nine, played inside-right, and son David, aged seventeen, was at inside-left for Stockport County at home to Hartlepools. Stockport won 2–0, with one of the goals by David Herd.

Chapter 6

Soccer in Europe

Ferenc Puskas juggled the ball on the left instep, flipped it on to the thigh and then forehead, let it roll down his back and backheeled it over the head again. He was on the centre spot just before the kick-off of the England–Hungary match at Wembley in 1953. The wizardry of the tubby Hungarian Army major held the 100,000 crowd in spellbound silence.

Within half an hour the crowd were realizing the greater significance of Puskas's flamboyant ball control. Although England included men like Stan Matthews, Billy Wright, Jimmy Dickinson and Stan Mortensen, they were trailing 4–1, outwitted, outpaced, outplayed. England were no longer the masters of football. The Continent had usurped us and we were now the pupils. It was the twilight of the gods.

Hungary were the first foreign side to win on English soil and the final score 6–3 did not reflect their superiority as accurately as the 7–1 margin in Budapest in the following May. There, reserve goalkeeper Ted Burgin of Sheffield United said in awe, 'They were like men from another planet.'

Fortunately the bitterness of defeat had a salutary effect. English players and clubs were willing to learn, and because they did so, England won the World Cup in 1966 and Liverpool dominated Europe in the seventies.

Long before 1953 Sir Stanley Rous, England managers-to-be Walter Winterbottom and Ron Greenwood and ace coach Jimmy Hogan had warned that our standards were slipping, and those on the Continent rising, because we concentrated on stamina and fitness at the expense of skill. We ignored these prophets, and failed to heed the red light of narrow escapes in matches against Yugoslavia, Austria and the rest of Europe. We cocooned ourselves in the cosy insularity that defeats abroad happened because they came at the end of an exhausting season.

Even leads given by Matt Busby with Manchester United and Arthur Rowe with Spurs were not followed. They insisted that there was no substitute for skill, and that close support should be given to the man with the ball, instead of aimless long passing. Rowe demanded: 'Don't kick the ball, pass it.'

Hungary's victory revolutionized our approach to the game. Kit became lightweight, heavy boots gave way to shoes, many discarded shinguards, medical supervision became more scientific and means were found to improve technique. Training altered: ball work replaced monotonous lapping and training centres had to be found because of the increased use of pitches.

OPPOSITE Wembley, 1953. Captains Billy Wright of England (left) and Ferenc Puskas of Hungary. (*Photo: Central Press.*)

England were bewildered at Wembley by the way Hungary turned team formation upside down. Centre-forward Nandor Hidegkuti dropped back to midfield, the wingers operated from a deep position and inside-forwards Puskas and Sandor Kocsis were the strikers. It was virtually a 4.4.2 formation and England centre-half Harry Johnston, accustomed to having the centre-forward at his elbow every Saturday, was so baffled that Hidegkuti capitalized on his freedom with a hat-trick.

Former England team manager Don Revie was centre-forward with Manchester City and adopted the Hungarian style in season 1955–56. His scheming took City to the FA Cup final, where opponents Birmingham made the same mistake as England three years before in not marking closely. Revie organized a 3–1 victory.

The Continental encroachment on our insularity was extended by the introduction of European club competitions, starting with the European Cup in 1955. The impact was all the greater because Real Madrid, one of the finest teams of all time, won the Cup in the first five years by playing superb and sophisticated football. They allowed full expression to individual flair and acknowledged that attack was the best form of defence. They scoured the world for men to maintain ascendancy.

Their greatest star was Alfredo di Stefano, a fair-haired, blue-eyed Argentinian nicknamed 'the White Arrow'. He was the complete player—arguably more complete than Pele—because he tackled, foraged, schemed and scored. Outside-left Francisco Gento terrified backs by his speed, as well as his club by bullfighting in Santander during holidays, and Santamaria was Uruguay's World Cup centre-half. Later came Raymond Kopa from France, Puskas after the Hungarian uprising of 1956, and Didì from Brazil.

The peak performance was a 7–3 victory over Eintracht Frankfurt in the 1960 final in Glasgow. Di Stefano scored three goals, Puskas four and the 135,000 crowd gave them a standing ovation.

Chelsea were the reigning champions when the European Cup was launched and the Football League typified the head-in-the sand, 'English is best' attitude when they forbade entry. Chelsea timorously obeyed but a year later Manchester United overrode the League's wishes and took up the gauntlet.

The Busby Babes (average age twenty) were emerging—youngsters who had been signed because of their skill, encouraged to use their initiative and groomed alongside fine players like Johnny Carey, Stan Pearson and John Aston. After scoring twenty-one goals in six games, including a 10–0 victory over Anderlecht, United yielded to the superior knowhow of Real in the semi-final.

They retained the League title and were heading for another confrontation with Real when they met disaster at Munich airport on returning from victory over Red Star Belgrade. Eight players were killed, including Duncan Edwards, surely destined to be one of the world's greatest players, Tommy Taylor and Roger Byrne; Bobby Charlton took several months to regain form. Busby was badly injured as well, and had a long convalescence before returning to Old

Trafford. He said: 'They were surely the greatest group of young players ever assembled in one team. I would have been able to sit back while they piled up a collection of trophies for years to come.'

United were set back a decade, while England's chances in the 1958 World Cup in Sweden were dealt a mortal blow. As a result neither United nor England was able to give a lead to the rest of the country in the bid to raise playing standards.

A sinister trend was developing in European competition, encouraged by the two-legged nature of the ties and the enormous rewards for success. The main objective was to obtain a 'good' result away from home, and that could be defeated by a one or two-goal margin. Teams went to matches with a blanket defence and instructions to everyone to get behind the ball when danger threatened.

The circumstances ideally suited the Italians, whose notorious *catenaccio* defence—a sweeper behind the back four—put goals at a premium in the Italian League. With manager Helenio Herrera weaving webs to entangle opponents, Inter-Milan had a spell of ascendancy and other dominating clubs were AC Milan, Roma and Fiorentina. Their influence encouraged the blight of negative football to come to Britain and retard our recovery for a time.

The first British club to win a European trophy was Spurs. It was in the Cup Winners' Cup, which, like the Fairs Cup (later UEFA Cup), had been launched

Manchester United, 1968, with that coveted European Champions' Cup. (*Photo: Colorsport.*)

following the success of the European Cup. It was in 1963, ten years after we had taken the road to recovery pointed out by Hungary. Spurs could match any foreign side in skill with free-scoring Jimmy Greaves, Danny Blanchflower, the late John White, Dave Mackay and Cliff Jones. But they also needed some old-fashioned physical challenges by Bobby Smith on Czechoslovakian international goalkeeper Schroif to turn a 2–0 defeat into a 6–2 aggregate win over Slovan Bratislava.

Liverpool found some unexpected obstacles in the European Cup in 1965. They stayed at Lake Como before the return leg with Inter after winning 3–1 at Anfield, and the players were kept awake by the bells of the church adjoining the hotel. Shankly said that 'one bell sounded like Doomsday', and asked the priest if something could be done. He even asked if Bob Paisley could 'put bandages on the bells to dull them'.

Shankly considered that two goals should not have been allowed in the match which Inter won 3–0. 'The first goal was from an indirect free kick which went straight into the net', he said, 'and for the second the ball was kicked out of Tommy Lawrence's hands'. Spurs, Derby and Leeds were other clubs who encountered dubious refereeing decisions abroad.

The stimulus of playing against foreign teams and the ambition to head Europe again brought a steady improvement in British football. The skill factor was being improved and brought into a framework which made full use of our traditional qualities of fitness, resolution and courage. It was still very difficult to overcome the superb organization and ability of the top teams, as England found in the World Cup and European Championship.

Alf Ramsey was hit very hard by Hungary's victory at Wembley. It was his thirty-second game for England at right-back. And his last. He was dropped and the humiliation served to fire the conviction that English footballers could again be the masters, provided their qualities were harnessed properly.

In his first tour after becoming manager of England in 1963 Ramsey talked to the team in the centre of the pitch in Bratislava. He held a football and said, 'Regard this as a precious stone. You must never give it away. You must protect it by moving to support a colleague with it. Make yourself available so that he can pass it to you easily.'

Ramsey used tactics which fitted the players, rather than force players into a style foreign to them. In the first three matches of the 1966 World Cup he tried wingers John Connelly, Terry Paine and Ian Callaghan, and discarded them in favour of a 4.3.3 formation—the 'Wingless Wonders' who won the trophy. With Bobby Moore, Bobby Charlton, Geoff Hurst (the only man to score a hat-trick in a World Cup final), Gordon Banks and Martin Peters, England could match any side in skill. Moreover Ramsey insisted on the midfield players getting into shooting positions whenever possible.

Successful sides always have imitators and many clubs who adopted 4.3.3 used the middle three to bolster the defence and overlooked the emphasis Ramsey put on attack. As a result English football took a sterile turn and the improvement in skill was not yet taking us to the top. A lead this time came not

OPPOSITE ABOVE Defenders become strikers at set-pieces in an effort to break down top defences. England's Dave Watson soars against Denmark. (*Photo: Press Association.*)

OPPOSITE BELOW Brian Talbot, of Arsenal, in action against Valencia in the 1980 European Cup Winners' Cup final. (*Photo: Syndication International.*)

from the Continent but from north of the border: Glasgow Celtic. Manager Jock Stein advocated complete support for the man with the ball by intelligent, non-stop running. He pushed midfield players Bertie Auld and Bobby Murdoch, and even the backs, to help the front runners, saying, 'The best place to defend is in the other team's penalty area.' Celtic reached the final of the European Cup at the first attempt in 1966–67.

The opponents in the final were Inter-Milan, winners in 1964 and 1965, and they had the start they wanted—a goal in seven minutes. They then retreated into their defensive shell, confident they could hold everything Celtic threw at them. But Celtic refused to panic and maintained aggressive, flowing football. Tommy Gemmell equalized with a tremendous shot and Steve Chalmers got the winner. Herrera was generous and factual in praise: 'It was a victory for football. The lessons are clear, a nine-man defence is not a substitute for skill and a positive attitude overcame our negativity.'

A prophet is often not appreciated in his own country. Celtic's insistence on the involvement of all ten outfield players in all facets of the game eminently suited British footballers' traditional virtues. But the first disciples of Celtic came from abroad: West Germany and Holland. They called the new style 'total football' and the credit for spreading the gospel is given to them, instead of the inventors Celtic. The Dutch and Germans integrated individuals, however brilliant, into well-organized teamwork. They too had stars: Holland, the incomparable Johan Cruyff, Rudi Krol, Wim Van Hanegem and Johan Neeskens; West Germany, 'Emperor' Franz Beckenbauer, deadly finisher Gerd Müller, ace-marker Berti Vogts and Rainer Bonhof.

Ajax of Amsterdam had a hat-trick of victories in the European Cup 1971–73. Although the Flying Dutchman Cruyff was their outstanding player, success was due to all-round teamwork. Their mantle was taken over by Bayern Munich who were superbly organized from the back by Beckenbauer. They, too, won the Cup three years in a row and provided the backbone for West Germany, who won the World Cup in Munich in 1974. Holland, who were Germany's opponents in the final, played most entertaining football and Germany recovered to win 2–1 after conceding a first-minute penalty.

Oddly, Bayern switched to cautious defence during their reign, and concentrated on soaking up Leeds's pressure in the 1975 final. If referee Michel Kitabjian had allowed a penalty when Beckenbauer brought down Allan Clarke and not ruled out a Peter Lorimer 'goal' for offside, the result would have been different. Bayern were equally cautious a year later in beating St Etienne of France.

Sound organization enabled the less powerful countries to set problems for the mighty. England had difficulty in overcoming Malta and Cyprus in the European Championship because they defended skilfully in the home legs. England manager Don Revie pointed out bitterly, 'If you stick eight dustbins in the penalty area it is difficult to get round them. How much harder with eight determined defenders! There are no minnows in Europe today.'

England were knocked out of the 1974 World Cup by Poland. Vital goals

OPPOSITE John Robertson scores the goal that gave Nottingham Forest their 1–0 victory over SV Hamburg in the 1980 European Champions' Cup final. (*Photo: Syndication International*.)

Horst Hrubesch heads in the goal against Belgium which won West Germany the European Championship in 1980. (*Photo: Popperfoto.*)

were conceded by errors by Bobby Moore in Poland and Norman Hunter at Wembley. Individual lapses are inevitable and in both these cases it is significant that the covering was inadequate.

If a well-built edifice was essential for a winning team Liverpool had the architect in dynamic Bill Shankly. He was assisted by a back-room staff with the burning ambition to bring glory to the club. He handed over to homespun Bob Paisley, who had the same knack of motivating players and of buying the right replacements at the right time.

They embarked on an unprecedented run of eighteen successive seasons in European competition, and were learning all the time. As they roamed from Athens to Malmö, Bilbao to Tbilisi, they absorbed suitable methods of leading foreign sides and added their own steely aggression.

Shankly's finest buy was Kevin Keegan from Scunthorpe for £35,000. Keegan acknowledged the way Liverpool put team before individual when he said, 'There are no stars at Anfield. We are all replaceable. If a player overreaches himself, he is brought down to earth in training the following week.' Proof of Keegan's statement came ten days after he had helped Liverpool win the European Cup in 1977 with a 3–1 victory over Borussia Moenchengladbach. He was transferred to Hamburg but, within a month, Liverpool signed his deputy, twenty-six-year-old Kenny Dalglish from Celtic.

Liverpool were now regarded as the leading side in Europe, if not the world. They retained the Cup a year later, beating Bruges at Wembley, despite making five changes compared with a year before. Out went Ian Callaghan, Joey Jones, Tom Smith, Steve Heighway and Keegan. In came Graeme Souness, Alan Hansen, Phil Thompson, David Fairclough and Dalglish. The newcomers slipped effortlessly into the well-oiled machine without impairing rhythm and understanding.

With Nottingham Forest, too, those supreme motivators Brian Clough and Peter Taylor demanded self-discipline in all players, whether great or ordinary. They knew that the outstanding lesson from competition in Europe is that the contribution of Ian Bowyer can be as valuable as that of £1 million Trevor Francis.

No player appreciates better than Emlyn Hughes the value of playing against top teams from abroad. As former captain of Liverpool and now Wolves he has played over eighty times in European competition, winning two UEFA Cup medals and two European Cup medals. He says, 'You have to go to Europe if you want to know if you really can play. And if you can't play you learn there how to improve yourself.'

Would You Believe It?

In March 1980 Manchester City became the first British club to have paid two separate million-pound transfer fees. That was when they signed striker Kevin Reeves from Norwich City—only six months after paying a seven-figure sum for Steve Daley from Wolves.

Nowadays goal difference decides Football League placings when two or more clubs have the same number of points. It used to be goal average (goals scored divided by goals conceded) and in 1927 a superior average of two hundredths of a goal (if you can imagine such a thing) earned Portsmouth promotion to the First Division. Going into the final match, they were level on points with Manchester City. On that last day Manchester City beat Bradford City 8–0, while Portsmouth defeated Preston 5–1. Only two clubs went up in those days, and Portsmouth collected second promotion place. Had present-day goal difference decided, Manchester City would have gone up instead.

Chapter 7

Memorable Matches

Magyar Magic

November 1953: England 3, Hungary 6

England played their first international match in 1872. For eighty-one years no foreign side succeeded in winning on English soil. Then Hungary, the Olympic champions, came to Wembley in November 1953. It was a foggy day, a grey day, in more senses than one. England, the nation that gave football to the world, were not only beaten at home for the first time; they were outclassed.

England's reign of the football world was over. No longer was prestige theirs by divine right. In future, status would have to be worked for, judgement based on the present and not on the past. Hungary's brilliant performance revealed that England had been overtaken by modern tactical thinking. England's traditional long-ball game was not enough, in itself, to rule the world against continental teams who possessed all the tricks, but not the ability to shoot. The shock of Hungary's electrifying football defused most English, and British, concepts of the game.

In retrospect, England should not have been taken so much by surprise. Hungary had won the Olympic title in Helsinki the previous year. They were unbeaten in twenty-five matches and, by eastern European standards, were professionals in all but name. They were led by Ferenc Puskas, an inside-left, who doubled as a major in the Hungarian army. Puskas had a roly-poly figure, one of the shrewdest of tactical brains and a left foot that was one of the most lethal in the game. It was said by those who envied Puskas his fame and fortune that he was a one-footed player. But with that one foot he could do more than anybody who might have been born with three.

Then there was right-half Bozsik, a member of the Hungarian parliament, tall, spare, and with an uncanny ability to split defences with passes that found the lurking Puskas or the menacing head of inside-right Kocsis. The prolific-scoring Kocsis was reckoned to have hit the net more often with his head than he did with his feet. But, between Kocsis and Puskas, in the programme at least, was the man who really turned England inside out. Hidegkuti was billed as a centre-forward but played alongside, or just in front of, Bozsik. He pumped balls through to Puskas and Kocsis, and also made a habit of pouring through the gap he had created for himself. Harry Johnston had been brought up, like every other British centre-half, on the precept that the opposing centre-forward

OPPOSITE England goalkeeper Gil Merrick tips one round the post against Hungary. (*Photo: Central Press.*)

played in the centre and up front, and the centre-half, using man-to-man marking, followed him wherever he went. The Hungarians killed the validity of that theory.

Just as few people can remember the names of the Brazil defenders who played behind Pele and his corps of brilliant attackers, so do the names of the other Hungarians fade. Given four world-class players in one team, that team will become the world's best, as Hungary did.

But all that lay ahead. England captain Billy Wright beamed a confident smile as he led his men on to the Wembley turf. No floodlights then. It was an afternoon match, to all intents and purposes lacking the drama now taken for granted on floodlight occasions. But only for less than sixty seconds. Within a minute Hidegkuti sold a dummy and scored. From that moment, Hungary's scoring attempts outnumbered England's by a ratio of 10 to one. When Jackie Sewell, who became England's most expensive player when sold by Notts County to Sheffield Wednesday for £34,000, snatched an equalizer, the respite was but temporary. Less than half an hour later, with Wembley's thousands gasping at the skill and intricacies of the Hungarians, their ability to mix long passes with short and their complete control of the ball, the magical Magyars, as they were dubbed, were 4–1 ahead. Hidegkuti scored his second, Puskas rolled the ball back from a tackle with the sole of his foot and scored with commensurate ease, and he also flicked in a Bozsik free kick with his head. England were in disarray. Stanley Matthews and his Blackpool partner Stan Mortensen played their hearts out, but a goal from Mortensen that allowed England to go in at half-time only 2–4 down was hardly spectacular encouragement. Within ten minutes of the start of the second half England, sad, bemused, England, were 6–2 behind. Bozsik had made it five and Hidegkuti had completed his hat trick. Alf Ramsey had the last word, taking England to 6–3 from the penalty spot.

Those who knew their football realized that England had a lot to relearn. Those who did not have such knowledge needed to carry their doubts for only six months. England went to the Nep Stadium in Budapest for the return match. Hungary won 7–1 . . . with the World Cup finals of 1954 only a few weeks away.

Real Perfection

May 1960: Real Madrid 7, Eintracht Frankfurt 3

Thousands of Scottish fans left Hampden Park, their national home of soccer, knowing there was little, if any, likelihood of their ever again seeing such a spectacular and satisfying game of football. Yet Scotland, their pride and joy, had not been playing.

A group of average German professionals had just surpassed themselves against some of the best players in the world and yet lost 7–3. It is in the record books as the 1960 final of the European Champions Cup, an apparently easy ride

for the Spanish club whose team Eintracht's manager, Ernst Berger, rated before the game as the best club side in the world.

Real, of course, were no ordinary Spanish club. Their players came from all parts of the world—di Stefano from Argentina, Puskas from Hungary, Santamaria from Uruguay, Canario from Brazil. Two years earlier, Didì had been Brazil's star in the 1958 World Cup final against Sweden, but he couldn't get in the side. Moreover Real had won the cup four times in a row; there were no doubts about making it five. But 130,000 turned up to see the execution. The televised genius of Puskas, di Stefano, Gento, Del Sol and the others was one thing. Football is lifeblood to the Scots, and the great men were there in the flesh.

The Scots were superbly rewarded. This was the last final in an era in which skills were supreme and not negated by cold tactics; no side of any generation would have marred the perfection that was Real Madrid. Eintracht had had a poor season in domestic football. Despite that, they had beaten Glasgow Rangers in the semi-final by 12–4 on aggregate. Even so, the Scots applauded them off the field for the part they had played in so magnificent a match. The most significant thing Eintracht did was to take the lead through Kress in the twentieth minute. It gave the match the lift it needed. Real had to fire on all cylinders. Di Stefano controlled the middle of the field, between the two penalty spots, like the master he was, demanding the ball and then giving it.

Alfredo di Stefano scores for Real Madrid against Eintracht.
(*Photo: Press Association.*)

Inside nine minutes, Eintracht had been put in their place. Real were a goal ahead, and di Stefano had scored the two. A minute from half-time Puskas, who had left Hungary during the 1956 uprising, angled in a classic goal from near the goal-line, the first of four he was to score in less than 25 minutes. Hampden acclaimed him. The rest was academic, or would have been except for di Stefano.

Stein had pulled two goals back for Eintracht and made it 6–3 when di Stefano took off from near his own penalty spot. It was almost as if somebody had whispered to him that his right to be regarded as the world's greatest footballer was to be challenged by Pele. Swapping passes with a variety of colleagues as he ran down towards the Eintracht goal, he left opponents sprawling before applying a graceful finishing touch to a goal that could hardly have been bettered at Hampden—or any other ground.

The following day, Real's aircraft was delayed four hours at Prestwick airport. It is generally accepted that the football-worshipping Scots did not want to lose them.

Busby's Triumph

May 1968: Manchester United 4, Benfica 1

British soccer has known few more emotional occasions than when Manchester United won the European Cup for manager Matt Busby. It mattered not to the players that they won it for the first time for England. It seemed to matter even less that they won it for themselves. No, it was the realization of a dream Busby had cherished from the day the Football League tried to stop Manchester United competing back in 1956.

The League had banned Chelsea from taking part in the inaugural tournament in 1955 on the grounds that participation would congest and disrupt fixture lists; and injuries could mean having to field weaker sides in League matches. Busby had to insist that United had at least eighteen players capable of holding down a First Division place before the League acceded to United's go-it-alone threat and gave grudging, formal permission.

Manchester United were stopped only at the semi-final stage by the mighty Real Madrid. Then came the Munich air disaster, wiping out the side that looked certain to become successors to Real as Europe's best. For ten years Busby toiled until at last there was only Benfica of Portugal standing between United and the trophy. The 1968 final, by rota, was at Wembley: it seemed impossible that United could be beaten. But they nearly were.

The tension was unbearable. There was too much pressure on the players. The first half was bad. Busby's message at half-time was: 'Keep on trying to play football.' Left-winger John Aston, son of the Johnny Aston who was United's left-back more than twenty years earlier, was having the game of his life, outshining even George Best and Bobby Charlton. But his work was being wasted until Charlton headed United into the lead just after the break.

That was all United needed surely? With a Wembley crowd willing them on, they battled away. Still the football wasn't good, but it was getting better, from United's point of view. With only nine minutes to go, Benfica equalized through Graca. The effect on United, not then an especially experienced team, was the same as on a boxer who takes a long count early in the fifteenth round of a title fight. Before the end, Eusebio, the great 'Black Panther', was to force a miracle save from United 'keeper Alex Stepney, but somehow United survived for a period of extra time. What could Busby say to revive his drained players? 'You're throwing the game away with careless passing', he admonished. 'You must start to hold the ball and play again.'

Not all the United players were in a state to get the message but suddenly George Best was evading one opponent and taking the ball round Henrique, the Benfica goalkeeper, before rolling it into the net. That was all United needed. Suddenly, the coolest men at Wembley were the United players. While bedlam raged on the terraces and in the packed stands, Brian Kidd celebrated his nineteenth birthday by getting a third and Bobby Charlton, skipper in the absence of the injured Denis Law, was the appropriate scorer of the fourth.

There were only two survivors from the Busby Babes era: centre-half Bill Foulkes, who had ignored Busby's 'stay back' instructions to dash upfield and score the winner in the semi-final against Real Madrid, and the skipper Charlton with his two goals in the final. Charlton and Foulkes both tried to persuade Matt Busby that he should precede them up Wembley's thirty-nine steps to receive the trophy, but the manager would have none of it, telling the players it was their day. Busby was the sole member of that 100,000 congregation who saw it that way.

George Best, in action for Manchester United against Benfica. (*Photo: Syndication International.*)

Keegan's Finale

May 1977: Liverpool 3, Borussia Moenchengladbach 1

At the end of April 1977 Liverpool were chasing a unique treble, the League Championship, the FA Cup and the European Champions' Cup. They cleared the first hurdle, winning the Championship, for the tenth time, by a point from Manchester City. When they went to Wembley for the FA Cup final, Manchester United were in the way, and won 2–1. It was a crushing disappointment for Liverpool to take to Rome where they were to play in the European Cup final four days later.

Lesser teams would have caved in, morale gone. Not Liverpool. Inspired by Kevin Keegan, they played the game of their lives. Keegan had good reason to put on a show. This was to be his last game for the club before joining SV Hamburg. Why did he leave Anfield where he was idolized? He has always said that he felt he had accomplished all he could there. Certainly the move proved the greatness of both Liverpool and Keegan. They survived without each other. With the eyes of Europe, and Hamburg specially, on him, Keegan gave one of his most memorable virtuoso performances. Despite being close-marked by Berti Vogts, one of the world's best defenders, Keegan achieved brilliant heights as Liverpool became only the third British club, after Celtic and Manchester United, to win Europe's premier club trophy. But, despite Liverpool's highly professional standards, the night was one of sentiment. Liverpool had been competing in Europe for thirteen years. Tommy Smith, the Anfield Iron, had played in most of those matches and had skippered the side in many. This was to be his last game.

They don't come any less sentimental than tough-tackling Tommy, a Scouser to his toe-nails with an accent you can cut with a knife. Could Liverpool win and crown his career? They could, and Smithy, who played most of his football at the heart of the back four, unbelievably, deliriously scored the goal that set up success. Terry McDermott, not long at Anfield from Newcastle, had scored the first. That clever Danish striker, Allan Simonsen, equalized. Liverpool battled on. It was their seventeenth game in six weeks, and the memories of defeat at Wembley were never far away. With twenty-five minutes to go and Rome's Olympic Stadium sounding like a huge Kop, Tommy Smith struck. He came up for a corner, and headed the ball in. Liverpool had cracked it. Phil Neal's third goal, from the penalty spot, merely emphasized the difference between the two sides.

It was a marvellous climax to Smith's 600th game for the club, and his last. Or so we all thought. But later Liverpool had second thoughts. They offered the old war-horse a lucrative contract he could not refuse.

It was Keegan's night, and Smith's night as well. To conform their status as Europe's No. 1 club, Liverpool won the Champions' Cup again the following year, beating Bruges 1–0 at Wembley in nothing like such dramatic circumstances.

OPPOSITE Kevin Keegan leaps over his 'shadow', Berti Vogts. (*Photo: Colorsport.*)

World Cup Wonders

July 1966: England 4, West Germany 2

Alf Ramsey said it first, in 1962, not long after taking over as England manager: 'We shall win the World Cup.' Four years later, on an unforgettable afternoon at Wembley, Nobby Stiles, the gap-toothed tiger from Manchester United, finished the script: 'Nobody can take this away from us.'

England won the World Cup by beating West Germany 4–2 after extra time in a final seared with thunder and lightning on the pitch as well as above it. And an entire nation went delirious with joy. After four unsuccessful attempts England, the fathers of football, were now the kings. It was a game to match the occasion. It could not have been more dramatic. A ninetieth-minute equalizer, a disputed goal, and last-minute effort in extra time that put the issue beyond doubt. But back to the beginning, and Bobby Moore, the England captain.

No man had ever walked up Wembley's famous thirty-nine steps to take a trophy three years in a row, but Moore was on this unique hat-trick. He had led West Ham United to triumph in the FA Cup final in 1964, and in 1965 was there again when his club won the European Cup Winners' Cup by beating Munich 1860 2–0. Moore was sure he was about to achieve his hat-trick, but did not dare to reveal his confidence. He went on the field looking as cool as ever. The hopes of a nation appeared a burden carried with ease, even when West Germany went in front in the thirteenth minute, the 100,000 crowd silenced by a goal from Helmut Haller that ranks as one of the softest ever scored at the home of English football.

Apart from a penalty to Portugal in the semi-final, England had not conceded a goal in the previous five matches. Yet a mis-hit shot went through Moore's legs and crept between central defender Jack Charlton and goalkeeper Gordon Banks as they left the ball to each other.

A rain shower was not inappropriate. But five minutes later, Moore restored some measure of sunshine, placing a free kick on to the head of Geoff Hurst who beat goalkeeper Tilkowski easily. Half-time came at 1–1. Extra time was looming with the score unchanged and only twelve minutes to go when Martin Peters, who with Moore and Hurst comprised the great West Ham triumvirate, put England in front with another header, a goal typical of Peters, who specialized in appearing on the blind side of defenders.

England were there, surely. The minutes ticked away. The crowd were whistling to the referee when winger Lothar Emmerlich backed into Jack Charlton, who cleared.

'I was shattered', said Charlton later, 'when the free kick was given against me. I was still trying to race back into position when it was taken but I wasn't worried when Siggi Held, their other winger, brought the ball down with his arms before centring it. Wolfgang Weber put it in the net, and we waited for the free kick that never came.'

There was no time left for England to get one back. They collapsed on the Wembley turf, shattered by the necessity of another thirty minutes. It was then

OPPOSITE Manager Ramsey 'lifts' his England team before they go into extra time. (*Photo: Syndication International.*)

that Ramsey made his most quoted utterance. 'You've won the Cup once', he said. 'Now you've got to do it again—and you can.'

They did. Alan Ball, still on the junior side of his twenty-first birthday, ran and ran and ran. And then there was Hurst, crashing a drive against the underside of the bar. It rebounded down—and out. Had it gone over the line? Yes, ruled the referee after consultation with a linesman, and it was the turn of the German heads to droop.

England still had a fight on their hands. Jack Charlton found himself tackling their full-backs as the Germans desperately sought an equalizer. It was then that the cool head of Moore caught them on the break. As he had done so many times for West Ham, the England skipper cleared to Hurst, on the left side of the halfway line. Hurst set off, and wasn't caught. He scored England's fourth with virtually the last kick of the match, and achieved immortality with a hat-trick in a World Cup final.

Manager Ramsey, who had been so right all along, wanted none of the glory. He refused when the players tried to lift him for a lap of honour. The honour came later—'services to football' the formal citation said. But Alf became a Sir because he gave English football the greatest day it has ever had.

Dutch Disappointment

June 1978: Argentina 3, Holland 1

In 1974 Holland, then widely regarded as the most stylish football-playing team in the world, lost the World Cup final to West Germany in Munich by 2–1. The Germans won the trophy, the Dutch gained most of the sympathy. Four years later, Holland again reached the World Cup final on foreign soil. Once more the uncommitted wanted them to win, and once more they lost, beaten 3–1 by Argentina after an encounter that was more a war of nerves than a football match. Maybe Argentina had the talent to win the Cup for the first time however the Dutch might have played, but the battle began before the kick-off.

Holland, with Rudi Krol and Johan Neeskens among the survivors from 1974, were without Johan Cruyff. The Dutch former skipper had announced a premature retirement from international football because he feared the possibility of kidnap in the politically-torn Argentina. He would have been in no danger at the River Plate Stadium, Buenos Aires. The Dutch came out first and waited, and waited. Argentina then appeared and immediately objected to a plaster bandage on the arm of Rene van der Kerkhof. The Dutchman had worn it in earlier rounds without any objection from opponents.

The entire Dutch team walked off the pitch while the plaster was changed. When they came back, ten minutes later, the mood had changed. When the game eventually started, the angry Dutch conceded four fouls in the first three minutes. The Argentinians responded with a couple in the same period, and the pattern was set. The teams were never going to be friends. Late tackles, body-checking, it was all there. But, their composure gone to the extent of even Krol

OPPOSITE ABOVE Geoff Hurst scores England's fourth goal.

OPPOSITE BELOW Holland's Krol and Argentina's Luque (striped shirt) challenge for the ball.

(Both photos: Syndication International.)

committing a yellow card offence, the Dutch played like a team feeling the world was against them. They were wrong, but conceded the first goal to the cynical Argentinians, to little Mario Kempes, a superb striker who came to Europe and did well in Spanish football.

The interval gave the harassed Dutch the chance to sort themselves out. They played the second half with much more positiveness and certainty. Nanninga came on for Johnny Rep, whose confidence had gone after missing an easy chance. He scored with nine minutes of normal time remaining from a centre by Rene van der Kerkhof, sweet revenge for the pre-match embarrassments to which he had been subjected. Seconds from the end, Robbie Rensenbrink hit an Argentinian post. It was an ominous sign that this was not to be Holland's day.

Extra time belonged to Kempes. Thirteen minutes after play was resumed, he dribbled past two opponents and trickled the ball into the net. The gesture had more than a suspicion of arrogance, but the eleven Argentinians on the field sensed long before the 80,000 crowd that the Dutch would-be masters had gone.

There were just five minutes left when Kempes the torturer laid on the third goal for Bertoni. By then the Dutch looked sick of football, sick of Argentina, and longing for the sight of a windmill. In 1974 and 1978 they had achieved unprecedented heights for a nation of their size. The orange shirt had become a symbol of what we called total football. More simply, they were all attackers and all defenders as the state of the game demanded.

Two members of that Argentina side came to Britain and experienced contrasting fortunes. Midfielder Osvaldo Ardiles, who was substituted after sixty-five minutes, brought his skills to Tottenham and became the hero of Spurs fans. Defender Alberto Tarantini took his powerful game to Birmingham with a different sequel. Birmingham were relegated from the First Division to the Second and Tarantini departed for home just before the end of the season.

Final Fantasy

May 1979: Arsenal 3, Manchester United 2

If you wanted a story about a cup final with three goals in the last four minutes and one team losing a 2–0 lead and then getting off the floor to win 3–2, you went to the fiction shelves of the local library. Or you did until the 1978–79 FA Cup final. Because that was when make-believe became barely credible reality.

An Arsenal-Manchester United confrontation at Wembley didn't thrill many people outside Manchester and North London. Arsenal had been there the year before when unexpectedly beaten 1–0 by Ipswich, and United, losers 1–0 to Southampton in 1976 and 2–1 victors over Liverpool in 1977, were making their third appearance in the final in four years.

Dreadfully predictable . . . those were the words that might have been used to describe the play before those last explosive minutes. The crescendo finish did the game a disservice by suggesting a classic. Most neutral observers found it all rather uninspired with the first eighty-six minutes, and the ninetieth, all

OPPOSITE
Arsenal captain Pat Rice hoists the FA Cup. (*Photo: Syndication International.*)

about one man, Liam Brady, who found himself in the minority when he insisted that Arsenal are not a one-man team.

There was enough talent on the field to have produced an intellectual thriller—in another place and at another time. Cup finals these days are not the ultimate that they once were. To have played in one was once the end. Now it is a passport, if you win, to European riches the following season. Arsenal fielded seven full internationals: Jennings, Rice and Nelson of Northern Ireland; O'Leary, Brady and Stapleton of the Republic of Ireland; and Brian Talbot of England. Manchester United countered with eight: Nicholl and McIlroy of Northern Ireland; McQueen, Buchan, Jordan and Macari of Scotland; Thomas, of Wales; and Coppell, of England.

United influenced most of the early sparring. It took the brilliant Brady thirteen minutes to extricate himself from the mass of population in the middle of the field, and it was hardly the long arm of coincidence that put Arsenal one up. Brady took the United defence out and Brian Talbot scored from just inside the penalty area. Talbot, a member of the Ipswich side twelve months earlier, was to go on to make history by becoming the first player to gain Cup-winners' medals with different teams in successive years.

United came back into the game and were preparing to go in at half-time and hold an inquest on why, precisely, it was that Arsenal were one up and not themselves. Then Brady struck again, and the inquest was on why are we two down. Brady went round left-back Arthur Albison, inside central defender Martin Buchan. From his foot the ball went into the net via Frank Stapleton's head. United's frustration grew as the second half aged. So did Arsenal's confidence, and with five minutes to go they took off midfielder David Price and replaced him with defender Steve Walford. But the plan to bolt the door didn't work because it was big defender Gordon McQueen who surprised everybody by coming from nowhere to sweep the ball into the Arsenal net. But Arsenal had only to defend for three minutes, so what was the problem? In two words, Sammy McIlroy. With two minutes to go, the Irish midfield man stunned one half of Wembley and transported the other into a frenzy of ecstasy. McIlroy, summoning strength from the depths of weariness, wormed his way past Walford and David O'Leary and forced the ball in off a post.

Two-two, and United, players especially, were on Cloud Nine. Unfortunately for them, Brady still had his feet on the ground. A positive run, a pass to Graham Rix, a centre to Alan Sunderland, and Arsenal had rescued themselves from the dead. Cup finals are an exercise in concentration. Brady's medal was the price United had to pay for losing theirs.

OPPOSITE ABOVE Brian Talbot scores Arsenal's winner in the 1980 FA Cup semi-final against Liverpool, a tie that went to four games before it was settled.

OPPOSITE BELOW West Ham's Geoff Pike (left) tackles Liam Brady, of Arsenal.

(*Both photos: Syndication International.*)

Well Hammered

May 1980: Arsenal 0, West Ham United 1

Soccer should have known better. West Ham had, after all, gone to Wembley twice in the previous sixteen years and won the FA Cup each time. But in 1980

they went as a Second Division club whose Cup successes had virtually cost them promotion.

Tradition, too, was against West Ham. Only six Second Division sides had ever won the Cup, four of them before the Second World War. Against the odds, Sunderland beat mighty Leeds by a solitary goal in 1973; in 1976 manager Lawrie McMenemy put unfashionable Southampton on the map with a similar win over another big club, Manchester United.

With Irish international Liam Brady parading his talents in front of a covey of coaches and agents from European clubs, England 'B' player Graham Rix, Brian Talbot seeking his third Cup-winners' medal in a row, and David Price, Arsenal were certain to have the edge in midfield.

True, West Ham had the elegant Brooking, a near-veteran of thirty-four games for England and one short of his five-hundredth for West Ham, and the exciting Alan Devonshire, whose experience of first-class football was less than two years. But they were joined in midfield by Paul Allen, who at 17 years and 256 days was the youngest player ever to appear in the FA Cup final, and the unhonoured and usually unsung Geoff Pike.

Defensively, Arsenal could hardly have been stronger. Pat Rice, Dave O'Leary, Willie Young and John Devine had aggregated sixty-six caps between them, and substitute Sammy Nelson could add forty-four more to the total. West Ham's Ray Stewart, Billy Bonds, Alvin Martin and Frank Lampard had just one international cap—Lampard's—between them.

Yet, astonishingly, West Ham triumphed. Arsenal, already fatigued, were not helped by the weather; Wembley Stadium became a cauldron of humidity. Neither were they aided by West Ham taking an early lead through a rare Brooking header. Their normal style, implanted by master coach Don Howe, was foiled. Simply, West Ham played it the Arsenal way.

It was a tactical victory for John Lyall, a manager steeped in West Ham. He withdrew Pearson into midfield and snuffed out Arsenal's major advantage by deploying five to their four.

Brooking responded with one of the best games of his notable career. Allen put a trap in the path of the weaving Brady, and the striking partnership of Stapleton and Sunderland, so effective throughout the season, was nullified. Brooking's goal proved enough.

It was the start of a catastrophic nine days for Arsenal. Defeat by West Ham ruled them out of the European Cup Winners' Cup. They lost the final of the UEFA Cup to Valencia on penalties four days later. Finally, needing to win their last match to finish third in the First Division and so qualify for a UEFA Cup place, Arsenal lost 5–0 at Middlesbrough.

Would You Believe It?

Aston Villa centre-half Chris Nicholl scored all four goals in the First Division match that resulted Leicester City 2, Villa 2 on 20 March 1976. Twice he put Leicester in front with own goals, but each time he equalized for Villa.

The Laws of the Game state that for a goal to be scored the whole of the ball must cross the goal-line between the posts (subject to there being no infringement of the Laws), but Alan Hudson was awarded a goal for Chelsea for a shot that went outside *the goal. It happened in a First Division home game against Ipswich Town on 26 September 1970. Hudson's sixty-sixth-minute shot hit the side-net, rebounded off the stanchion on to the pitch, where goalkeeper David Best collected the ball to take the goal kick. But referee Roy Capey signalled a goal, convinced (after checking with both linesmen) that the shot had entered the net. Despite frantic Ipswich protests, the goal stood and Chelsea won 2–1. Television evidence subsequently proved that Hudson's shot had hit the side netting, but although Ipswich asked for an enquiry the League dismissed their protest by pointing out that 'the Laws of the Game state that the referee's decision on all matters is final'. Even when he is proved wrong!*

Arsenal left-back Dennis Evans was the victim of one of the strangest own goals on record, in a First Division match against Blackpool at Highbury on 17 December 1955. With the game running into injury time, a whistle blew and Evans, assuming the ninety minutes were up, kicked the ball into his own net. But that whistle had been blown by someone in the crowd, not by referee F. Coultas, so it was a case of 'Evans own goal'. The result: Arsenal 4, Blackpool 1.

Clean sheet contrast: Goalkeeper Ray Clemence kept twenty-eight clean sheets in Liverpool's forty-two matches in their 1978–79 League Championship triumph. Stoke City failed to score in twenty-four of their forty-two First Division games when relegated in season 1976–77.

Seventeen goals is the record aggregate for a League fixture since the Football League was founded in 1888. The match, in December 1935, resulted Tranmere Rovers 13, Oldham Athletic 4 (Division 3 North).

Liverpool used only fourteen players in forty-two matches when they won the Football League Championship in 1965–66.

In a Mexico League match, Carlos Zompa scored four times for Atlanta against Los Apaches. As Zompa left the ground, a Los Apaches fan shot him four times in the legs—a bullet for each goal. Zompa never played again.

Chapter 8

Players I Will Never Forget

A golden thread of memories runs through the tapestry that represents my lifetime involving football. Including boyhood days, it is a span of more than thirty years. In that time I've been able to watch and meet some of the greatest players. When I'm not writing, putting together a television feature, or sweating through another coaching session, I occasionally have time to sit back, put my feet up, and think. . . .

First of all, of Bert Trautmann. Because, had there been no Bert Trautmann there might not have been Bob Wilson, professional goalkeeper. When I was a boy, growing up in Chesterfield, there was only one goalkeeper who mattered to me, the German prisoner-of-war who had arrived in Britain as a reluctant guest and had stayed to become the hero of a nation by playing on in an FA Cup final with a broken neck. Years later I found I was in good company. Big blond Bert was also the hero of Gordon Banks, seventy-three times an England goalkeeper, when he was a schoolboy in Sheffield.

Trautmann, who succeeded where Hitler failed, by conquering Britain, played his pre-war football in Germany as a centre-half. He went in goal after hurting himself in a prisoner-of-war match, and stayed there. His is a unique story in football. When in 1948 he was released from the prisoner-of-war camp just outside Manchester, he had parents to return to in Germany but decided to spend another twelve months in Britain working on a farm. By the end of the following year, he had established himself as the permanent successor to Frank Swift as Manchester City's goalkeeper and top personality.

Diving, swooping, leaping, Trautmann stayed with the Maine Road club until he was nearly forty-two, and, though national caps were obviously not for him, he was honoured with the captaincy of the Football League against the Irish League, and was Footballer of the Year in 1956. He received the trophy a few days before playing for Manchester City, beaten finalists the year before, in the FA Cup final against Birmingham City, in which match he broke his neck diving, with typical courage and agility, at a Birmingham forward's feet. The Maine Road men, who had lost the 1955 final 3–1 to Newcastle United, beat Birmingham by the same score. Ironically, the first clue Bert had that his injury was more than just a ricked neck was when Frank Swift gave him a congratulatory slap on the back at the civic reception and Bert slumped to the floor in pain. Subsequently he spent four months in a plaster cast, encasing his chest, back, neck and head. He came back and played

OPPOSITE
ABOVE, LEFT TO RIGHT Bert Trautmann, Denis Law (*photos: Colorsport*), Bobby Charlton (*Photo: Syndication International*).
CENTRE, LEFT TO RIGHT George Best, Bobby Moore (*Photos: Colorsport*), Frank McLintock (*Photo: Syndication International*).
BELOW, LEFT TO RIGHT Franz Beckenbauer, Sepp Maier, Gerd Müller (*Photos: Colorsport*).

on for another six years, a story without a parallel in the history of soccer.

In playground and schools games, he was the man I imagined I was. I believed that, if I could become half as good a goalkeeper as Bert, I would settle for that. I reckon I just about made it.

Maine Road . . . Denis Law. Yes, I know he is automatically associated with Manchester United, but Denis's first big transfer, from Huddersfield, took him to Manchester City in 1960 for the then British record fee of £55,000. Denis stayed with City until going to Turin and then on to United. Surprisingly given a transfer by Manchester United manager Tommy Docherty, he went back to Maine Road to play out his last couple of seasons.

I was lucky when playing against Denis. He did not have the successes at my expense that he achieved against other goalkeepers. And I'm glad, because, if ever a player's game reflected his own personality, it was Denis's. He bubbled so much with nervous energy that all a manager had to do was wind him up and let him go. As a striker, he was lethal in the box. His fifty-five caps were a Scottish record until overtaken by Kenny Dalglish, and his career in the national side lasted fifteen years from 1959 until the 1974 World Cup finals.

Bobby Charlton was undoubtedly the most popular of the Manchester United players as far as the occupants of the grandstands were concerned, but for those on the Stretford End terraces Denis was the King. By Johan Cruyff standards, Denis wasn't naturally gifted. Who is, it might be asked, but I make the point to emphasize how vital was Denis's own enthusiasm. Yet there was a feeling that Denis didn't take that enthusiasm into his *football* relationships with the English.

When he is among his neighbours in Manchester, Denis rates the Sassenachs as all right. Put a white shirt of England on them, and Denis bristles. That July afternoon in 1966 when the British stayed in front of their television sets to see England win the World Cup, Denis, disgusted at Scotland's failure to reach the finals, flung his golf clubs across his shoulders and marched off, ignoring the screen and England for whom his Old Trafford team-mates, Charlton and Nobby Stiles, were playing.

During his action days, Denis could never bear to watch a football match. It was play or push off. Now he admits to a great thrill from his work as a radio commentator for the BBC.

Old Trafford . . . and I can't think of Law without Charlton and George Best. Bobby had one of the hardest shots I ever faced. Like most goalkeepers of my time, I was glad that he didn't play farther upfield than he did. Those big, booming shots of his look spectacular from the stands but, from a goalkeeper's view, there was time to see them coming. Whether they could be saved or not, was a different matter. Bobby's reputation as a sportsman was exemplary, but he still knew how to look after himself. Without any doubts, his greatest assets were the accuracy with which he could play long balls and the inspiration he gave to his colleagues. As a golfer, he never had a lesson in his life. Yet, despite the limited amount of opportunities for play (United were always travelling somewhere) he got down to a thirteen handicap without any trouble.

George Best is undoubtedly a contender for being the best all-round forward produced in Britain in the last forty years. Not only could be score goals, he could make them. No other player of my time had the facility for dribbling with both feet; most good dribblers are known to have a stronger and weaker foot, and that knowledge usually gives defenders some chance. But not in George's case. We planned to contain him. Then we hoped. Not many players of his size had George's courage. It is tough in the penalty area, even for a goalkeeper. An attacker as slightly built as George might have tried to dodge the flying boots. But he never did.

Bobby Charlton . . . on to Bobby Moore, one with 106 caps and the other with 108. They went through so much together for England, the World Cups of 1962 in Chile, the 1966 triumph and Mexico in 1970. They were colleagues with a massive respect for each other, and it showed when Charlton's United met Moore's West Ham.

Moore utterly destroyed the idea that captains must make a lot of noise to get results. He led by example. He was merely brilliant in the 1966 World Cup finals, but in Mexico in 1970 he surpassed himself. Pele says he was the best defender he ever played against. Who am I to argue against that?

Bobby Moore won his last England cap in 1973. I watched him playing some six years later, and I couldn't believe that he wasn't still playing at top level. The old economy was there. He seemed to have all the time in the world. Everybody else appeared to be tearing round twice as fast. Is it purely game reading? Absolutely.

When Arsenal played against West Ham, we tried to isolate Bobby, the idea being that somebody could run at him with the ball. Bobby was a shade one-paced; he could be beaten that way. But he would see the signs, hang back behind the other central defender, and then come in to nick the loose ball away. He had a unique positional sense and he passed the ball with superb accuracy. A player with those two attributes just has to be made skipper. He was never outgoing or demonstrative. But I've seen the occasional hard look flashed at West Ham and England colleagues, and that was enough.

Captains . . . The greatest I ever played under was Frank McLintock, who led Arsenal when we won the League championship and FA Cup double in 1970–71. It will always be something of a mystery to me and, I think, to Frank himself, why he was restricted to no more than nine caps during a Scotland career that stretched, intermittently, from 1963 to 1971. Frank was the total opposite to Moore. He couldn't stop talking. Frank was so demonstrative he would be bullying and encouraging at the same time. Towards the end of his Arsenal days, when he was not playing quite as well, he had to be kept in the side because of his qualities of leadership.

He is probably the most instinctive person I have met—so depressed when we lost badly, but the first to pick himself off the floor and promise us what we'd do to the opposition when we met them next time.

Captains . . . Moore had only one rival of comparable stature: Franz Beckenbauer of Bayern Munich who, in 1974, followed Moore as a World Cup-winning captain. They were remarkably similar men, on field and off. Emperor

Franz, as the media christened him, had Moore's sense of timing and occasion. The more important the match, the cooler he became and the better he played.

The young Beckenbauer came to England for the 1966 World Cup finals as a defensive midfield player, and was given the job of marking Bobby Charlton. Though Beckenbauer did it adequately in one sense, certain England players, notably Alan Ball, were granted more space and freedom than they expected and England won. Beckenbauer lost that battle, but was to win the next war. When Bobby Charlton was substituted in the quarter-finals of the 1970 World Cup at Leon in Mexico, Beckenbauer used his freedom to haul Germany from a 2–0 deficit to a 3–2 win.

Moore and Beckenbauer got on extremely well with each other. They visited each other's homes and, had they been able to play together, I imagine Beckenbauer would have operated slightly in front of Moore. Franz would have played as the deep-lying defender of the midfield three, the sweeper in front of the back four, and the supplementary central defender all in one. I can see him surging forward towards the centre of the field looking to find somebody with that unique pass of his, a sort of off-the-outside-of-the-foot just plonking the ball in the place where it would make life so simple for a grateful team-mate. It was all done with an almost arrogant, nonchalant Bavarian flourish.

Bayern Munich . . . and Beckenbauer's two team-mates at club and national level, goalkeeper Sepp Maier and striker Gerd Müller. I know something about goalkeepers, and Sepp was different. He proved that a keeper doesn't have to go by the textbook to be good. It just helps to have Maier's talent for goalkeeping and his sense of the extrovert. Maier, whose career was ended by a car crash in the late seventies, was a goalkeeping gambler. I was not averse to taking the calculated risk, but Sepp was worse. It worked for Sepp. I'll never forget Don Howe coming back from seeing Bayern overwhelm Coventry City in a European game and saying, 'I've seen the best goalkeeper for years. His command of the air is superb. He makes up his mind very quickly and thinks nothing of careering out almost to the edge of the penalty area.'

Maier had a flair for publicity. No wonder he has done well in various business ventures. Even if Bayern's club games were so one-sided, and many of them were during the time Beckenbauer, Maier and Müller were winning European champions' medals, fans would come away remarking on Maier's shorts down to his knees, the gloves big enough to signal aircraft to their parking spot on the runway, the outsize sweater he always wore.

While all that was going on at one end, down at the other was the reason for Maier's idleness and almost permanent win-bonuses—Gerd Müller, the smallest but most successful striker in European football in the past fifteen years. Müller, one of the stockiest of men, averaged around a goal a game for the West German national side, and more than in all first-team matches for Bayern. He shot the winning goal in the 1974 World Cup final; no other scorer would have been nearly so appropriate. Without suggesting that West Germany's striking force was a one-man band, Müller was so exceptional that, had he been in the England team in Mexico in 1970, England would have been capable of winning the World Cup for a second time. Instead, Müller scored the goal that knocked England out at Leon. This goal revealed all the talents of Müller, whose business successes in Munich rival those of Beckenbauer and Maier. He was entirely off the ground and he had connected with a ball that distraught and disappointed English defenders argued should have been cleared. They were doing themselves no favours. Only Müller would have turned that situation into a goal.

He was built more thickly than Jimmy Greaves, and where Jimmy placed most of his scoring attempts, Müller's philosophy was to hit them hard. He could see space long before the ball arrived there and, having as likely as not called for it, could put it in the net before defenders realized what was going on.

Strikers ... Müller's only challenger, once Greaves had departed the international scene, was Eusebio, the Black Panther from Portugal or, to name his birthplace, Mozambique. He scored nine goals, more than any other striker, in the 1966 World Cup finals. He was a world-class player in a world-class Portugal side when his club, Benfica, were ruling the European club scene. But I often wonder how he would have fared playing for less successful sides.

I played my first game for Scotland against Portugal at Hampden Park in 1971. We won 2–1 and had a particularly useful side, but Eusebio left the proceedings at half-time. I shall always be convinced, too, that that great save of Alex Stepney's, a few minutes from the end of normal time in Benfica's 1968 European Cup final against Manchester United at Wembley, was really more of a Eusebio miss. Nevertheless, Eusebio was one of the supreme strikers. He could hit a ball so suddenly out of nothing that it was like an explosion. And he had one trick that I've seen only Pele do so often. Instead of feinting or body-swerving opponents, Eusebio would run at them, play the ball on to their legs, take the rebound off the astonished defender and run past. He did it fantastically well.

From Portugal to Holland ... and two Dutchmen who share the sad distinction of being captains of losing sides in a World Cup final, Rudi Krol in Argentina in 1978 and Johan Cruyff in West Germany in 1974. Cruyff? Well, what is there to say about the man who has almost everything? He has to be in the same class as Alfredo di Stefano and Pele.

By common consent, each of the trio was regarded at his peak as the best player in the world. Yet, though they were different types of players, they had this in common: their teams, national or club, revolved around them. Pele never captained a side. In that capacity, Cruyff was in the same category as di Stefano. Cruyff, strong-willed, had his battles with Dutch soccer authority. He was left out of the side as a youngster, punishment for a misdemeanour. In the traumatic months before Holland's players settled their pre-1974 World Cup finals demands with the Dutch soccer authorities, Cruyff was the most influential figure in the negotiations.

But no skill in negotiations round a table could match Cruyff's achievements on the field. Tall, beautifully proportioned and with enough weight to make it count, Cruyff didn't so much play in matches as run them. Sometimes, when things were going exceptionally well, he would patrol just inside the left touchline with a foot here, a push and a prod there and the occasional shout of directive to ensure that the winning position that had been built up would not be thrown away. Cruyff has a good business brain. It was also apparent on the field. When Cruyff had the game won, he refused to take undue risks. There may never have been a player whose value to his teams was so high.

Real Madrid could play without di Stefano and win. Puskas, Gento and Kubala or Del Sol, they were all match-winners. Brazil could get on without Pele, as they did, apart from one match, and win the World Cup in 1962. Garrincha and Didì, among others, were there to sort it out. But Ajax and Holland? Cruyff, whose exceptional abilities were the sighting of space seconds before any other players and then the touch to be able to deliver the precisely weighted pass into it, was a Svengali figure. With him, Holland reached a peak they will probably, as a small nation, never reach again. They were an exceptional side, in 1973 and 1974. Most of Europe called their game total football. In reality it was a system that allowed players either to defend or to attack as the situation demanded. Or as Cruyff decreed.

For the 1978 World Cup finals, Cruyff had been succeeded by Krol, who was overshadowed in Cruyff's line-up. So, were the other nine. But I played against Krol quite a lot for Arsenal and as the Dutch football after Cruyff's retirement was not quite so total, it is fair to judge Krol as a defender-captain. In that category, I'd give him a bronze medal behind Moore and Beckenbauer. He is a good passer of a ball, his technical qualities are excellent, and he has a mind of his own. If he could have had his way, I'm sure he would have pulled the Dutch team out of that World Cup final discourtesy when they were kept waiting for ten minutes or so by hosts Argentina. That was gamesmanship of the highest order. Or lowest, depending which way you look at it. By the time the Argentinians had used up a few more minutes complaining about a plaster case on the arm of Rene van der Kerkhof that had been permitted in earlier matches, Krol, I've since gathered, was ready to advocate a walk-off on the basis that the Argentinians would have had to follow them and be made to return later. I think it was then that Holland knew that they'd got another strong captain.

Recognition . . . Krol is not the only player to fail to get the acclaim he deserves. I will always feel that Sandro Mazzola, of Italy, was unlucky too. As a midfield player cum striker, Mazzola always had problems in being a contemporary of Gianni Rivera. It seems a pity they couldn't strike a partnership but it was probably yet another instance of Italian temperaments not being compatible.

Mazzola had astonishing ball skill. It was inherited from his father, who was one of the ill-fated Torino team whose aircraft, in fog, crashed into a mountainside nearing Turin. Vittorio Mazzola had always taken his boy to matches and, when he went to the dressing-rooms to change, he left the young Sandro by the touch-line to entertain the crowds with ball skills. On one of my tours of Italy with Arsenal, we went up the mountainside and laid a wreath in the monastery into which the plane crashed. After that, I followed Sandro's career perhaps more intently than most.

OPPOSITE
ABOVE, LEFT TO RIGHT
Eusebio, Johan Cruyff (*Photos: Colorsport*), Rudi Krol (*Photo: Syndication International*).
CENTRE, LEFT TO RIGHT
Sandro Mazzola, John Charles, Dino Zoff (*Photos: Colorsport*).
BELOW, LEFT TO RIGHT Peter Shilton, Ray Clemence, Pele (*Photos: Syndication International*).

Italy . . . John Charles. The big Welshman's name is still revered in Turin where he became Britain's most successful soccer export to Italy. In the years from 1957, when the Wales captain was sensationally transferred from Leeds to Juventus, John Charles, the gentle giant, was fêted wherever he went. He even became part-owner of a night-club, and made a pop record before it became the custom of personalities to exercise tonsils and tape.

On the same visit that included the pilgrimage, one of the clubs we played was allowed to include a guest player—John Charles. It was terrifying to keep goal against him. I went up with a wing and a prayer, with hardly a chance, against such a big and talented opponent, of getting to the ball. Shopping with John was quite an experience. Charlo appeared at the end of the street. There were cries of: 'Charlo is here.' And when we reached the end of the street, Charlo had acquired, as gifts, three suits and several shirts and ties. He wasn't allowed to refuse them.

Later, playing in a charity match at Fulham, I was much happier to find myself on the same side as John, then a lot heavier and not so mobile. But, to give the crowd more excitement, he played up front instead of in defence. Across came a corner, not a good one. It was too low to head, too high to volley. The young agile John would probably have turned it into a diving header. The old John simply threw out that great chest of his and the ball crashed into the inside junction of crossbar and post. He has to be the best player Wales have ever produced.

Italy . . . goalkeepers. Dino Zoff, who kept through eleven consecutive international matches before conceding a goal to little Haiti in the first match of the 1974 World Cup. A monumental record, and doesn't that make him the best goalkeeper of them all? No. I think that distinction is for my old friend Gordon Banks.

Leaving aside that most famous save of all time from Pele at Guadalajara in the 1970 World Cup, Banks's attitude was the one that started taking the concept of goalkeeping well beyond the obvious business of just saving shots. Banks, with his study of angles, and intensive practice, was an extra full-back, always a potential attacker when throwing from goal, and a splendid interpreter of the play in front of him. The car crash in which he injured an eye probably cost him four years of a magnificent playing career. The magic century of international caps may not have been beyond him. He was twenty-seven short at the time of the accident, and averaging around nine England games each season.

Goalkeepers . . . Peter Shilton and Ray Clemence. Shilton started his League career under Banks at Leicester and then moved to Stoke City and Nottingham Forest. Clemence, a legend of Liverpool, was at Scunthorpe before going to Anfield. Lucky England to have such a pair. They both show consistency. They have both attained heights of perfection. Clemence is the better at coming off his line. Shilton is supreme in the six-yards box.

Shilton's greatest achievement was convincing Leicester, so early in his career, that they could afford to transfer Banks, then an automatic England choice, to Stoke. Clemence's was going through forty-two First Division

OPPOSITE International soccer star Kevin Keegan. (*Photo: Colorsport.*)

matches in 1978–79 and conceding only sixteen goals as Liverpool, not surprisingly, won the championship.

On to Gerson, and the Brazilians of 1970. I regard them as the best side of all. Apart from the goalkeeper Felix, whose style and method were decidely hit and miss, they were the complete team. The most underrated player was Gerson in the middle of the midfield three. One argument is that there was so much talent in front of him that he could hardly fail. But Pele, Tostao, Jairzinho, Rivelino and Clodoaldo had their lives made easier by the piercing passes from Gerson. I shall never forget one he flicked right on to Pele's chest. Pele kept the ball in the air and then volleyed it past the goalkeeper. Some years later, I played in an indoor tournament with Gerson who was still striking the ball with frightening accuracy.

Everything that side did was fabulous, nothing more so than the goal Tostao made for Jairzinho against England in the qualifying round. It was a master goal, from a man who scored in every game in the finals, and was enough to beat England. But the abiding memory of that side came later in a hotel in London and confirms that by the side of Pele we are all but mere mortals. I had been in Pele's room conducting an interview, and he had autographed a copy of his book. Hovering outside as we left was a cleaning lady, dustpan and broom to the fore. She knew it was Pele's room and hoped to meet the great man. Looking at me and the book, she said: 'Are you Mr Pele?' She had no idea what Pele looked like. The name itself was enough . . . total, complete, ultimate fame.

Would You Believe It?

On 9 September 1956, a fifteen-year-old boy, Edson Arantes do Nascimento, made his debut for the crack Brazilian club Santos and scored in a 7–1 victory against Corinthians of Santo Andre. Pele, as he was to become known, scored his 1,000th goal in senior football in October 1969— a penalty against Vasco da Gama of Rio de Janeiro. That was Pele's 909th match. His most prolific year was 1959, when he scored 125 goals.

Denis Law once scored seven goals in an FA Cup tie, but failed to reach the next round. This bizarre situation occurred in January 1961, when Manchester City faced Luton in the fourth round. Heavy rain preceded the match at Luton, but Law provided ample evidence of why he was regarded as one of the greatest of all British strikers, scoring six times before the referee was forced to abandon the game in the sixty-ninth minute because the pitch was waterlogged. In the replay, Luton produced their best form and won 3–1. City's scorer? Denis Law, of course.

On 13 December 1942, in a wartime French League match between Racing Club de Lens and Aubry-Asturies in Lens, a striker named Stanis scored sixteen goals.

OPPOSITE ABOVE England's Trevor Brooking and Paul Mariner in fierce competition with Wales's Ian Walsh during the 1980 home internationals.

OPPOSITE BELOW Italy *v.* Spain, European Nations Cup, 1980.

(*Both photos: Colorsport.*)

Chapter 9

Great Postwar Managers

The hardest part of writing about the great postwar football managers is knowing when to stop. Because the game has developed into a branch of showbusiness, because the media now report its every cough and sneeze, because the quality of leadership has become vitally important, the manager's rise to prominence in the postwar era has been every bit as meteoric as that of the player. In contrast to the prewar period, when there were virtually just Herbert Chapman in England, Vittorio Pozzo in Italy and Hugo Meisl in Austria, managers of exceptional ability and unmistakable charisma have abounded since the war. So many names clamour for inclusion here, in fact, that it is necessary to draw the line somewhere. But where? What, after all, constitutes greatness?

That will always be a matter of opinion. Many, for instance, consider Arthur Rowe to have been a great manager because he introduced a new style of play, 'push-and-run', and because he laid, in the 1950s, the foundations of the Tottenham Hotspur side which, under Bill Nicholson, won the English League and Cup double in 1960–61, and subsequently much else besides. But not even Nicholson himself, creator of a team of all the talents and mentor of Greaves, Blanchflower, White and Mackay, can measure up to the stringent criteria we are compelled to use to keep this assessment within manageable proportions. Nor, for that matter, can Stan Cullis of Wolves, Joe Mercer and Malcolm Allison of the old Manchester City partnership, Don Revie of Leeds, Bela Guttmann of Benfica, Udo Lattek of Bayern Munich, Cesar Luis Menotti of Argentina '78, or even Brian Clough and Peter Taylor of today's Nottingham Forest.

Greatness, for our purposes, becomes principally a matter of honours won. The period under review is an intensely competitive one—Pozzo, for one, lamented the proliferation of competitions in the 1960s—so finishing top of the heap marks a manager out as something special. And if he can steer a team to triumph in the World Cup or European Cup, nothing less, then he is entitled to be considered one of the greats. But there is more to it than that. Greatness in a manager is also a matter of endurance, of personality, of influencing in some way the course of the game of football. No doubt many will disagree, but the names which follow, I think, satisfy more than most the requirements for greatness. They cover the world, and I have taken them in a rough chronological order.

Ironically, the first profound influence on European club football after the war was not a manager at all, but a president. Santiago Bernabeu joined Real Madrid's juniors at the age of fourteen and served the Spanish club as player, captain, secretary, scout, manager and director, as well as president. Long before he died in 1978, Bernabeu had made Real the most famous club on earth. In the summer of 1953 Bernabeu, who had then been president for ten years, made three signings which transformed Real from a good side into one that was to set unimaginably high standards for the rest of the world in the postwar era. The three players Bernabeu had the great good sense to recruit were Alfredo di Stefano, 'Paco' Gento and Hector Rial.

What followed is well known—or ought to be. Real proceeded to win the first European Cup, in 1955–56, and retained it for the next four years. By the time they overcame Eintracht Frankfurt 7–3 at Hampden Park in 1960, the most memorable European Cup final of all, they were an institution and Miguel Munoz, their former wing-half, had been appointed manager.

Munoz's contribution to the legend of Real was considerable. In the first place, he took over as manager at a time when nothing but spectacular success was acceptable from him. Secondly, he managed to handle di Stefano, who had an extremely awkward temperament to go with his divine gifts as a footballer, and he succeeded in blending Ferenc Puskas and Luis Del Sol, one of his own signings, into the team. Backed wholeheartedly by Bernabeu, Munoz also coped manfully with the eventual break-up of the first great Real side. The European Cup was not regained until 1966, but the important thing was that Bernabeu and Munoz, between them, had given everyone a glimpse of a dazzling, attacking, free-scoring heaven, and had shown others just how a football club should be run.

Football, or foreign football at least, was a delight to watch in the 1950s. In addition to Real Madrid there were the Hungarian and Brazilian national teams. Puskas, of course, had been a member of the Hungarian side which shattered all illusions about British supremacy by winning 6–3 at Wembley in November 1953 and 7–1 in Budapest six months later.

Then there was Pele. In 1958, the man who was to develop into the greatest player the world has ever seen was eighteen and making his World Cup debut for Brazil in Sweden. He did so with devastating effect, alongside those other gods of the game, Garrincha and Didì. As in the case of di Stefano, Puskas and Gento at Real, it could be argued that players of the immeasurable quality of Pele, Garrincha and Didì did not really need a manager. That belief was shown to be demonstrably false, however, by Vicente Feola, the huge plump man who steered Brazil to World Cup triumph for the first time and thereby began his country's exciting domination of the international scene.

Before 1958, Brazil had tried five times, without success, to become world champions. What Feola did that none of his predecessors had managed to do, in 1950 and 1954 certainly, was harness the extraordinary talents of his country's footballers without discouraging them from expressing themselves fully. To a large extent, it was a question of finding the most suitable playing formation for them. A disastrous tour of Europe in 1956 had shown Brazil to be incapable of making the third-back game work for them. So Feola decided to introduce the system which, though it may sound quite unexceptional now, was completely revolutionary then.

That is not entirely true: 4.2.4 was not in fact Feola's own invention. It had originated at the Flamengo club of Rio when they were coached by Fleitas Solitch, a Paraguayan. Feola, however, had the perception and courage to use it in a fiercely competitive situation. His reward was the World Cup and imitation by the rest of the world.

That same year, 1958, English football had suffered a savage blow. A crash at snowbound Munich Airport had decimated the 'Busby Babes', the second of three great Manchester United teams built by Matt (now Sir Matt) Busby and arguably still the finest club side to have emerged in the Football League since the war. How different the history of English and world football might have been if United's plane had taken off properly we shall never know. All that can be said is that without the late Duncan Edwards, Roger Byrne and Tommy Taylor, England drew with Brazil in Sweden and failed narrowly to reach the quarter-finals of that World Cup. With them . . . we can only speculate.

Busby himself was so gravely injured at Munich that, for a time, his life hung in the balance. Happily, he recovered, and his courage in returning to Old Trafford to build yet another marvellous team endeared him forever not only to the British public but also to the world at large. That third team of Busby's, a potent blend of expensive signings and youngsters brought through the productive Old Trafford nursery, typified all that he believed in and stood for in football. Bursting with naturally gifted individuals, it played the game positively and with style.

It also gave a fairytale ending to Busby's trend-setting, twenty-four-year career as United's team manager. When, in 1968, United beat Benfica 4–1 at Wembley to become the first English club to win the European Cup, Charlton, Best and company offered the final vindication of Busby's farsighted decision in 1956 to enter the competition against the wishes of the Football League.

The honour of being the first *British* side to win Europe's major club competition had gone to Jock Stein's Celtic the year before. That Stein had taken over at Parkhead only two years prior to Celtic's triumph over Helenio Herrera's Inter-Milan in Lisbon gives some measure of his ability of the manager known to Scottish football as the 'Big Man'. Winning the European Cup must have given Stein enormous satisfaction on levels other than the purely personal. One of his great ambitions, for instance, has always been to rid Scottish football of its crippling parochialism, and he has pursued it harder than ever since he became manager of Scotland in 1978.

No one is more dedicated to the job, or to football, than Stein. His thirst for knowledge and his willingness to learn from others make distance no object when there is an informative match to be seen. At Celtic his punishing work schedule finally landed him in the coronary ward of Glasgow Infirmary. That was three years after the club, Scottish champions ten times during his thirteen-year reign, had proved their enduring quality by reaching the final of the

OPPOSITE ABOVE Vicente Feola, the former manager of Brazil. (*Photo: Syndication International.*)

OPPOSITE BELOW LEFT Sir Matt Busby and the European Champions' Cup. (*Photo: Colorsport.*)

OPPOSITE BELOW RIGHT Jock Stein of Celtic and the Scottish FA Cup. (*Photo: Syndication International.*)

European Cup for the second time. In 1970, however, Celtic were beaten 2–1 by the Dutch champions, Feyenoord. When, in 1972, Celtic also reached the semi-finals of the competition, no other club in Britain had a record to compare with theirs. It showed what can be achieved by a deep knowledge of the game, hard work, an astonishing memory and an overriding humanity and humility.

Helenio Herrera's approach to management was altogether different from Stein's. Chronically flamboyant, he believed implicitly in the value of self-induced motivation. At Inter, where his considerable reputation was made, the players were encouraged to dance about, shouting slogans, in all kinds of hysterical pre-match rituals. On leaving Inter in 1962, a relieved Gerry Hitchens, the former England centre-forward, said it was like being demobbed from the Army. Nevertheless, during the eight years under Herrera, Inter won the Italian Championship twice, the European Cup twice and the World Club Championship twice. When they finally parted company in 1968, the year after Inter had lost to Celtic in Lisbon, Herrera was reported to be earning more than £50,000 a year. By the time Roma sacked him in 1971 his salary had shot up to an estimated £140,000, a staggering sum even now.

In addition to being the highest-paid manager of his era, Herrera was one of the most influential. Dave Sexton, who has managed Chelsea, Queens Park Rangers and Manchester United, is one of the many who have sat at the feet of the high priest of *catenaccio* defence and the sweeping counterattack.

Those tried and trusted tactics profited Inter little, though, when they went to Anfield in 1965 for the first leg of a European Cup semi-final. Bill Shankly's resurgent Liverpool won 3–1, and it might easily have been a rout. The second leg was a completely different matter, Inter winning 3–0 in extremely suspicious circumstances. What really counted, though, was that Liverpool had been launched on what was to become a European career of amazing continuity considering the fierce competition to represent the English First Division.

Typically, Shankly built at Liverpool a system that would endure. Its basic ingredients were commonsense, selflessness, determination, dedication and teamwork. Look at any Liverpool team now, twenty years after Shankly took over at Anfield, and you will see that the recipe for success remains in principle unaltered. If there has been any change at all it is one of refinement. Bob Paisley, Shankly's faithful lieutenant for so long, polished his inheritance so brightly that, by winning the European Cup twice in succession, Liverpool have surpassed in the last six years their many notable achievements during Shankly's fourteen years in charge.

Even so, much of the credit for Liverpool's towering reputation in Europe must go to the gritty little Scot who dragged them out of the Second Division and up to the heights. Under Shankly, the inspired motivator, Liverpool began to set the standards of play which Ron Greenwood, the England manager, regards gratefully now as the foundation of his own team.

Only twice have Liverpool been truly outplayed by foreign opponents. Red Star Belgrade have done it and so have Ajax Amsterdam, more traumatically. In the European Cup of 1966–67, Ajax shook Liverpool rigid by winning 5–1 in

OPPOSITE, MAIN PICTURE Bill Shankly of Liverpool and the UEFA Cup.

OPPOSITE, INSET Helenio Herrera with his Inter-Milan players.

(*Both photos: Syndication International.*)

Amsterdam and then drawing 2–2 at Anfield despite all Shankly's psychological warfare. A certain up-and-coming youngster called Johan Cruyff was the most obvious cause of the damage, but it soon became evident that Ajax had also discovered a manager of unusual ability when they appointed Rinus Michels to succeed Vic Buckingham, the much travelled Englishman, in 1965.

Michels's strict discipline was not always popular with his players, but the success he achieved quickly won them over. Three Dutch titles in a row were followed, in 1969, by the club's first appearance in the final of the European Cup. Ajax were overwhelmed 4–1 by AC Milan on that occasion, but consolation was not long delayed. Two years later Ajax overcame their nerves and Panathanaikos at Wembley to record what was to be the first of three successive victories in the European Cup final.

If Michels sowed the seed of Ajax's pre-eminence and of Holland's major contribution to the development of the game, 'total football', it was a then obscure Romanian, Stefan Kovacs, who brought the plant to full flower in 1972 and 1973. Taking over from Michels, who left to manage Barcelona immediately after Ajax's first European Cup triumph, Kovacs adopted a less authoritarian approach than his predecessor, encouraged the attacking *catenaccio* defence and gave full reign to the talents of Cruyff, Keizer, Neeskens and Hulshoff.

It was to Michels that Holland turned when they qualified for the finals of the 1974 World Cup. He kept the spirit of 'total football' alive to such an extent that the Dutch dazzled the world with their fluidity on the way to disappointing defeat in the final by West Germany, the hosts.

That victory, by two goals to one, established beyond doubt that Helmut Schoen of West Germany was one of the great managers of his time. Even though West Germany had finished second in the 1966 World Cup and third in 1970 under Schoen, there were still critics of his policies. A tall, courteous and kindly man, Schoen was not a strict disciplinarian like his predecessor Sepp Herberger, who had guided West Germany to an unexpected World Cup triumph in 1954. Indeed, he was criticized, particularly in 1974, for allowing senior players such as Beckenbauer to dictate tactics.

The secret of Schoen's more relaxed approach to running the national side was that he could lead and guide dedicated professionals without regimenting them. Herberger's methods were there to be copied, because Schoen had been his assistant from 1956 until he took over full control in 1964, but the newcomer elected to tackle the job in his own quiet way.

Schoen's great adversary was, of course, Sir Alf Ramsey. Ramsey, then plain Alf, won the first round in their battle of wits by discovering a team capable of overcoming almost bottomless West German resilience in the 1966 World Cup final at Wembley. When they confronted each other again, in the quarter-finals of the 1970 World Cup and in the quarter-finals of the European Championship in 1972 (which West Germany went on to win), it was Schoen who came out on top. In Mexico he exploited Ramsey's excusable misuse of substitutes and, two years later, he exposed the negativity into which the England manager had lapsed by then.

Sir Alf Ramsey and Helmut Schoen after the World Cup game at Leon, Mexico, 1970, in which West Germany beat England 3–2. (*Photo: Syndication International.*)

Nevertheless, Ramsey remains a prominent outline on the landscape of international football. Above all, he gave back to England, the original masters of the game, a belief in themselves that had been steadily eroded by the way former pupils elsewhere in the world had not only absorbed their lessons but improved upon them. To do that, Ramsey had to be an innovator. What he devised, in the four years between becoming manager of England and winning the World Cup for the first and only time in the history of English football, was the concept of playing without the orthodox wingers on whom English clubs had relied traditionally. Ramsey it was who gave the seal of approval first to the 4.3.3 formation and then, when his innate caution asserted itself even more, 4.4.2. Those who were in Leon that fateful day back in 1970, when a 2–0 World Cup lead ended in 3–2 defeat, will tell you, though, that England's performance before they were overtaken by West Germany was an unforgettable example of controlled, attacking football.

Most important of all, perhaps, Ramsey ended the selection of the England team by committee. He agreed to take over as England manager, after a startlingly successful eight years at Ipswich, only on condition that he be allowed full autonomy. And managers great or small have reaped the benefit of that historic stand.

Would You Believe It?
In 1960–61 Chesterfield met Doncaster Rovers in the first round of the FA Cup and Oldham Athletic in the second round. Chesterfield's opponents in the first two rounds of the Cup the following season? Doncaster and Oldham.

Chapter 10

World Soccer Stars

Osvaldo Ardiles

In Argentina he is known as 'the Panther'. At Tottenham he is recognized simply as one of the best midfield schemers in the world. Yet the climb to acceptance in Britain has not been easy, especially for a man riding the success of his country's World Cup triumph.

Shortly after that victory in Buenos Aires in the summer of 1978, Keith Burkinshaw, the Tottenham manager, completed what some described as the transfer deal of the century by signing Ardiles and Ricardo Villa in a joint deal valued at £700,000. At the time, experts considered that Villa's direct centre-forward style would be better suited to British soccer than Ardiles's slinky, cultured ball-play. How wrong they were! Villa struggled to maintain a senior place, making twenty-six League appearances plus six as substitute, whereas his little Latin team-mate took the First Division by storm. The intelligent running and incredible ball skills of Ardiles quickly made him a huge box office attraction on whichever English ground he played.

Ardiles has been accustomed to the adulation of crowds since the days when he helped his first professional club, Instituto, to win the Cordoba League title in 1972. Shortly afterwards he joined Huracan in the Argentinian Metropolitan League, the country's premier competition, where he won two national Championships. Next came the supreme prize: victory in the 1978 World Cup, and Ardiles understandably looked to Europe to extend his footballing triumphs.

In only his fourth game for Spurs, he must have wondered if he had made a mistake in moving from his homeland. Spurs went to Anfield and were thrashed 7–0 by Liverpool, a defeat which meant they dropped to twenty-first position. Poor results at home and away followed, and almost inevitably, people began to cast doubts about the South America ability to fit into the English League scene. They argued that their temperament and style of play was not suitable to the demanding needs of a long British season.

Yet slowly but surely Spurs' playing results improved, and Ardiles soon showed his critics how well he had adjusted. Although Villa at first failed to adapt, 'Ossie' produced a series of stunning displays. Even the usually phlegmatic Bob Paisley, manager of Liverpool, described him as 'a world class performer any club would love to have'.

Photo: Syndication International.

In Ardiles's first season at Tottenham, Arsenal won the North London derby at White Hart Lane by five goals to nothing. That game was the Argentinian's first taste of the white-hot rivalry between the two clubs, and it took place just two days before Christmas Day 1978. On Christmas morning Ardiles went next door and told his neighbour with a wry smile, 'You've ruined my Christmas.' The neighbour? Alan Sunderland, Arsenal's striker who had scored a hat-trick in that 'derby' clash.

On field Ardiles, who is loyal by nature, shows an immaculate concentration and, probably most important of all, an instinctive ability to adapt to any situation including some glutinous British pitches. Away from soccer he is an articulate man, who is eager to learn about his adopted homeland. Indeed, he takes regular English lessons and is training to become a lawyer. British crowds have taken him to their hearts. There can be no greater tribute to this unassuming player who has so impressively met and mastered the challenge of the world's most demanding League.

Roberto Bettega

A swift, low cross from the left wing by Benetti glided across the face of the England goalmouth. Before the danger could be averted, a darting header from the flying Roberto Bettega had literally finished England's 1978 World Cup hopes.

Before that hot day in Rome, when Italy beat England in group II of the World Cup qualifying competition, the name of Bettega may have meant little to the soccer world. Subsequently, he has become one of the game's most exciting goalscorers. Few, however, knew the story of despair that almost ended his career before it had had a chance to prosper.

Bettega joined Juventus from school, and in 1968 signed professional terms. But he saw little chance of finding a first-team place, and when an opportunity arose to spend a year with Second Division Varese he quickly accepted. Varese promptly gained promotion, and Bettega, playing on the left side of the attack, finished the season as their top scorer with thirteen goals in thirty games.

His success gave Juventus a sharp reminder that they had a readymade striker for first-team action. He made an immediate impact on his debut for them in October 1970, once again ending the season as top scorer. This success brought international recognition with appearances for both the Under-twenty-three and Under-twenty-one sides.

He was the Golden Boy of Juventus, and the following season he began as everybody had hoped, scoring ten goals in his first fourteen games. But then tragedy struck. He contracted a lung infection that not only finished his season, but threatened to end his career. The young Bettega spent many anxious days in hospital under medical care. Not surprisingly he began to consider the possibility of quitting the game. But with the encouragement of Juventus chairman Giampiero Boniperti he resumed training, and all through the summer of 1972 he worked desperately at regaining football fitness.

Photo: Syndication International.

Meanwhile, Juventus had won the League Championship so that, when the new season began, Bettega was not an immediate choice. Indeed he had to wait until January 1973. Could he find the flair—the natural skill and brilliant heading which had made Italians liken him to the giant Welsh star John Charles?

The answer came swiftly enough. Bettega began scoring again and eventually the Italian manager Enzo Bearzot recognized his talent. He was chosen for the senior international side in June 1975 against Finland in Helsinki. Italy won that match 1–0 and Bettega's reputation was complete. Such courage and perseverance deserved their reward and Roberto Bettega has now assured himself a place among the great strikers of European soccer.

Kenny Dalglish

When Kevin Keegan moved from Liverpool in July 1977 to face—and conquer—fresh challenges in West Germany, the gap he left in the Merseyside attack seemed impossible to fill, at least from within Britain.

Many felt that Liverpool would have to go shopping in a continental football market for the replacement. They were wrong. For in Kenny Dalglish from Celtic the Merseyside club found a footballer with deadly pace, fine balance, an abundance of skill, and the ability to shoot with either foot. The cost was a mere £440,000, a bargain purchase by today's prices, and Dalglish quickly replaced Keegan in the hearts of the fanatical 'Koppites'.

With Celtic, his only other club, he scored a staggering 112 goals in only 204 League games, and those figures exclude the wealth of Scottish Cup and League Cup goals he scored during the Parkhead club's rampage through the honours north of the border.

When Dalglish was at Celtic, one of his best friends both on and off the field was Sandy Jardine of Glasgow Rangers. The two players went into business together, and made a record called 'Each Saturday', which surprisingly was all about football! But Dalglish's hopes for massive sales were not realized: 'I don't think anyone bought it. Still, one day Arthur Negus might get round to valuing it', he jokes.

His contribution to Liverpool's success has been phenomenal. In his first season at Anfield (1977–78) he scored the winning goal of their first League game against Middlesbrough. He proceeded to score in the next two games, and after six League games had been completed he had scored five goals. Was it just a flash in the pan? Dalglish quickly shattered that thought. He just kept on scoring and by the end of the season his tally had reached thirty. That thirtieth goal will be remembered for some time. Liverpool had reached the European Cup final for the second successive year, and faced the Belgian champions Bruges before a crowd of 92,000 at Wembley Stadium.

The Belgians immediately threw up a tight defensive wall and appeared concerned only with forcing a draw. But, after an hour of football almost totally dominated by Liverpool, a searing pass from Terry McDermott was controlled by Dalglish who beat the off-side trap and put Liverpool into the history books as the first British club to win the trophy for a second time.

The following season he scored a further twenty-five goals as Liverpool won the League Championship for the eleventh time.

Despite Scotland's poor record in the past two World Cups, this small but sturdily built Glaswegian has continued to appear for his country and has broken the Scottish appearance record. In addition to his inherent ball-playing skills, he has shown astonishing consistency and staying power. In November 1979 he recorded his 100th consecutive League appearance for Liverpool. Everywhere he is a marked man, yet he still rides tackles with supreme judgement, and remains one of the game's most ruthless finishers.

BELOW LEFT Liverpool's Kenny Dalglish is marked by Mark Lawrenson of Brighton.

BELOW RIGHT Rudi Krol in a duel with Asa Hartford.

(*Both photos: Syndication International.*)

Rudi Krol

Only a handful of footballers attain world stardom. Most are strikers. For them scoring goals provides the ultimate glamour. Rarely does another position gain the same sort of acclaim. Yet Rudi Krol, as a defender, has achieved a status previously enjoyed by the German, Franz Beckenbauer.

Rudi Krol, sweeper *extraordinaire* for Ajax and Holland, and Dutch captain in the 1978 World Cup finals, has attracted so much praise that it is difficult to believe he is not a free-scoring forward. He spent ten years at the top with Ajax of Amsterdam before joining Vancouver in the North American Soccer League.

In 1969–70, his first season with Ajax, he was ever-present, but after twenty-five games of the following season he broke a leg, and was prevented from appearing in the 1971 European Cup final against Panathanaikos at Wembley. But the great Ajax of the early seventies provided him with two further opportunities to help win the most prestigious of club competitions, in 1972 and 1973. Alongside Cruyff and Neeskens at club level, Krol performed

with such flair and consistency that it was hard to conceive him producing any greater performances. Nevertheless, he was a dominating personality in Holland's two World Cup finals. At Munich in 1974 he showed sufficient initiative and skill to participate in the heart of attacking movements.

Although Holland provided the most thoughtful, attacking and fresh football of the tournament, they came face to face with the host nation, West Germany, in the final—and lost.

Sadly for Krol and the Dutch, it was to prove the same story in the following finals in Argentina in 1978. Despite showing superior skills in an unfamiliar climate, Holland were unable to surpass the Argentinians, though no fault could be laid at Krol's feet. He was almost infallible at the centre of Holland's defence.

Unfortunately for Ajax, Krol decided to follow the American trail in the summer of 1980, when he joined Vancouver Whitecaps. But one thing is certain: should Holland call on the brilliant Dutchman, Krol will cross the Atlantic without the slightest hesitation to perform for his country the only way he knows how—with world-class style.

Hans Krankl

Born in Vienna, Hans Krankl has scored consistently for Rapid Vienna, Barcelona and Austria. Yet he could have been born in Manchester, Liverpool or any other birthplace of the traditional English centre-forward, for he possesses the typical aggression of such great English goal-scorers as Dixie Dean, Ted Drake, Tommy Lawton, Nat Lofthouse, Malcolm Macdonald, Geoff Hurst and company. His goal-scoring feats speak for themselves.

Krankl's best season to date came in 1977–78 when he scored forty-one League goals in only thirty-four games for Rapid Vienna to win an award made by a firm of football manufacturers. His consistency in front of goal reached a peak during the Argentinian World Cup finals when he scored four goals.

His footballing talents first emerged as a nine-year-old with Vienna junior club Strassenbahn. When age permitted he was accepted into the Rapid Vienna Youth team and, by the time he was eighteen, it was clear he would soon be ready for the big time, but a year's loan with a lesser club was thought desirable for experience. He went to WAC, and after a year he returned to Rapid to be offered a professional contract. But all the time he was scoring goals he had his eyes firmly set on another career—as a professional motor racing driver. Indeed, he held a part-time job as a car mechanic before being offered terms in Vienna. The fame he gained from hitting the target time after time allowed him to establish a friendship with Nicki Lauda, a man whom he had idolized as a youngster. Fortunately for soccer enthusiasts, his loyalties kept him on the football pitch rather than the race track.

His brilliant form for Rapid gained many admirers, including Spanish giants Barcelona, who had been watching him for some time. In 1977 they had been put off by the £280,000 price-tag. But a brilliant World Cup performance

OPPOSITE Hans Krankl.
(*Photo: Bob Thomas.*)

boosted their interest, and they were not frightened away this time, even by an increased asking price of £475,000.

Such is his fame that, though an innocent party, he was once mentioned during a divorce case. An aggrieved husband told the court that his wife so idolized Krankl as a footballer that she had papered the entire house with posters and photographs of him!

Robbie Rensenbrink

When Johan Cruyff declared he was leaving Holland for the financial security of America, many likened it to pulling the bung from a boat, with the Dutch national team as the sinking ship. Happily, in Robbie Rensenbrink they found a man with the ability not only to replace Cruyff, but also to add a new dimension to Dutch football.

Rensenbrink had already played with distinction for the Belgian champions Anderlecht, after joining them in 1970 from FC Bruges. But in his performances for Holland he had not always produced the style and class that he possessed. He appeared inhibited by Cruyff's presence. Nevertheless, during the 1974 World Cup finals, he grew in international stature and became a national hero alongside Cruyff as Holland played their way to the final, where they were beaten by West Germany. Four years later, with Cruyff gone, Rensenbrink was the inspiration behind Holland's marvellous controlled performances that once again took them to the final, this time to lose to the host country, Argentina.

But those who knew the Dutchman were not surprised at the rave notices he received during that summer of 1978. He had, after all, taken part in three successive European Cup Winners' Cup finals for Anderlecht. The first in 1976 pitted the Belgian team against the English FA Cup holders, West Ham United. Unfortunately for West Ham, the destination of the final—Brussels—was chosen before the 1975–76 competition began and was therefore literally a home game for Anderlecht. Despite a concentrated effort by the Londoners, Anderlecht won an exciting final 4–2, Rensenbrink scoring two of the goals. They returned to the final as holders, against the West Germans SV Hamburg, but gave a below-par performance and lost the Cup 2–0. But they regained the trophy in 1978 in devastating style.

The final, in Paris, presented Rensenbrink with an opportunity to show the world his prowess before the Argentinian World Cup finals. He rose to the occasion in the manner of a proven star as Anderlecht beat Austria WAC 4–0, Rensenbrink scoring two of the winners' goals.

His virtues are many. He possesses an experience gained over the best part of ten years with Holland, plus many European campaigns with Bruges and Anderlecht. He has style, grace, power and the physique to match.

Rensenbrink demonstrated the multiplicity of his gifts against Austria WAC in the 1978 European Cup Winners' Cup final. The Austrian defenders attempted to stop him by every means they knew; they hustled and harried him, sandwiched him and tried their best to prevent him from seeing goal.

OPPOSITE Ardiles and Rensenbrink, two of the world's most outstanding players (Argentina *v.* Holland, World Cup, 1978). (*Photo: Colorsport.*)

Rensenbrink kept his cool and provided the best answer—with his deft left foot.

Paolo Rossi

To many soccer critics, Paolo Rossi is the perfect striker. He combines a litheness with skills and vision beyond his years. In his native Italy he has been labelled with an unbelievable £3 million price-tag.

Rossi emerged during the Argentian World Cup finals in 1978. Before the competition, few had heard of the slim twenty-one-year-old Tuscan. By the end of it few people doubted that he was one of the best attacking players in the world. His rise to the fore of Italian and world soccer has a Hans Andersen fairy tale quality about it.

Rossi began his playing career with Cattolica Virtus, who are virtually the nursery for the Italian giants Juventus. Once he reached the age of sixteen, it was accepted that he would be promoted to the Juventus Youth sides. But an agonizing list of injuries prevented him from achieving his number one aim—a place in the Juventus team. He underwent three cartilage operations, and also broke a wrist. When he reached fitness again it was decided he should be loaned to Third Division side Como in the hope that he could gain some valuable experience.

After a handful of appearances for Como during an eight-month spell, he was loaned by Juventus to Lanerossi Vicenza who, realizing they had acquired a bargain deal, promptly bought a half share in him, as Italian soccer rules permit.

OPPOSITE ABOVE Spain *v.* Brazil, World Cup, 1978. (*Photo: Syndication International.*)

OPPOSITE BELOW Laurie Cunningham, one of the increasing band of English soccer stars whose attachment to a great continental club has proved mutually beneficial. (*Photo: Colorsport.*)

BELOW LEFT Holland's Robbie Rensenbrink tries to find a way past Scotland's defender Donachie.

BELOW RIGHT Rossi of Italy is chased by Dietz of Germany.

(*Both photos: Syndication International.*)

At Lanerossi, he was positioned on the right wing, very wide and often in deep-lying positions. As he was chosen in this position for the Italian Youth team, one could understand his perplexity when he was told by Lanerossi that he would be switched to centre-forward. He accepted the change and soon began scoring goals again. Indeed, he ended the first season with twenty-one goals and Lanerossi were promoted to the Italian First Division.

Despite his successes Juventus failed to show any interest, so it was with Lanerossi that he continued to score. He produced another twenty-four goals, but by this time Lanerossi needed capital and it was decided to auction Rossi. To the surprise of everybody in Italy, Lanerossi's president Signor Farina personally took over the half share for a staggering 2.5 billion liras, worth £1½ million at the rate of exchange then current.

When the 1978–79 season ended, Lanerossi were relegated, and Farina was forced to put his half share in Rossi up for sale. But all the big clubs came to an agreement not to pay a price that Juventus's half share took to £3,000,000.

So when Rossi threatened to retire Signor Farina made another remarkable move with Juventus's permission: he hired him to Perugia at the beginning of the 1979–80 season for just £600,000 for two years.

But in May 1980 Rossi was banned from football for three years—reduced to two on appeal—by the Italian Football Federation, as one of the players involved in alleged match-fixing. It meant his absence from the European Championship the following month—and how host country Italy, with only two goals in four games before their own fans, missed him.

Allan Simonsen

He stands 5 ft 6 in and weighs a little under 9 stone. But Allan Simonsen is no weakling on the football field. The diminutive Dane has confounded some of the game's finest defenders with his pace and intelligent running and in 1977 he was European 'Player of the Year'.

He began his footballing career with Vejle, a small club situated some 150 miles from Copenhagen. Until 1977 Danish football was still amateur, which gave Simonsen the opportunity to represent his nation in the 1972 Olympics in Munich. He gave some fine performances, which attracted the attention of Borussia Moenchengladbach. With the recommendation of fellow Dane, Henning Jensen, a former Borussia player who later went to Real Madrid, the German club decided to take him on their staff, although they wondered whether his apparently delicate physique would stand up to the strain and stresses of the Bundesliga. Simonsen quickly dispelled their qualms and became an important part of the Borussia attack. Indeed, he was a major reason for their three League title successes from 1975 to 1977.

In 1975 Borussia reached the final of the UEFA Cup, and Simonsen scored two of the five goals in the second-leg victory over Twente Enschede. So to 1977 and the ultimate honour a week after his twenty-fifth birthday: Simonsen, against all the odds, had risen from the relative unknown backwaters of Danish amateur football to become the European Footballer of the Year.

OPPOSITE Allan Simonsen. (*Photo: Colorsport*).

In addition to his part in the hat-trick of League championships, the busy little Dane had frightened more than a handful of Liverpudlians in May 1977 when he scored a stunning goal that put Borussia on level terms in the final of the European Cup. Liverpool went on to win 3–1, but Simonsen's contribution to a memorable game was enormous.

For much of that 1977 season, with Jupp Heynckes injured, Simonsen was virtually a one-man forward line for Borussia, teasing opposing defenders with his skills on the ball and sustaining his class throughout the season.

Had Simonsen been born in Manchester, Munich or Amsterdam, he would have a mantlepiece crowded with international trophies. Yet for all that he remains one of the world's deadliest strikers.

Would You Believe It?

Transfers have been conducted in some strange places, few less likely than the meeting point when England Under-twenty-one goalkeeper Alan Stevenson moved from Chesterfield to Burnley in a £50,000 deal in January 1972. The parties concerned met in a cafe on the M1, and the actual signing took place over sandwiches and coffee.

Real Madrid, the Spanish club who won the European Champions' Cup in each of the first five years in which it was played, were unbeaten in home League matches from February 1957, when they lost 3–2 to Atletico Madrid, to March 1965, when Atletico, again, beat them 1–0. During this time they played 122 matches, winning 114 and drawing eight. Tottenham Hotspur began the 1960–61 season, in which they won the Football League Championship and FA Cup 'double', with eleven consecutive victories. Leeds United went twenty-nine games at the beginning of season 1973–74 before losing 3–2 at Stoke, after leading by two goals. It was the longest undefeated run from the start of a Football League season.

The oldest footballer to play in the Football League was New Brighton manager Neil McBain. When his team arrived two men short at Hartlepool on 15 March 1947, he played himself in goal, at the age of fifty-two years and four months.

A soft-drink can cost Borussia Moenchengladbach their place in the European Cup in the 1971–2 season. The can was thrown at Roberto Boninsegna of Internazionale Milan during the first leg of a second-round match. Borussia played brilliantly and won 7–1, but they were fined £1,000, banned from playing European matches at home and made to replay the game on a neutral ground, in Berlin. The Italians, 4–2 ahead from their home leg, forced a 0–0 draw, and Borussia were out.

Chapter 11

Black is Beautiful

Only in comparatively recent years have coloured footballers begun to make an impact on the game in Europe. The frequently forecast Black Revolution in England was a long time coming, but now it is normal to see at least one coloured player in most English matches.

The skills and stylish grace of a player such as Pele are rarely found in a white man. Do racial differences affect sporting performances? Black men are more naturally equipped to function in a hot climate. Africans lose heat rapidly, and tend to have slimmer frames and shorter bodies than white men. A greater proportion of their weight is taken up by muscles and tendons in the arms and legs, an important factor in speed and agility.

Coloured players have a natural aptitude. They are lissom athletes, with control, touch and pace. It is not thought strange that tall men make the best basketball players, or small men the best jockeys. Yet there is no uniformity of view over the ideal shape for a footballer. England manager Ron Greenwood says: 'I like to think the balance that coloured boys possess is almost inherent in them. It is amazing the way they can adjust their bodies to any situation which controlling a ball demands. This is something that the Nordic races haven't got.'

Bertie Mee, former Arsenal manager and a professional physiotherapist, does not agree. 'There are various ethnic theories', he says, 'but I cannot accept there are differences. It is true that members of certain coloured communities have a joint mobility greater than that of Europeans. But this is not an inherent factor; it is a result of the coloured people's way of life.'

Whatever the physical differences, coloured players have one major hurdle to overcome, the belief that when the going gets tough they wilt. It is no more so in the black man than the white. Soccer, to West Indies people in Britain, has come to mean as much as their favourite cricket, and to them as well as others ambition was fired because football offered so much.

Brendon Batson, a Grenadian who began with Arsenal and moved on to Cambridge United and West Bromwich Albion, says: 'I can make a better living at football than anything else. And from the social point of view I will be more readily accepted.'

Cyrille Regis, born in French Guyana, plays with Batson at West Bromwich. He could have played for France, but he is glad he won honours for England. He says: 'In the coloured areas of London and Birmingham, lots of black kids come up to me and say: "Well done, Cyrille—keep it going." All of them are so eager for me to do well that I can never escape the responsibilities I feel for them. You realize that your progress could help a whole lot of people on the way up. All sorts of rubbish has been spoken about black players not having enough heart or courage for the game. I don't think anyone believes that any more, now that they've seen a few of us do so well.'

Few have done better than Laurie Cunningham, who left Batson and Regis at West Bromwich and moved to Real Madrid. Cunningham is in some ways defiantly black. A winger with superb skills, control and acceleration, he, like Regis, knew that if he made the breakthrough to become the first really successful black footballer in England he would light a torch for thousands of immigrant youngsters.

The first coloured man to play for England's senior team was right-back Vivian Anderson, Nottingham born, who at the age of twenty-two and after seven notable performances for the England 'B' team, faced Czechoslovakia at Wembley in November 1978. Anderson had been rejected as a sixteen-year-old by Manchester United. Their loss was Forest's gain. A defender who loves to dash down the wing, he grew in self-confidence and stature. His England debut was an unqualified success.

There is a saying that black fighters are best because they are hungry fighters. A coloured boy, with perhaps the experience of a tough background to draw on, has more incentive to make the grade than his white counterpart. Pele, who was born into a poor Brazilian Negro family, had a simple option: the chance of playing football or becoming a shoeblack.

Racism may be officially frowned on, but it remains in some societies today. For a Negro boy it is easier to be accepted if he chooses sport, stage or medicine. As one American athlete said: 'A white kid tries to become President of the United States, a black kid tries to become Jesse Owens.'

The emergence of black African countries as international soccer nations is still only in its infant stage. Their first representatives in the World Cup finals were Zaïre, who achieved that distinction in 1974. Their efforts captured the sympathy of the West German crowds. In their first match, they lost to Scotland by only 2–0. But a few days later they were overwhelmed 9–0 by Yugoslavia, and were then beaten by Brazil 3–0. Yet it is certain an African side will eventually become a world power, as soon, that is, as their natural skills are harnessed to team organization and determination.

Morocco took part in the 1970 World Cup finals and won a point off Bulgaria. The preliminary rounds of the African group of nations tournament now includes teams from Tunisia and Sudan in the north, and Kenya, Mauritius, Tanzania, Togo and Zaïre in other parts of the continent. What Zaïre have accomplished, nations such as Kenya, Nigeria and Ghana are seeking to emulate.

The most successful coloured footballer in the game's history has been Pele, a world-class player right from his first World Cup in 1958 in Sweden, when he was the seventeen-year-old prodigy of a team bursting with top-class skills. Pele proved himself to be as exciting as any of them, scoring two goals in Brazil's 5–2 win in the final against Sweden.

At the heart of Pele's game was a pursuit of the impossible. He also continually strove to improve his football, a lesson for the many thousands less talented than himself. In scoring around 1,200 goals and creating everlasting memories, he dominated world football as no man had done before. When he retired from Brazil and Santos, his club side, he joined New York Cosmos for a razzmatazz final fling that did much to establish soccer in the United States. As a person, he retained his modesty always. Pele will be remembered as a footballer with a grace and style that made him a player apart.

The footballer who was Europe's answer to Pele was Eusebio da Silva Ferreira, who found fame with Benfica and Portugal. Born to poverty in Mozambique, Eusebio made a sensational start, scoring a hat-trick against Juventus at the age of seventeen. In Britain, he is best remembered for his magnificent performances for Portugal in the 1966 World Cup finals in England. When Portugal lost their semi-final against England 2–1, Eusebio left the field in tears, yet with nine goals, the distinction of being leading scorer in the competition—and a £1,000 cheque for his efforts. 'The Black Panther' had left his mark.

Though never matching Pele's earnings, Eusebio lived well. His skills ensured that. They were superb control, marvellous acceleration, and explosive finishing. Like Pele, he was forced to live with some ferocious tackling.

Flying winger Laurie Cunningham has twice entered the record books as Britain's costliest black footballer, first when he moved from Orient to West Bromwich for £110,000 in March 1977, and then when in June 1979 he left The Hawthorns to go into European football with Real Madrid after being capped by England. The fee £950,000. He was soon popular with Spanish crowds.

Others seem destined to attract offers from abroad. Some of the growing nucleus of coloured players currently established in British football are listed below.

Viv Anderson

Right-back Viv Anderson became the first coloured player to represent the senior England side in November 1978, against Czechoslovakia.

Anderson joined Forest in 1975, having been rejected two years previously by Manchester United. Under the guidance of manager Brian Clough and assistant Peter Taylor, he never looked back. His forthright tackling and turn of pace are features of his play, and he is known by team-mates as 'the Extension' because of his long legs.

After helping Forest to promotion in 1977, he played a major part in their Championship and League Cup double the following year. In 1979 and 1980 he gained European Cup Winners' medals, when Forest beat first Malmö and then SV Hamburg, as well as further League Cup honours. His elevation to the full England team became certain after fine displays during the 'B' team tour of Malaysia, New Zealand and Singapore, in May and June 1978.

Brendon Batson *(West Bromwich Albion)*

Albion's rise as one of the most attractive teams in the First Division in recent years has been attributed largely to their two coloured strikers, Laurie Cunningham, now with Real Madrid, and Cyrille Regis. But an equally important figure has been Brendon Batson, their Grenada-born full-back. His calm yet competitive displays in defence, coupled with an ability to increase the width of the attack with right-flank overlaps, have made him one of the most effective full-backs in England.

Batson had a brief spell with Arsenal before moving to Cambridge United, where he played 163 League games. He was transferred to WBA for £30,000 in February 1978, and has proved one of the best transfer bargains in recent years.

George Berry *(Wolves)*

West German-born, West Indian father, Welsh mother, Berry made his international debut for Wales against West Germany in May 1979. He began with Ipswich but did not make the first team there and signed professional with Wolves in December 1975.

A central defender, he emerged through the Youth team at Molineux to become their 'Player of the Year' in season 1978–79. An integral part of Wolves' revival, he forged an effective defensive partnership with former England captain Emlyn Hughes last season. Hughes's influence has helped to shape the career of the composed youngster, who starred in Wolves' League Cup triumph last season.

Luther Blissett *(Watford)*

This Jamaican-born striker began season 1978–79 as a Third Division reserve but finished it as an England Under-twenty-one international, playing against Wales in February 1979.

A lithe and skilful product of Watford's youth scheme, he burst into the headlines during their League Cup run that season. Blissett scored two goals in three consecutive Cup-ties, the most memorable being against Manchester United in the third round. He got another in the semi-final, but Watford went out to the holders, Nottingham Forest. To Watford's promotion that year to Division Two Blissett contributed a total of twenty-one League goals (plus seven in the League Cup), joining Ross Jenkins in one of the season's most prolific scoring partnerships in British club football.

John Chiedozie *(Orient)*

Over in East London, Orient have given a chance to more young coloured players than most other clubs, and one of the benefits they have reaped has been the discovery of talented winger John Chiedozie. He was born in Owerri,

OPPOSITE
CLOCKWISE FROM TOP LEFT
Viv Anderson, Brendon Batson (*Photos: Syndication International*),
Luther Blissett, George Berry (*Photos: colorsport*).

Nigeria, in April 1960 and learned his football on sand pitches. Then he was caught up in the Biafran war, and came to Britain with his parents, settling at Forest Gate, East London, close to West Ham's ground.

Chiedozie was watched in schoolboy football by Orient scouts and joined the club as an apprentice. His idol at the club was another coloured winger, Laurie Cunningham, and when he was transferred to West Bromwich Albion for £110,000, Orient knew they already had his replacement.

He made his League debut in the Second Division at home to Millwall in March 1977 and signed professional on his seventeenth birthday. At 5 ft 7 in, he is a brave, hard-working, goal-scoring winger, and a regular crowd-pleaser.

Terry Connor *(Leeds United)*

Terry Connor made an immediate impact for Leeds, scoring the winning goal on his debut against West Bromwich Albion in November 1979. Then only seventeen, he had been at Elland Road for just under a year, and got his chance after some prolific scoring in the junior and reserve teams.

Born of Guyanan parents, he made progress at a remarkable rate on arrival at Leeds. Tireless running, deft footwork and ability to find team-mates with well-weighted passes makes him Leeds' most outstanding coloured prospect since Albert Johanneson in the sixties.

Connor followed his debut success with further goals against Manchester United and a brilliant individual effort in Leeds' 1–0 victory against Arsenal at Highbury, proving himself not only a scorer of fine goals, but in action against top opposition as well.

Garth Crooks *(Tottenham Hotspur)*

Garth Crooks possesses all the characteristics of the coloured striker: he is fast, powerful and skilful. These qualities made him one of the most respected players in the First Division and a strong candidate to extend the list of coloured footballers to represent England at full international level.

Crooks made his League debut for Stoke (where he was born) against Coventry in 1976. He has appeared for England Under-twenty-one and scored a hat-trick for them against Bulgaria in November 1979. In three seasons with Stoke (1977–80) he scored 46 goals, and in July 1980 Spurs paid £600,000 to play him alongside their other new striker, Steve Archibald from Aberdeen.

Justin Fashanu *(Norwich City)*

Among the 'goals of the season' that illuminated Match of the Day in the 1979–80 season was an absolute spectacular by powerful Norwich striker Justin Fashanu. Moving in from the right against champions Liverpool, he hit a rising shot from some 25 yards that arrowed past Ray Clemence's stretching right hand and swerved just inside the far post.

OPPOSITE
CLOCKWISE FROM TOP LEFT
John Chiedozie, Terry Connor, Justin Fashanu, Garth Crooks (*Photos: Colorsport*).

At 6 ft 1 in and 12 st 7 lb, Fashanu is built like a light heavyweight boxer, which indeed he was before professional football claimed him full-time. He was a finalist with a knockout punch for England Schools Under-sixteens and ABA Junior Under-seventeens.

Fashanu was born at Hackney, London, on 19 February 1961. As a small boy he was cared for by Dr Barnardo's before being fostered by a Shropham, Norfolk, family. It was in Norfolk schools football that Justin was noted by Norwich City Youth team manager John Sainty. A trial was quickly followed by the offer of an apprenticeship, and he signed as a full professional on Christmas Day 1978.

Fashanu made his First Division debut in January 1979, and scored his first senior goal at Leeds two months later. By the time he was eighteen he had won England Youth caps against Belgium and Italy, followed by a 'B' International appearance against New Zealand.

Bob Hazell *(Queen's Park Rangers)*

Born in Jamaica, Hazell became the first coloured player to represent England Youth, scoring his country's only goal against Wales in March 1977. In December the same year this strapping centre-back made his League debut for Wolves at Newcastle. At 6 ft 1 in he established himself quickly as a first-team regular, and in the process was capped at Under-twenty-one level.

In September 1979 he was transferred to Queen's Park Rangers for £240,000, one of Tommy Docherty's major outlays after becoming manager at Loftus Road. A lithe athlete and powerful tackler, he enjoys forages into the opposition penalty area.

Vince Hilaire *(Crystal Palace)*

If Crystal Palace live up to the prediction of becoming one of the 'teams of the Eighties', there is little doubt that Vince Hilaire will have been an important contributor. As a stylish attacker, he played a notable part in their Second Division Championship triumph in 1978–79, and then showed that he could take the First Division in his stride.

At only 5 ft 6 in and 10 st 4 lb he is both small and brilliant, taunting opposing defenders with pace and mazy dribbles. He was born at Forest Gate, near West Ham, on 10 October 1959, of Dominican parents, and was spotted for Crystal Palace by their ace talent scout Arnie Warren.

Hilaire signed professional from schoolboy in October 1976, and the way was open to a splendid career. He was in Palace's FA Youth Cup winning teams of 1977 and 1978, by which time he was already looking the part in first-team football. He shields the ball well, strikes from deep positions.

He is an all-round sportsman. At school he played basket-ball and cricket, and in athletics shone in the triple jump and 400 metres. As an aggressive left-hand batsman, he played for Essex Under-nineteens when only seventeen.

Ricky Hill (*Luton Town*)

Ricky Hill exploded into League soccer as a seventeen-year-old midfield player at Easter 1976. He was signed as an apprentice by Luton after some impressive displays for Cricklewood Schoolboys in North London. An injury gave him his first opportunity and he grabbed it at once. Making his debut as a substitute with twenty-two minutes to go in a League match against Bristol Rovers, he created one goal and scored another. He was rewarded with an England Youth cap the same year.

Hill's strength lies in his close ball control and powerful shooting and he quickly became established in Luton's first team—clearly another good advertisement for the coloured player in League football.

Chris Hughton (*Tottenham Hotspur*)

Chris Hughton did not become a full-time professional with Tottenham until the start of the 1979–80 season, because he preferred first to complete a four-year apprenticeship as a lift engineer. But he quickly made up for lost time with a series of impressive performances at full-back.

Hughton, whose brother Henry plays full-back for Orient, joined Spurs as a part-time professional in June 1977 and became a regular member of the reserve

ABOVE LEFT Bob Hazell.

ABOVE RIGHT Vince Hilaire.

(*Both photos: Colorsport.*)

team. And when he turned full professional his commanding displays were recognized by an international debut for the Republic of Ireland against the United States in October 1979. He was born at West Ham, but qualified for Eire because his mother comes from the Republic.

Cyrille Regis *(West Bromwich Albion)*

This strong, purposeful centre-forward joined West Bromwich from Berger Isthmian League side Hayes in May 1977 for £5,000. Scoring twice on his debut against Rotherham in the League Cup, he finished his first season with eighteen goals. That year Albion came fifth in Division One and reached the semi-finals of the FA Cup, losing to the eventual winners, Ipswich Town. Regis scored a magnificent goal in the sixth round to beat the then First Division leaders Nottingham Forest.

The following year his performances caught the attention of England manager Ron Greenwood, and he won his first international honour when he played for the 'B' side against Czechoslovakia in Prague. Season 1979–80 began badly for Albion largely because it also began badly for Regis. He needed a knee operation, but after a delayed return was quickly among the First Division goals again.

Garry Thompson *(Coventry City)*

When Garry Thompson, Coventry's Birmingham-born striker, broke a leg during the 1978–79 season, football was temporarily deprived of one of its most promising talents. He had gained a regular place in Coventry's first team and his powerful foraging in front of goal brought him ten goals in his first twenty-six League appearances. Then an accident in training halted his career. He did not recover sufficiently to reappear in the League until midway through the following season, but it was soon evident that his absence had caused him to lose none of his sharpness.

Thompson, a product of Coventry's youth policy, signed professional in June 1977 and was capped for England Youth.

Would You Believe It?
One of the strangest goals ever scored was Chelsea's second in a 3–1 home win against Leicester City on 18 December 1954, the season Chelsea became League champions. A shot by Johnny McNichol rebounded off the crossbar. The ball fell between two Leicester defenders, Stan Milburn and Jack Froggatt, who both lunged at it and connected simultaneously. The ball flew into the net. It went down officially as 'Milburn and Froggatt shared own goal'—the only known instance of a goal being recorded in this way.

OPPOSITE
CLOCKWISE FROM TOP LEFT
Ricky Hill, Chris Hughton
(*Photos: Colorsport*), Garry
Thompson (*Photo: Bob Thompson*), Cyrille
Regis (*Photo: Syndication International*).

Chapter 12

Great Clubs of My Time

Benfica

Benfica's claim to world recognition is their record in the European Cup. They have reached the final on no fewer than five occasions, and have won the trophy twice.

Since the war, the 'Eagles' from Lisbon have dominated the Portuguese Championship. Despite an amazing run by neighbours Sporting Lisbon, who won the title seven times during an eight-year spell (1947–54), Benfica have been champions of Portugal almost twice as many times as their nearest rival. They have also dominated the Portuguese Cup. Yet it was in European competition during the 1960s that they gained so many admirers for their enterprising and entertaining play which produced so many spectacular goals.

In 1961, the second time they took part in the European Cup, Benfica reached the final. On the road to it they scored twenty-three goals, but their last opponents, Barcelona of Spain, appeared to be a much tougher side than any of the others they had overcome in previous rounds. This proved to be the case, but Benfica triumphed in Berne thanks largely to an own-goal from Barcelona's Ramallets, the second of Benfica's three in a five-goal thriller.

Benfica returned to the final the following season after again scoring heavily in the earlier rounds—seventeen goals in six games. Goals were plentiful in the final, too, when against five-times holders Real Madrid they scored five, cancelling the three by the legendary Hungarian Puskas. Two of Benfica's goals were scored by a young black striker who himself was to become a legend. His name was Eusebio.

Eusebio da Silva was born in the Lourenço Marques quarter of Mozambique on 25 January 1942, one of a family of eight children. His father died when he was only five, and his mother had to bring up the family single-handed. Although he was a junior champion at 400, 200 and 100 metres, Eusebio already knew where his destiny lay. He joined the Lourenço Marques Sporting Club from school, and, by the age of seventeen, football was his livelihood.

He scored a hat-trick on his debut for Sporting Club, and it was not long before the Portuguese clubs had their eyes on him. Benfica acted quickly and Eusebio donned their colours for the first time on 23 May 1961, scoring three goals in a private game. His official debut was less exhilarating. He played in the second leg of a Cup-tie against Setubal, with Benfica leading 3–1 from the first

OPPOSITE Eusebio, about to score for Benfica against AC Milan in the European Champions' Cup final in 1963. Milan won 2–1. (*Photo: Central Press.*)

leg: by half-time they were losing 3–0. Eusebio netted to level the aggregate score, and then Benfica were awarded a penalty. Eusebio was elected to take the kick but missed; Setubal scored again, and Benfica were out.

The 1962 European Cup final against Real Madrid was probably the highlight of Eusebio's career. His next three European Cup finals were less fruitful. At Wembley in 1963 he put Benfica ahead against AC Milan, but the Portuguese failed to prevent the Italians from scoring twice. Two years later Benfica won the Portuguese League for the third consecutive time, but AC Milan's rivals, Inter, beat them 1–0 in the European Cup final.

In 1968, back at Wembley, they faced Manchester United, but Eusebio was so well marked by Nobby Stiles that they lost again—this time 4–1 in extra time. But, while these European setbacks were undoubtedly a tremendous disappointment, Benfica continued to produce top-class performances in the League. Indeed, when the 'Eagles' won the title in 1972, they added the Cup as well, thus recording a remarkable number of five League and Cup 'double' successes in their history.

Portugal have not been the greatest soccer nation in Europe. But Benfica have thrilled lovers of thoughtful, intelligent football around the world. They have produced so many players with all-round ability, not just Eusebio, but Cruz, Augusto, Neto, Germano, Pereira, Santana, Aguas and Coluna. Yes, Benfica have been a credit to Portugal and to football.

Benfica: Postwar Honours

PORTUGUESE LEAGUE CHAMPIONS: 17 times – 1950, 1955, 1957, 1960, 1961, 1963, 1964, 1965, 1967, 1968, 1969, 1971, 1972, 1973, 1975, 1976, 1977.
PORTUGUESE CUP WINNERS: 13 times – 1949, 1951, 1952, 1953, 1955, 1957, 1959, 1962, 1964, 1969, 1970, 1972, 1980.
EUROPEAN CUP WINNERS: twice – 1961, 1962.

Juventus

Juventus are known in Italy as La Vecchia Signora—The Grand Old Lady, which is an apt description for the country's most famous club. But despite the domination held by Juventus at club level they have failed to make as much impact on the European scene as their Italian rivals AC Milan and Internazionale.

Not only have they governed the Italian League for a long time, but they imported some of the world's outstanding players, notably Welshman John Charles, and the Argentinian Enrico Sivori. But a paradox of Italian football has deprived Juventus of the mass of local support. Although the most popular club throughout the country, they are second in the hearts of most fans in their city of Turin. Torino are closer to the working classes there, most of whom work in the city's main factory, Fiat, home of the country's giant car works. Ironically, Juventus have for many years been heavily subsidized by the Agnelli family, who own Fiat. Despite this local rivalry, Juventus have always been the team to beat. Indeed, when a star player, almost anywhere in Europe, is available for transfer, it is most likely that the name of Juventus is the first to be suggested as a possible home for the player. Such is the magnetism of The Grand Old Lady.

Juventus were original members of the Italian League in 1929, and totally dominated Italian football for the next few years. Much of the success of that period was due to South American players, notably three Argentinians: Cesarini, Orsi and Monti. But Juventus's best season during those early years was yet to come. It came in 1933–34 when they finished the season unbeaten at home, and provided nine players to the Italian team that beat Hungary 1–0 in Budapest. Yet, surprisingly, that team failed to hold any control on the domestic scene, and it was not until 1950 that they regained the Italian Championship. Their success, it is true, was attributable in great part to the demise of Torino following the Superga air crash.

Juventus were then managed by an Englishman, Jesse Carver, who brought Danish strikers John Hansen and Carl Paest to the club, along with a brilliant Argentinian called Martino. But in 1951 Carver was sacked, and replaced by former Juventus centre-forward, Sarosi. He took Juventus to the Championship title again in 1952, with the inclusion in the team of a third Dane, inside-right Karl Hansen.

Possibly the outstanding postwar player to wear the black and white stripes of Juventus was Giampiero Boniperti, who played at centre-forward, inside-right and outside-right, and was eventually promoted to captain. 'Boni', as he was affectionately known throughout Italy, was capped thirty-eight times for Italy and was a member of Juventus's side when they won the League title on no less than five occasions. On the last three, 1958, 1960 and 1961, he was joined by giant Welshman John Charles, who signed for Juventus from Leeds United in 1957, at about the same time as a little Argentinian called Enrico Sivori. In 1959 they won the Italian Cup for a third time, and they retained the trophy the following year to become the first Italian side to record a League and Cup 'double'.

Financially, Juventus have never been the poor relations in Italian soccer. They have proved this in recent years and as long ago as 1968 they paid £440,000 to persuade twenty-year-old central striker Pietro Anastasi to leave Varese. That was just a year after they had won the League title for the thirteenth time. But in Europe, Juventus, while always respected, have failed to dominate in the way they have in domestic competitions. They lost the Fairs Cup 1–0 to Ferencvaros in 1965, and again reached the final in 1971, but lost on the away goals rule to Leeds. Their first success in European competition came in 1977, when an away goal in the second leg against Atletico Bilbao by Roberto Bettega, one of a new breed of superstars at Juventus, was enough to secure the UEFA Cup.

The Italian national side have always relied on Juventus to supply a large number of their players. In fact no fewer than ten of the twenty-two-strong squad that travelled to Argentina in the summer of 1978 for the World Cup finals were Juventus players. This in itself shows the debt Italian football owes to The Grand Old Lady.

Juventus: Postwar Honours

ITALIAN CHAMPIONS: 11 times – 1950, 1952, 1958, 1960, 1961, 1967, 1972, 1973, 1975, 1977, 1978.
ITALIAN CUP WINNERS: 4 times – 1959, 1960, 1965, 1979.
UEFA CUP WINNERS – 1977.

Manchester United

Manchester United have always been something special to me. They were the club I wanted to join as a youngster. In fact in 1957 I was asked to become an apprentice at Old Trafford. Bert Whalley, their coach at the time, watched me play for England Schoolboys against Northern Ireland and at several other games. One night he invited me over to watch the Charity Shield match between Manchester United and Aston Villa. Nigel Sims was in goal for Villa and played an absolute blinder. After the game, which United won 4–0, Bert asked me what I thought of Sims's display and I replied that I thought he was brilliant. At that Bert said I could be twice as good a goalkeeper as Sims if I joined United. I dare say he was giving my morale a boost because he was keen for me to sign. But my father would not agree. Those were the days of the £20-a-week footballer and he insisted I qualified in other things.

Manchester United have captured the imagination of the world with their passionate attempt to become its most successful club. The yearning for such success has brought spectacular triumph; it has also brought heartbreak.

United's first big prize was gained in 1908—the League Championship. They followed that with the FA Cup in 1909 and the League title again in 1911. That was to be their last major victory for thirty-seven years, when once again they won the FA Cup, beating Blackpool 4–2 at Wembley. But United's most famous period began in the 1950s, and has continued to this day.

At a board meeting held at Old Trafford on 15 February 1945 the most important item on the agenda was the appointment of manager. The man they chose was the former Scotland and Manchester City wing-half, Matt Busby. There was to be no wiser decision in the history of this famous club.

Busby's first season in charge ended with United fourth in 1945–46 in the wartime League North. A full League programme was renewed the following season and four times in those first five postwar seasons United ended as runners-up in the League as a prelude to winning the Championship in 1952. By then Busby was in the process of creating a team that will always be

OPPOSITE ABOVE Anastasi scores for Juventus against Leeds in the UEFA Cup final of 1971. They lost the trophy on the away-goals rule. (*Photo: Syndication International.*)

OPPOSITE BELOW Jimmy Greenhoff scores in the 1977 FA Cup final against Liverpool, and Manchester United are on their way to another trophy. (*Photo: Colorsport.*)

remembered as the 'Busby Babes'. He began to introduce a number of youngsters into the first team shortly after United won the 1952 title, and harnessed them to the proven talents of Johnny Carey, who could play in almost every position including goal, centre-forward Jack Rowley and full-back Johnny Aston. These were just a handful of players who helped Busby to plant the seeds of success.

The real key to the future, however, lay with the United juniors, who made the FA Youth Cup their own property in five successive seasons from 1953 to 1957. United's explosion, if it can be called that, began in 1956, when they won the League title by a record eleven-points margin with a side that included youngsters such as Duncan Edwards, Dennis Viollet, Eddie Colman and David Pegg. They confirmed their strengths the following season by retaining the Championship and reaching the FA Cup final in which they lost 2–1 to Aston Villa. They also reached the semi-final of the European Cup. The 1956–57 season, in fact, was the greatest that United had enjoyed.

Understandably, they began the 1957–58 campaign in buoyant mood. Indeed, they looked likely to win the European Cup. They drew 3–3 in Yugoslavia against Red Star Belgrade, after winning the first leg 2–1, and so were in the semi-finals. But the plane carrying the United team home to Manchester crashed in the snow in Munich, on 6 February 1958. Eight players were killed in the disaster: Roger Byrne, Geoff Bent, Eddie Colman, Mark Jones, Duncan Edwards, David Pegg, Tommy Taylor and Liam Whelan. Trainer Tom Curry, coach Bert Whalley and secretary Walter Crickmer also died, as did eight newspaper representatives, including Frank Swift, the former England and Manchester City goalkeeper.

Astonishingly, with a makeshift and hurriedly rebuilt team United reached the FA Cup final that season, but were beaten 2–0 by Aston Villa. While Matt Busby, seriously injured in the air disaster, fought for his life, assistant-manager Jimmy Murphy took charge at Old Trafford. United overcame the appalling effects of the tragedy miraculously well, and Busby, later to be knighted, took the team to new heights—and the greatest night in their history: 29 May 1968. With such personalities as Bobby Charlton, Denis Law and George Best in their side, United beat Benfica 4–1 in extra time in an exhilarating European Cup final at Wembley. The 1970s brought them the FA Cup for the fourth time and even a spell in the Second Division. Yet such are the magnetic qualities of Manchester United that in the past decade their average gate was a little under 50,000. Can you wonder that I was keen to join them!

Manchester United's Honours List

FOOTBALL LEAGUE CHAMPIONS: 7 times – 1908, 1911, 1952, 1956, 1957, 1965, 1967.
FA CUP WINNERS: 4 times – 1909, 1948, 1963, 1977.
EUROPEAN CUP WINNERS – 1968.

Bayern Munich

During the 1970s, Bayern Munich controlled West German domestic competitions, and their name was revered in every corner of Europe. In fact their success began in 1967, when they beat Glasgow Rangers in the final of the European Cup Winners' Cup, in Nuremberg. Included in their side were Sepp Maier, Franz Beckenbauer and Gerd Müller, players who were to haunt many top clubs for a decade.

Bayern's victory in that tournament (they won 1–0 in extra time) was not greatly impressive, but it set them on the road to a series of triumphs which no West German club had previously achieved. Already, in their own country, Bayern were a good side, and had provided a constant source of players for the national team.

Everyone knew what the Germans could do. The 1966 World Cup final at Wembley was proof of their ability, with Beckenbauer an integral part of their advance in that tournament to a place as runners-up in the greatest football event on earth. But Bayern's record of three successive European Cup victories between 1974 and 1976 built a platform on which West German football could justifiably be extolled at club level.

Their first success in the European Cup was in 1974, in the Belgian capital of Brussels. Bayern were lucky in the first round when a penalty-kick shoot-out brought them victory against the comparative Swedish unknowns Atvidaberg. They found their second-round opponents equally difficult, finishing the eventual winners by seven goals to six against Dynamo Dresden. A 4–1 home win against CSKA Sofia assured them of a place in the semi-finals, and a match against Ujpest Dozsa and three goals in Hungary were sufficient to take them to the final. There they faced Atletico Madrid, the champions of Spain, and a side that many felt would be too good for Bayern. They drew 1–1, but in the replay Bayern surprised many by winning 4–0. Scorers were Gerd Müller (2) and Uli Hoeness (2), names that would crop up time and time again on score-sheets.

As holders, Bayern were expected to put up a bold show in the 1974–75 tournament. But, when the final matched them with Don Revie's solid Leeds United, the champions of England, the Germans were considered the underdogs. Leeds dominated the game for long spells but, with Maier in brilliant form in the Bayern goal, the Germans held on. Then in the seventy-second minute they caught the Leeds defence off guard, and went ahead through Franz Roth. The victory was complete when, ten minutes from time, Gerd Müller again lived up to his reputation as Europe's most dangerous finisher by cracking home a marvellous drive.

So Bayern returned to Munich with the trophy. Although few outside their own city believed they could retain the European Cup for a third time, Bayern confounded the sceptics once again. This time they disposed of formidable challenges from Benfica and Real Madrid en route to Hampden Park, scene of the 1976 European Cup final. By then they were expected to walk over their opposition, the French champions St Etienne. But the French proved to be far more difficult than expected. Twice they hit the post and went close to creating one of the great upsets in European football. In the end a goal by Roth in the fifty-seventh minute provided Bayern with their hat-trick of European Cup victories.

Bayern's football has not always been the most attractive in the world but they have provided West Germany with some of its greatest players. Beckenbauer, sweeper supreme, is many people's conception of the greatest defender in the history of the game. Gerd Müller combined a stunning accuracy with a pace and vision that ruined England's 1970 World Cup hopes in Mexico. And Sepp Maier, a likable goalkeeper with giant gloves, often seemed unbeatable. Bayern Munich have set standards that will be difficult to surpass, certainly in West German domestic football.

Bayern Munich: Postwar Honours

WEST GERMAN LEAGUE CHAMPIONS: 5 times – 1969, 1972, 1973, 1974, 1980.
WEST GERMAN CUP WINNERS: 5 times – 1957, 1966, 1967, 1969, 1971.
EUROPEAN CUP WINNERS: 3 times – 1974, 1975, 1976.
EUROPEAN CUP WINNERS' CUP WINNERS – 1967.
WORLD CLUB CHAMPIONS – 1976.

Real Madrid

Real Madrid, like Barcelona, are not just a football club. The great virtue of both is that they have created magnificent sport complexes in which the whole family can be part of the social scene. There are facilities for lawn tennis, hockey, basketball, cycling, swimming and other recreational pursuits. The scale and imagination of these centres makes the set-up at British soccer clubs look antiquated by comparison.

OPPOSITE ABOVE Bayern Munich are about to become 1974 European champions. Hoeness scores in the 4–0 win over Atletico Madrid. (*Photo: Colorsport.*)

OPPOSITE BELOW England's Laurie Cunningham showing his skills for Real Madrid against Barcelona. (*Photo: Bob Thomas.*)

Real Madrid were the first club to attract European acclaim, and the way they did is a story that is unique in football history. Long before the Spanish League began in 1928, Real Madrid had secured their niche in Spanish football. The 'championship' in Spain during the first few years of the twentieth century took the form of regional leagues, with the winners of each league playing against the other for the right to be called 'champions'. Real won the tournament four times in a row from 1905 to 1908. Indeed, by 1979, their honours list included nineteen Spanish League successes and thirteen cup victories. But it was in European football that they were to reach the heights of success never previously attained. In fact it is doubtful whether a club side will ever achieve the domination Real imposed throughout Europe.

When the European Cup began in the 1955–56 season only a handful of clubs participated. Very few of them took it seriously. Two clubs did, namely Real and French champions Stade de Reims, who quite fittingly reached the first final in 1956. The French were without any imported players. Real included

two Argentinians, inside-left Hector Rial and the legendary Alfredo di Stefano at centre-forward.

Di Stefano was born in the Argentina capital of Buenos Aires and played for the Colombian side Millionarios. Both Real and Barcelona wanted the striker and both clubs thought they had, in fact, signed him—indeed, they had. Millionarios had sold him to both clubs! So a meeting was held in Spain to settle who should have him. It was decided that he should spend alternate seasons with each club, beginning with Real. But he started poorly, and Barcelona sold their share to Real. Di Stefano promptly replied in his next game by scoring four goals in a 5–0 win—against Barcelona!

Many critics claimed that Real relied too heavily on the foraging, scheming skills of di Stefano. They were sometimes called a one-man team, but they did have many other great players. Miguel Munoz at wing-half, who captained Real for some time, Jose Marie Zarraga, and goalkeeper Alonso were all major assets to the cup-winning Real of the 1950s. Another player they depended on a great deal was Francisco Gento, known as Paco, who spent eighteen years at Chamartin, Real's home in Madrid.

Real's first European Cup win took place in Paris with the Spaniards winning 4–3. They returned to the final the following year against Fiorentina after beating Manchester United in the semi-final. By then interest in the competition had increased considerably. So much so, that their 2–0 win in the final in Madrid was watched by a crowd of 124,000.

Victory number three was a sad affair. Real reached the final in Brussels after beating Vasas Budapest in the semi-final. AC Milan, the other eventual finalists, beat a new Manchester United team. The 'old' United team had been decimated in the Munich air disaster after United's quarter-final second-leg game against Red Star of Belgrade. Predictably, Real won the 1958 final against AC Milan, but only after they had been forced to extra time, with the winner coming from Gento, to make the score 3–2. As Real's success gathered momentum, so did the competition, as more and more clubs tried to dethrone the kings of Europe.

The 1959 final, in Stuttgart, gave Reims the opportunity of revenge. The 1956 finalists from France had fielded Raymond Kopa in the first final. In 1959 they were to come up against him, for he joined Real prior to the 1959 tournament. Mateos and di Stefano secured a fourth championship, and Real were well and truly etched into the history books.

But the fifth successive European Cup win by Real is the victory still best remembered. It has been described as 'the greatest game of all time'. Indeed, few among the 135,000 people would disagree, for on the night of 18 May 1960 Real beat German champions Eintracht Frankfurt by seven goals to three. The stage, at Hampden Park, Glasgow, was set alight by two men: di Stefano, and the unparalleled genius of the Hungarian Ferenc Puskas. He scored four of the seven, di Stefano getting the other three. That was the last of Real's record-breaking run of victories, but in 1966 they won the European Cup for a sixth time with a 2–1 victory over Partizan Belgrade in Brussels. I wonder if we shall see their like again.

Real Madrid: Postwar Honours

SPANISH LEAGUE CHAMPIONS: 18 times —1954, 1955, 1957, 1958, 1961, 1962, 1963, 1964, 1965, 1967, 1968, 1969, 1972, 1975, 1976, 1978, 1979, 1980.
SPANISH CUP WINNERS: 7 times—1946, 1947, 1962, 1970, 1974, 1975, 1980.
EUROPEAN CUP WINNERS: 6 times – 1956, 1957, 1958, 1959, 1960, 1966.
WORLD CLUB CHAMPIONS – 1960.

AC Milan

When AC Milan were founded in 1899, jointly by Englishmen and Italians, they were known by the improbable name of the Milan *Cricket* and Football Club. Nine years later, Milan produced another football team, Internazionale, known throughout the world as Inter-Milan. Ever since their rivalry has been intense. The first AC Milan team included several foreign players, notably Englishmen, among them Dr John Kilpin, a powerful centre-half, and an elegant Belgian forward, Louis Van Hege, who spent many years with Milan. By the time Inter were born, Milan had won three titles all with the help of Kilpin.

Surprisingly six British players were included in the 1900 championship-winning team, but Kilpin was the only survivor in the teams that won the competition again in 1906 and 1907. That was to be Milan's last championship until 1951. There is little doubt that the creation of Inter had a great deal to do with that fact.

Milan reappeared among the front runners in 1950 when they finished second to Juventus in the Italian Championship. In 1951 their famous all-Swedish trio of Gunnar Gren, Gunnar Nordahl and Nils Liedholm, won them their fourth Italian Championship, their first for over forty years. They scored 107 goals, the same as Inter who finished one point behind.

The power behind Milan was the millionaire publisher Andrea Mizzoli, and although money was spent liberally Inter continued to succeed in the Championship. Indeed it was not until 1955 that Milan regained the title. They still fielded Nordahl and Liedholm, and were now inspired by the brilliant inside-left Juan Schiaffino, who joined them from Hungary. But the pressures of managing a top side in Italian football at that time took their toll. During the 1954–55 season Milan manager Bela Guttmann, who later gained European Cup triumphs with Benfica, was dismissed during a brief loss of form, despite Milan's top-of-the-table position at the time. But they did win the title that year, and again in 1957 and 1959.

Milan's successes in the League tended to occur every three or four years, but in Europe success seemed to follow them throughout each campaign. They entered the European Cup for the first time in 1955–56, but were beaten by Spanish giants Real Madrid in the semi-final. Real knocked them out again the next time they met, in 1958. This time it was in the final of the tournament in Brussels, where an extra-time goal from Paco Gento took the trophy back to

The goal that won the European Cup Winners' Cup for AC Milan in 1973. It was scored by Chiarugi against Leeds United.
(*Photo: Colorsport*.)

Spain. But Milan eventually won that most coveted of soccer prizes in 1963 against Benfica of Portugal, who fielded the brilliant Eusebio. He shook Milan in the eighteenth minute when he put Benfica ahead, but two goals from Milan's Brazilian centre-forward Altafini secured the Cup for the Italians. One member of the winning side was a nineteen-year-old inside-forward, Gianni Rivera. This young man went on to take part in four World Cup tournaments, and to be a member of Milan's championship-winning side sixteen years later.

Milan's next European Cup success came in 1969. In that competition they needed to beat only three clubs before they were faced with a final game against Ajax in Madrid. AC won 4–1, more comfortably than anybody could have expected. A hat-trick from Prati ensured the trophy for Milan for the second time. This victory gave them a chance to win the World Club competition, but the series proved to be a frightening experience against Estudiantes de la Plata of Argentina. In Buenos Aires, Combin, Madrid's Argentinian centre-forward, had his nose broken, and Prati was kicked in the back while having treatment. Afterwards several Argentinians were given long suspensions and a few were even sent to prison. Nevertheless Milan won on aggregate, though their League season was seriously affected by injuries.

In addition to Milan's European Cup success, they have won the European Cup Winners' Cup twice, in 1968 and 1973, and were beaten finalists in 1974. Milan's success in Italian domestic soccer may not match up to that achieved by Inter, but their European conquests have gained them many admirers throughout the world. They continue to succeed. Indeed they won their tenth League title in 1979. They enjoy rivalry with Inter that may appear volatile on the surface but, with both clubs attracting large attendances, that rivalry is good both for the clubs and Italian football in general.

> **AC Milan: Postwar Honours**
>
> ITALIAN CHAMPIONS: 7 times – 1951, 1955, 1957, 1959, 1962, 1968, 1979.
> ITALIAN CUP WINNERS: 4 times – 1967, 1972, 1973, 1977.
> EUROPEAN CUP WINNERS: Twice – 1963, 1969.
> EUROPEAN CUP WINNERS' CUP WINNERS: Twice – 1968, 1973.
> WORLD CLUB CHAMPIONS – 1969.

Arsenal

The first time I walked into Highbury I was nineteen and was training to be a school-teacher at Loughborough College, but Arsenal said they were interested in signing me. So I travelled down and as I approached the ground the stands appeared enormous. I had never seen any soccer stadium quite so impressive. When I went out on to the pitch with Billy Wright, the Arsenal manager, I found it hard to credit that anyone could have had the foresight to build stands like that as long ago as the 1930s. Nor, indeed, could a small group of workers from a government armaments factory in Woolwich have visualized such an imposing stadium when they had a whipround and collected ten shillings, sufficient to buy a football in 1886. That was the start of a football club, known then as Royal Arsenal, which was to become admired throughout the world.

Those factory workers were unable to find enough cash to buy kit, but a member of their team, a former Nottingham Forest goalkeeper called Fred Beardsley, persuaded his former club to send down a complete set. Arsenal have worn that same red ever since.

In 1893 they moved to Manor Fields, Plumstead, their first permanent site, and there they remained until 1913 when they moved again, this time to their present home at Highbury.

Arsenal struggled financially, and failed to make a great impact on the Second Division. But in 1925 Herbert Chapman, after a brilliant spell of success with Huddersfield Town, came south to transform them into one of the most famous clubs in the world. Chapman's managerial influence on the team was immediate. Arsenal finished second in his first season with fifty-two points, and in the following year they reached the FA Cup final only to be beaten 1–0 by Cardiff City. The only occasion, incidentally, that the trophy has left England.

Chapman lifted Arsenal to an unparalleled run of success, and, despite his sudden death in 1934, the momentum he introduced was sustained first by George Allison and then by Tom Whittaker, Chapman's trainer and chief disciple.

Chapman guided Arsenal to the League Championship title in 1931, 1933, and 1934, though he died before that title was secured, and they won it again in 1935, 1938, 1948 and 1953. The FA Cup went to Highbury in 1930 and 1936. In 1950 the 'Gunners', captained by Joe Mercer, beat Liverpool 2–0 to win the Cup

again. But the 1953 League title was the last trophy to grace the boardroom of Highbury for seventeen years.

During that barren period Arsenal in 1969 completed fifty years as a First Division side. There were, of course, many fine players during that time, including George Eastham, David Herd, Derek Tapscott, Tommy Docherty, Mel Charles, Terry Neill and Dave Bowen. They were all internationals but Arsenal occupied a mid-table position for much of that period.

The triumphs of Spurs winning the 'double' in 1961 and their European success, and the rise of Chelsea and West Ham, made the job at Highbury difficult for Billy Wright, the former Wolves and England captain. He had taken over in 1962 without any managerial experience, and was replaced by the physiotherapist, Bertie Mee, in 1966. Mee was a brilliant organizer, and he set Arsenal on a new road to success. They reached the final of the League Cup in 1968 and 1969, though failing to win that trophy which still remains elusive to them.

The worst moment of my footballing career happened on 15 March 1969. Arsenal had beaten Tottenham in the two-legged semi-final of the League Cup, and faced Swindon Town (of the Third Division) in the final at Wembley. History records that we were beaten 3–1 but not how bad I felt after the game. The Arsenal players were invited back to Claridge's in London's West End. I sat near to Jack Kelsey, the best Arsenal goalkeeper of my generation and now commercial manager at Highbury. Soon I was pouring my heart out to him.

'For goodness sake', he said. 'I played for Arsenal for ten times as long as you have, and I would have given anything to go to Wembley with them. What are you worrying about?' He was right, of course—and how was I to know that I would return to Wembley for the 1971 FA Cup final, and finish on the winning side?

In 1970 Arsenal reached the final of the European Fairs Cup, but trailed 3–0 away to Anderlecht in the first leg before substitute Ray Kennedy pulled a goal back. On an emotional night at Highbury, Arsenal won the second leg 3–0. The famine was over.

Next came the coveted 'double' in 1971 when we won the League Championship and FA Cup. Arsenal were once again a force to be considered in the world of football.

A former Arsenal player, Terry Neill, took over as manager when Bertie Mee resigned in 1976, and with the help of such talented youngsters as Liam Brady, Graham Rix, David O'Leary and Frank Stapleton the club reached the 1978 FA Cup final. They were beaten 1–0 by Ipswich Town. But Arsenal returned the following year for their tenth Wembley FA Cup appearance, and millions of people, watching the televised coverage, enjoyed one of the most exciting finals seen at Wembley. After leading 2–0, Arsenal relinquished the lead as Manchester United drew level with only minutes left. A replay looked a certainty but Alan Sunderland slipped in to score Arsenal's late, late winner and give the club yet another cup to add to the long list of trophies.

When translated, the Latin inscription on the Arsenal motif reads: 'Victory

OPPOSITE Liam Brady bursts between Manchester United's Joe Jordan and Lou Macari in the 1979 FA Cup final, won 3–2 by a Brady-inspired Arsenal.
(*Photo: Colorsport.*)

Upon Unity'. There can be no better way to describe the tradition that is Arsenal—despite their losing the 1980 FA Cup Final, their third in successive years, 1–0 to West Ham.

Arsenal's Honours List

FOOTBALL LEAGUE CHAMPIONS: 8 times – 1931, 1933, 1934, 1935, 1938, 1948, 1953, 1971.
FA CUP WINNERS: 5 times – 1930, 1936, 1950, 1971, 1979.
THE DOUBLE (League Championship and FA Cup) – 1971.
EUROPEAN FAIRS CUP WINNERS – 1970.

Liverpool

I have always had a great affection for Liverpool. As a goalkeeper going to Anfield, I always wanted to produce that little bit extra. Not many teams succeed there, though, curiously, when I was with Arsenal we beat them three years running in front of their own fanatical supporters. Each time it was as though we had won the World Cup, the FA Cup, the European Cup and every other major prize rolled into one.

Walk down the tunnel from the dressing-rooms and you come face to face with a sign which reads: 'This is Anfield'. And, in my visits there as a player, standing underneath would be Bill Shankly (a legend in his own lifetime), adding to the pre-match psychological warfare which every team faces when they play at Anfield.

'Shanks' never missed a trick. On the Friday before Arsenal met Liverpool in the 1971 FA Cup final we went out to examine the Wembley pitch. When we came off I saw Shankly sitting at the side of the tunnel. 'Good afternoon, Mr Shankly. The pitch is looking great, isn't it?' I said. 'Ah, I don't know about that, son', he replied, 'it's very slippery for goalkeepers out there.'

Liverpool, first under 'Shanks', and more recently guided by Bob Paisley, have maintained a consistency throughout the last fifteen years that has never before been achieved in this country. Arsenal in the 1930s, Manchester United in the fifties, and Tottenham in the sixties, were all clubs which dominated for some time. But not one of them was able to sustain excellence of performance over a comparable period or, indeed, to produce so many world-class players as have emerged from the Liverpool 'factory'.

OPPOSITE Franz Beckenbauer playing for New York Cosmos – soccer is rapidly growing in popularity in the US, and fans bring customary American enthusiasm to the game, as the inset shows.
(*Photos: Colorsport.*)

How have they achieved this remarkable continuity? A major factor must be that so many of the backroom men at Anfield today were stars there in their playing days. Bill Shankly, Ronnie Moran, Bob Paisley, Joe Fagan and Geoff Twentyman were all Liverpool players and now they pursue the club's success behind the scenes. Even Tommy Smith, scorer of one of Liverpool's three goals when they won the European Cup in 1977, is back at Anfield, as youth coach.

Although they were elected to the Football League in 1893, Liverpool's

success has reached a real peak only in comparatively recent years. They were a First Division club between 1905 and 1954, having won the Second Division Championship three times before they were promoted. They returned to the First Division in 1962, when Roger Hunt scored forty-one League goals, and since then they have not finished a League season in lower than eighth place.

Liverpool won their first Championship under the magical managership of Bill Shankly in 1963–64. 'Shanks', who took control in December 1959, remained at the helm until July 1974, when he retired. Since then Bob Paisley has carried on the Liverpool success story. Shankly preached a simple lesson to his players. He continually stressed how lucky they were to play for Liverpool. He told them what an honour it was to play for such a great club, and reminded them that, if they misbehaved, or failed to give 100 per cent performance, they would be cheating their pals.

The 1970s undoubtedly belonged to Liverpool. They won the Championship four times, and from 1973 to 1980 they did not finish lower than second place. The FA Cup was not a competition they were able to dominate so comprehensively. They won it only once during the decade, in 1974, but also finished twice as runners-up.

But it was on the European stage that Liverpool gave their greatest performances, and to much wider audiences. Their first success came in 1973 when they beat Borussia Moenchengladbach 3–2 on aggregate in the UEFA Cup final. And in 1976 they took the trophy back to Anfield by beating FC Bruges 4–3 over two legs. Little did those two clubs know they would feature again in Liverpool's greatest victories.

In 1977 Liverpool won the League Championship, and reached the final of the FA Cup. They had also reached the final of the European Cup, a competition that had so far eluded them. So Liverpool were on course for an incredible assault on football's three most glittering prizes. Their FA Cup final opponents at Wembley in May 1977 were Manchester United, who so often produce something special on Cup occasions. So it proved again this time. Stuart Pearson put United ahead, but Jimmy Case equalized with a superb goal. Then, just as Liverpool were getting back into the game, they were dealt a cruel blow. Lou Macari attempted an opportunist shot which deflected off the chest of Jimmy Greenhoff, and past the despairing clutches of Ray Clemence, to ruin the chance of an historic treble for Liverpool.

Bob Paisley now faced the difficult task of preparing his players for the European Cup final, just four days later. But he need not have worried, for the luck that had eluded them at Wembley returned in Rome. And it was against a team they knew only too well, Borussia Moenchengladbach. Terry McDermott put Liverpool ahead, but Allan Simonsen responded with a brilliant goal for the Germans. When Liverpool regained the lead it seemed fitting that 'old faithful' Tommy Smith should be the one to rise and head the goal because he had given such marvellous service to the club. Finally, a penalty by Phil Neal brought the coveted trophy to Merseyside.

By now Liverpool were feared throughout Europe and it was no real surprise

OPPOSITE Two European soccer greats: above, Wilfried Van Moer (Belgium); below, Rudi Krol (Holland). (*Photos: Colorsport.*)

when they reached the final again the following year. This time they overcame the negative tactics of the Belgian champions FC Bruges.

Kenny Dalglish, the man who replaced Kevin Keegan in 1977, scored the goal that sent Liverpool into the football history books as the first British club to win the European Cup twice. Who can doubt that more rich rewards are in store for this remarkable club?

Liverpool's Honours List

FOOTBALL LEAGUE CHAMPIONS: 12 times (record) – 1901, 1906, 1922, 1923, 1947, 1964, 1966, 1973, 1976, 1977, 1979, 1980.
FA CUP WINNERS: Twice – 1965, 1974.
EUROPEAN CUP WINNERS: Twice – 1977, 1978.
UEFA CUP WINNERS: Twice – 1973, 1976.
EUROPEAN SUPER-CUP WINNERS – 1977.

Ajax

I have good reason to remember Ajax. After winning the League title in 1971 Arsenal qualified for the European Cup the following season. We were progressing well in that competition and had high hopes of winning it. But in the quarter-finals we were drawn against Ajax. We took the lead in Amsterdam through Ray Kennedy, but Ajax replied with a low shot from the edge of the area from Gerrie Muhren that found its way into the net past me via Peter Simpson. Worse followed for us. Ajax were awarded a penalty after Dick Van Dijk was felled in the area, and from the spot Muhren put the Dutch side into the lead.

So to Highbury for the second leg. We needed to win by one goal to nil, on the away goals counting double rule, to progress to the next round, but it was just not our night. After only sixteen minutes we were another goal down. Rudi Krol hit a long pass which looked harmless enough. I moved to the edge of the area to gather it, but George Graham got there first, and under pressure from Arie Haan, headed the ball past me. There was no further score and Ajax went on to retain the Cup they had won in 1971.

Not one club in Europe can boast such an overwhelming monopoly of domestic competitions as Ajax. Their strength has dwindled slightly in recent years, but they remain the most feared club in Holland. Few teams, as we discovered, are happy to find themselves drawn against the Dutch masters in European competitions.

Despite the slow emergence, generally, of Dutch football on the international scene, Ajax were quick to gain the notice of the world. Professional football was initiated in the Netherlands in 1953 and since then Ajax have produced championship-winning performances, the type which has been approached in Holland only by Feyenoord and PSV Eindhoven. In fact, it was Feyenoord who

OPPOSITE ABOVE Liverpool keep the European Cup. The goal by Kenny Dalglish that beat Bruges 1–0 and meant that Liverpool were European champions in successive seasons. (*Photo: Colorsport.*)

OPPOSITE BELOW Johan Cruyff beats a Panathanaikos defender in the 1971 European Cup final at Wembley. Ajax won 2–0 to begin a three-year reign as European champions. (*Photo: Syndication International.*)

gained the acclaim of the footballing populace when they took the European Cup to Holland for the first time by beating Celtic 2–1 in Milan in 1970. A year earlier, Ajax had surprised many by beating the Portuguese champions Benfica in the three-match quarter-final, but were convincingly beaten themselves by AC Milan in the final, when Prati scored three in a devastating 4–1 win.

Ajax reached the final again in 1971, when they beat the Greek champions Panathanaikos 2–0. That game at Wembley introduced to the world a young player who was to become a household name—Johan Cruyff. In addition to winning the European Cup that year, Ajax carried off the KNVB Cup, the Dutch equivalent of the FA Cup.

As I have already recounted, they reached the final of the European Cup again in 1972 and won 2–0, in an exciting game against Inter-Milan, the incomparable Cruyff scoring both goals. Could they win the competition for a third time? Only Real Madrid had been able to master every club in Europe and win the European Cup six times, five in succession. But those five came during the first five years of the competition. A first-round bye preceded a second-round tie against Bulgarian champions CSKA Sofia. Ajax won 6–1 on aggregate, met Bayern Munich in the quarter-final, and once again proved their strength with a 5–2 aggregate victory. Real Madrid were the next obstacle, but the power of Ajax was enough to carry them to the final 3–1 on aggregate, and an intriguing encounter with Italian champions Juventus. The match proved disappointing, although many onlookers in Belgrade claimed that Ajax should have won by more than the one goal, scored by Johnny Rep.

Three European Cup successes, World Club Champions in 1972, Super Cup holders in both 1972 and 1973. That is Ajax's record. Moreover they have won the Dutch Championship and Cup competitions a record number of times, and produced many of the stars who took Holland to within ninety minutes of World Cup success in both 1974 and 1978.

Perhaps the biggest blow to Ajax was the departure of Johan Cruyff to Spain and Barcelona. His £900,000 transfer in December 1973 stunned Ajax. Indeed, they began the 1973–74 season without Cruyff and were knocked out of the European Cup at the first attempt, by CSKA Sofia. In fact, they won nothing for three years. But, with Neeskens and Krol staying loyal to their championship cause, they regained their old form eventually, and took the Dutch Championship in 1977 for the seventeenth time. They continue to be *the* football club of Holland: long may their splendid flair grace the European scene.

Ajax: Postwar Honours

DUTCH CHAMPIONS: 12 times – 1947, 1957, 1960, 1966, 1967, 1968, 1970, 1972, 1973, 1977, 1979, 1980.
DUTCH CUP WINNERS: 6 times – 1961, 1967, 1970, 1971, 1972, 1979.
EUROPEAN CUP WINNERS: 3 times – 1971, 1972, 1973.
WORLD CLUB CHAMPIONS – 1972.
EUROPEAN SUPER-CUP WINNERS: Twice – 1972, 1973.

Celtic

It took Britain twelve years to produce its first winner of the top European club competition. From its inauguration in season 1955–56 the European Cup was accepted as the ultimate in club competitions, and for a long time Britain failed to produce a team good enough to bring the trophy back to the country where soccer supposedly took its roots. But at last, in May 1967, Celtic beat Inter-Milan 2–1 in the Portuguese capital of Lisbon and won the European Cup. To the vast Celtic support it seemed fitting that their team, with its great history and tradition, should be the first British club to win the competition. Indeed it was in 1967, in that year when Celtic first played in the European Cup, that so many of today's memories and today's attitudes were forged at Celtic Park.

But Celtic's first great victory, other than in the domestic competitions, came in 1938, when they were one of eight clubs to play in the Empire Exhibition Cup. Four Scottish and four English clubs took part: Aberdeen, Celtic, Hearts and Rangers of Scotland, and Brentford, Chelsea, Everton and Sunderland of England. Celtic beat Everton 1–0 in the final against the odds, putting the seal on their jubilee year.

Their victory fifteen years later in the Coronation Cup of 1953 was still more famous. Celtic had not won an honour for two years, which in Scottish soccer is a long time to go without a major triumph. Eight clubs competed, four each from England and Scotland. Scotland's representatives were Rangers, Hibernian, Aberdeen and Celtic. From England came Arsenal, Manchester United, Tottenham and Newcastle. Once again, Celtic overcame all the odds by beating Arsenal, Manchester United and Hibernian. Since that competition, Celtic have become the more feared team in the Celtic–Rangers dominance of Scottish soccer.

They have had only five managers since their first official match (against Rangers) in 1888. Willie Maley spent fifty-two years at the club as both player and manager. Jimmy McStay followed for a short spell. Then Jimmy McGrory, one of the most famous players Celtic ever had, took over. Jock Stein was the architect behind Celtic's modern success, and was eventually replaced by another former Celtic player, Billy McNeill, the present manager.

Under Stein's command they became one of the most feared teams in Europe, if not in the world. In his thirteen years as manager of Celtic, he achieved an astonishing number of honours. He won a total of ten Scottish League Championships, including the world record—nine titles in a row (1966–74); he had eight Scottish Cup successes and six League Cup victories. But, above all, he masterminded that famous European Cup victory.

That is still the major accomplishment in the history of Celtic Football club. But the final against Inter in 1967 started badly for Celtic. After only seven minutes Jim Craig was penalized and a penalty was awarded to Inter-Milan, with which Mazzola made no mistake. Now Celtic had to overcome Inter's renowned iron defence. They did so with a thundering goal from Tommy Gemmell. Then Steve Chalmers deflected in the winner. Celtic proudly returned with the European Cup to a wealth of praise echoed around Britain. They had achieved something no other club in these islands had done, and earned the respect of Europe in doing so.

Celtic's Honours List

SCOTTISH LEAGUE CHAMPIONS: 31 times – 1893, 1894, 1896, 1898, 1905, 1906, 1907, 1908, 1909, 1910, 1914, 1915, 1916, 1917, 1919, 1922, 1926, 1936, 1938, 1954, 1966, 1967, 1968, 1969, 1970, 1971, 1972, 1973, 1974, 1977, 1979.
SCOTTISH FA CUP WINNERS: 26 times – 1892, 1899, 1900, 1904, 1907, 1908, 1911, 1912, 1914, 1923, 1925, 1927, 1931, 1933, 1937, 1951, 1954, 1965, 1967, 1969, 1971, 1972, 1974, 1975, 1977, 1980.
SCOTTISH LEAGUE CUP WINNERS: 8 times – 1957, 1958, 1966, 1967, 1968, 1969, 1970, 1975.
EUROPEAN CUP WINNERS – 1967.

Would You Believe It?

The city of Manchester has seen both the highest and lowest attendances in Football League history. The highest was 83,260 for the First Division match between Manchester United and Arsenal on 17 January 1948, played at Maine Road (City's ground) because Old Trafford was still under repair from extensive bomb damage during the war. The lowest—just thirteen spectators—was at Old Trafford for a Second Division fixture between Stockport County and Leicester City on 7 May 1921. The game was switched there because Stockport's own ground had been closed by the FA for disciplinary reasons.

Ted Drake, the former Arsenal centre-forward who was later to become manager of Chelsea, scored all his club's goals in their 7–1 victory over Aston Villa at Villa Park on 14 December 1935. During the match he had just eight shots at goal. The other one struck Villa's crossbar. Drake scored a hat-trick in the first half, and had doubled his total by the 58th minute.

In season 1925–26 Cardiff City had a record seventeen internationals on their playing staff—nine Welsh, four Scottish and four Irish.

Goalscorers are hardly more prolific than Dixie Dean or Jimmy Greaves. Remarkably, they were exactly the same age—23 years and 290 days— when they scored their 200th League goals. Dean played for Tranmere Rovers, Everton and Notts County in the 1920s and 30s. Greaves wore the colours of Chelsea, Tottenham Hotspur and West Ham United in the 1950s and 60s.

OPPOSITE Celtic (hooped shirts) against their old rivals Rangers in the Scottish FA Cup final, 1980. Celtic won 1–0. (*Photo: Colorsport.*)

Chapter 13

The Rise of Eastern Europe

Soon after the Second World War the Football Association, prompted by the Foreign Office, invited the Russians to send a team to tour Britain. They brought their champions, Moscow Dynamo, who had just finished their league programme and, if their visit aroused unexpected interest among the British fans, the tour also stirred up ill-will on both sides.

It opened on 13 November 1945, against Chelsea at Stamford Bridge, and two hours before the kick-off the ground was full. With the gates locked, fans climbed over walls, and pressure from behind forced spectators on the terraces to flood over on to the dog track. When the match kicked off, spectators lined the pitch and space had to be made for players to take corner kicks.

No one knew how many people got into the Chelsea ground that day, but it must have been over 100,000, with 20,000 shut outside. After being two goals down early on the Russians recovered and finally drew 3–3. Then came a 10–1 victory against Cardiff City, a Third Division side; a 4–3 win against Arsenal at White Hart Lane, and a 2–2 draw with Glasgow Rangers.

The most remarkable match was that against Arsenal, for it was played in impenetrable fog. Players and spectators alike could see no more than ten yards but the Russian referee refused to cancel or abandon the game. One of the stars of the Dynamo team was the acrobatic goalkeeper Alexei Khomich, who died just before his country staged the Olympic Games. The British took him to their hearts and nicknamed him 'Tiger'.

Technically the Russians were inferior at heading but exceptionally good in attack, though all their goals were scored from close range. Centre-forward Konstantin Besov withdrew towards midfield, and in possession the Russian attack exchanged neat, quick, short passes while the inside-forward trio constantly switched position by intelligent running, and the ball was invariably played into space for a runner. The imaginative and skilful combined play of the Russian forwards was remarkable in 1945; then followed seven years during which Stalin cut off the Russian game from all international contact and they fell behind.

Yugoslavia underlined her political independence when, in November 1950, she accepted an invitation to meet the full England eleven and drew 2–2 at Highbury. Vladimir Beara, the Yugoslavia goalkeeper, pulled off a string of fine saves and when it was later revealed that he had studied ballet it was even suggested that English professional players should have dancing lessons!

OPPOSITE ABOVE A section of the huge crowd that packed Stamford Bridge to see Moscow Dynamo play Chelsea.

OPPOSITE BELOW Moscow Dynamo defending against Chelsea at Stamford Bridge, 1945.

(*Both photos: Syndication International.*)

Although no team from Eastern Europe has ever won the World Cup, they have totally dominated the Olympic Games soccer tournament. This is because they insist that all their players are amateurs. For the 1952 Olympics in Helsinki six teams from Eastern Europe took part. The Russians emphasized how much they had declined by struggling to beat Bulgaria 2–1 after extra time in the preliminary round. In their next game they drew 5–5 with Yugoslavia and lost the replay 3–1. Hungary took the title with an outstanding team that was to do even better against England the following year, and introduced for the first time the revolutionary 4.2.4 tactics. At the time, as in the Wembley game, many people commented that, in a team of master craftsmen, left-half Josef Zakarias looked a poor player. In fact he was playing as a defender, alongside centre-half Gyula Lorant.

As the list of finals shows, teams from Eastern Europe have taken a firm grip on the Olympic Games soccer tournament:

1952	Helsinki	Hungary 2, Yugoslavia 0
1956	Melbourne	Russia 1, Yugoslavia 0
1960	Rome	Yugoslavia 3, Denmark 1
1964	Tokyo	Hungary 2, Czechoslovakia 1
1968	Mexico City	Hungary 4, Bulgaria 1
1972	Munich	Poland 2, Hungary 1
1976	Montreal	East Germany 3, Poland 1
1980	Moscow	Czechoslovakia 1, East Germany 0

In the European Championship Russia has been more successful than in the Olympics, winning the 1958–60 competition in which countries like England, West Germany and Italy did not participate. In the final they beat Yugoslavia 2–1 in Paris after extra time.

Russia reached the final again in 1964 (in Madrid) and in 1972 (in Brussels) but were beaten on both occasions by Spain 2–1 and West Germany 3–0. The years of Russia's splendid isolation ended in 1954. They hammered Sweden 7–0 in a friendly and, being careful to invite Arsenal to play in Moscow in August when they were preparing for the new season, they thrashed the London club 5–0.

That same year, Hungary, Czechoslovakia and the always independent Yugoslavia took part in the final stages of the World Cup. Russia declined to enter while FIFA obligingly placed all the teams from Eastern Europe in two exclusive groups: Czechoslovakia, Romania and Bulgaria in one, Hungary and Poland (who withdrew) in another.

The Czechs failed to score a goal in final-round matches against Uruguay and Austria, and Yugoslavia reached the quarter-finals before losing 2–0 to West Germany. Hungary would probably have won the competition if Ferenc Puskas had not been injured in the first round. Puskas talked himself into the team for the final against West Germany and scored as Hungary went 2–0 up, but the trophy went to West Germany by 3–2. From 1958 onwards the World Cup was entered by all the teams from Eastern Europe, but Russia's debut in Sweden was remarkable only for the appearance of goalkeeper Lev Yashin. Dressed completely in black, and topped by a black cap with an enormous brim, Yashin had replaced 'Tiger' Khomich in the Moscow Dynamo goal in 1953 and proved to be an exceptionally gifted player.

To date, however, the Russians have flopped more often than not and were most successful in the 1966 series. Then they reached the semi-final, in which West Germany defeated them 2–1 and Portugal beat them for third place by the same score. Against professional opposition, Russia's only success was when Dynamo Kiev carried off the European Cup Winners' Cup in 1975. Other clubs from Eastern Europe have won international trophies, but none has been consistently successful. FC Magdeburg captured the Cup Winners' Cup for East Germany in 1974, Ferencvaros took the UEFA Cup to Hungary in 1965, and in 1967 the Yugoslav side, Dynamo Zagreb, also won the UEFA Cup.

Overall, the most successful country from Eastern Europe has been Czechoslovakia, even if they have never matched the brilliance of Hungary in the period 1953–55. Though no club from Eastern Europe has yet collected the European Cup, which is regarded by all as 'the big one', Slovan Bratislava became the first club from Eastern Europe to win the Cup Winners' Cup in 1969 when they beat CF Barcelona 3–2 in the final. At full international level the Czechs reached the World Cup final for the second time in Chile in 1962 and won the 1976 European Championship when it was staged in Yugoslavia.

In 1962 the Czechs faced Brazil in the World Cup final at Santiago. They had a brilliant attacking player in left-half Josef Masopust, and a fine left-back in Ladislav Novak, who is still, with seventy-five caps, the most honoured Czech player of all time. But, though the Czechs played some neat football and had a tight, compact defence, they lacked one essential ingredient that all great teams must have—a consistent goalscorer.

Early on, the Czechs were in command and Masopust, dribbling into the penalty area, gave them the lead with a shot from close range. Largely through the skills and speed of right-winger Garrincha, Brazil got back into the game. But they needed the unintentional help of the Czech goalkeeper, Viliem Schroiff. He was at fault when Brazil equalized. He went out to a cross, failed to make contact with the ball and left Amarildo, standing in for the injured Pele, to score a soft goal. Schroiff was at fault again when he dropped a ball lofted into the penalty area, so handing the Brazilians another gift and they eventually won 3–1.

Masopust became the manager-coach of First Division club Zbrojovka Brno after ending his playing days in Belgium. He was one of four players from Dukla, the Czech Army team, to play in the final, and loves to tell a story relating to that 1962 World Cup. A few days after the Czech team returned home, the four Chile veterans were ordered to report to Hradcany Palace to see the Dukla chairman who was also in political charge of the Army as Minister of Defence. 'At last', Masopust said to his colleague Svatopluk Pluskal, 'we are going to get some money for reaching the World Cup final.' That afternoon the players were ushered into the Minister's office, and, after a lengthy speech in

Masny, the best-known of recent Czechoslovakia players, beats two West Germans in the 1980 European Championship. (*Photo: Syndication International.*)

which he thanked them for their splendid showing in Chile, he handed each player an autographed copy of his own book *The Importance of Sport in Modern Society*.

In the 1976 European Championship Czechoslovakia had first to eliminate England from the qualifying competition. Then in the quarter-final they beat Russia 2–0 at home and drew 2–2 away, to reach the finals. There, in the semi-final in Zagreb, the Czechs beat Holland 3–1 after extra time despite the fact that the Dutch had most of their spectacular 1974 World Cup final team on duty, including full-backs Rudi Krol and Wim Suurbier, Johan Neeskens and Wim Jansen in midfield, and Johan Cruyff and Robbie Rensenbrink in attack.

In the final Czechoslovakia were winning 2–0 after twenty-six minutes, with Jan Svehlik scoring from close range and Karol Dobias beating Sepp Maier with a low cross shot from the edge of the penalty area. Dieter Muller got one back for the Germans on the thirty-minute mark; then, with the Czechs defending and counterattacking, they hung on for almost an hour. In the dying seconds West Germany forced a corner and as the ball came across Bernd Holzenbein fouled the Czech goalkeeper Ivo Viktor, who had been brilliant in the final stages, and went on to head an equalizer.

Extra time brought no further score and each side was called on to take five penalty kicks. Neither goalkeeper had any chance with any of the spot-kicks until, with the Czechs ahead at four penalties to three, Germany's Uli Hoeness blasted his kick high over the crossbar. The Czechs now had to score with their remaining penalty and this threw tremendous pressure on the fifth man. But manager Vaclav Jezek had anticipated just such an eventuality and kept Antonin Panenka, a regular penalty-taker, until last. Panenka hit a dipping, swerving shot, and Maier dived underneath the ball as it passed into the net. Panenka disappeared beneath a pile of jubilant team-mates and Czechoslovakia were champions of Europe.

Would You Believe It?

On Christmas Day 1940 two players turned out for two different Football League clubs on the same day. Tommy Lawton played for his own club, Everton, in a Merseyside derby against Liverpool in the morning, and after lunch made a guest appearance for Tranmere Rovers against Crewe Alexandra. Len Shackleton played for the two Bradford clubs, his own side, Park Avenue, and as a guest for Bradford City.

When Denmark met Mexico in the final of the 1971 Women's World Cup, 108,000 people filled the Aztec Stadium, Mexico City to see the Danes win 2–0 and retain the trophy. Many paid up to five times the face value for tickets to see a match which featured girls wearing hot-pants, and goal-posts painted pink.

In 1888–89, Preston North End won the Football League Championship without losing a match and the FA Cup without conceding a goal.

On Easter Monday 1936, when Luton Town were playing at home to Bristol Rovers in Division Three (South), manager Ned Liddell had problems. Both his recognized first-team centre-forwards were out of action. After some deliberation, Liddell decided to draft Joe Payne in to fill the main striking role. The move was a sheer gamble, because Payne had played only a handful of games for Luton, and those as a defender. By half-time Payne had scored a hat-trick and netted seven more in the second half. Ten goals in one match—a record for the Football League—from a man who turned up to the ground not even expecting to play.

Arnold Birch, a goalkeeper with Chesterfield, scored five times for his club in 1923–24. All were penalties and Birch's total is a record for a goalkeeper in a season.

When Preston North End reached the final of the FA Cup in 1888, they asked for permission to be photographed with the trophy before the game, so confident were they of victory. The referee, Major Marindin, told them: 'You'd better win the Cup first.' They didn't. West Bromwich Albion beat them 2–1 at Kennington Oval.

Pele exchanges his shirt with Bobby Moore—'the best defender I ever played against'—after England's match with Brazil in the 1970 World Cup finals in Mexico. (*Photo: Syndication International.*)

Chapter 14

South American Soccer

The dark blue Cadillac squeezes past other limousines double-parked in Rockefeller Plaza, New York City, and halts outside the skyscraper numbered 75. The young Brazilian chauffeur releases the doorlocks with the electric switch, walks to the sidewalk and opens the rear door. Out steps Pedro Garay, a thirty-year-old Cuban exile, the official bodyguard and assistant appointed by Warner Communications to work alongside the VIP still seated in the back and to whom the Cadillac and chauffeur come as fringe benefits with the post of PR consultant.

As he appears, Edson Arantes do Nascimento shows he wears his latest crown as naturally as Pele wore all the others of a rewarding life. The well-organized arrival is predictably interrupted by the request of another Cadillac chauffeur—a black New Yorker—for an autograph. 'It's for my gal who plays soccer at High School'—and Pele, being Pele, forsakes the demeanour of businessman, rests his briefcase on the sidewalk, asks for a pen and signs. The message is in English. 'Good luck—Pele.'

He smiles that famous smile, heads through the swing doors, and, by the time he reaches the elevators, his mini entourage has increased to include two teenagers, two members of the New York Cosmos staff and a uniformed security guard who wants to know if Pele enjoyed his most recent trip to Brazil. Pele repeats the smile, says he did and then moves up to the fifteenth floor, just short of halfway up in the headquarters of the one-billion-dollar Warner Corporation, where Robert Redford has an office; where approval is given to the latest Warner Bros movie budget, and where Cosmos have a lofty administrative suite and a basement ticket office.

In his own office, the hub of a small suite which also houses a bilingual secretary, a receptionist, Pedro Garay, and Roberto Xisto, the Brazilian who is his world business manager, Pele steps across the zebra-skin rug, walks round the oval table to his chair, gets a quick business update from his secretary, removes his jacket and finally ponders on the question:

'Why is South American soccer so good . . . ?'

Ever candid in private, but never seeking public controversy, he presents his answers diplomatically and thoughtfully.

'When Argentina won the last World Cup, I was pleased as a South American, even though a Brazilian like me had to have some disappointment. I was lifted by the style of Argentina who, whatever may be said about the different controversies that surrounded their victory, gave some fresh air to a game that tends to be tactically strangled these days.

'Even if Argentina had lost the 1978 Final to Holland, as well they might, the memory of their positive football would have remained. In a sense it would then have been the same as the '54 Final (when I was still at school) and the West Germans Sepp Herberger and Fritz Walter beat the Hungarians who had defeated Brazil en route to the Final.

'It is the magical play of Hungary we remember mostly from that tournament and era, a time when Puskas, Hidegkuti and others were painting tapestries around some of the world stadia. Likewise, I suppose, Brazil's great presence leading to the 1950 Final defeat by Uruguay in Rio de Janeiro is what we most remember—well, what I most remember, anyway!—in what was undoubtedly as big a world upset as four years later when the Germans took the trophy from the tired Hungarians.'

Pele walked to the record player in a corner of the office and started a disc of Sergio Mendez and the Brazilian group he sometimes 'borrows' for relaxation. He kept the volume low and then returned from World Cup history to more modern times and the question in hand: well, how good is/was/will be the South American player? The world's greatest goalscorer-turned-executive played with the question as if juggling with a ball from famous foot to famous foot. He wasn't sidestepping the issue, either. Answering the question these days can lead only to compromise and some contradiction.

'He's good, the South American player. He can be very good. Even as a boy he loves to play with the ball as if it were more than his toy, as if it were his possession. When I was a boy, like so many the world around, we could not find the money, the *cruzeiros*, to buy a ball, so we made our own. In our case, we got old newspaper, rolled it up, added some rags and stuffed it all into an old sock. To hold it all together we tied the ''ball'' with string and then we'd play. Of course, we had already learned to kick almost any object that moved because Brazilian boys, and I guess you could say South American boys almost all over that Continent, except places like Venezuela, where they push others sports ahead of football, yes, Brazilian boys educate themselves to kick a ball, with their fathers watching, before they can run. Or walk. You could say their fathers demand it.

'Football is basically a simple game, too often complicated by those who seek lofty status as ''football intellects''. If you master the basics when you are a boy, it should have the same results as doing your school homework every night: in other words a better chance in later life! One of the essential techniques is ball control, which gives you and your team greater chance of retaining possession.'

This statement of the very simple and obvious steers Pele into his theory that, overall, the South American player has better technique than most Europeans, repeat most. Some think it comes from having the sun on his back more, or for the other climatic reason that harder playing surfaces demand greater control than the self-controlling softer pitches of most European countries where the game is often played in deep winter. Pele accepts more the

OPPOSITE ABOVE A save by Fillol of Argentina in the 1980 match against England.

OPPOSITE BELOW Valencia's Bonhof and Arsenal's Talbot, European Cup Winners' Cup, 1980.

(*Both photos: Syndication International.*)

view that the South American works harder at those basics earlier in life than others and, therefore, benefits more. In six colour films which he made for Pepsi-Cola, entitled 'Pele: the Master and his Method', he aims at a young audience and sidetracks the tactical side of the game to emphasize the priority of learning those basics.

It does not end with the boys at school or on the beaches which Brazilians use as playing fields when they're relaxing. As Pele confirms: 'Physical conditioning is important to the South American, but in training he is accompanied by a ball more than not. It becomes almost his permanent companion. He doesn't eat it. He doesn't drink it. He doesn't sleep with it. But the South American possesses the football from an early age and never lets go. I know there have been many great ball artists produced by European football, but they're at a premium. Players who are considered little more than ordinary in South America are still masters of the ball.'

Pele interrupts to take a 'welcome back to New York' phone call from Steve Ross, President and top man of Warner Communications, and then returns to his platform:

'What I'd like to be able to say for South Americans and Europeans, since together they represent the world's best, is that there were many more better players and more coaches prepared to let them become better players. I do not believe that great players emerge as great whatever the circumstances. There has been evidence to the contrary and a coach, by insisting that players follow his tactics rigidly, can half strangle ability. Let's return to that basic of ball control and possession. The reason I question the validity of defensive football is that it generally throws ball control out of the window. It trades ball control for caution, and I argue that to score goals to win you mostly have to be in possession of the ball. Clearing the ball aimlessly, as so many goalkeepers and other defenders do, is guaranteed to lose that possession more times than not. Lose possession and you're on defence again. Retain it and you're in command.'

Pele, of course, is all too aware of Brazil's fall from the prestigious heights their great skills acquired for them in the '58, '62 and '70 World Cup tournaments in Sweden, Chile and Mexico. Regrettably he concedes Brazil deserved nothing more than the defensive labels given them in the '74 and '78 competition in West Germany and Argentina, even though they finished third in that last tournament.

'As I was saying,' he went on, 'a coach can suffocate talent by demanding that forward players resort to defensive responsibilities as a priority. We saw it happen with Brazilians of all people. Yes, Brazilians, the world masters who once gave a lot of joy to the gloom of the game. First, go back to 1974. The Brazil team, coached by my friend Zagalo, included flair players like Rivelino, Jairzinho, Paulo Cesar. You may have seen plenty of their technique in back positions, but hardly noticed their flair. The tactics—the heavily defensive, over-cautious tactics—did not allow it. They wore chains around their gifted feet.'

Pele stopped to consider why this was. He has never been slow to criticize

OPPOSITE Joe Jordan in action for Scotland; inset, in Manchester United strip, in characteristic pose. (*Photos: main picture, Colorsport; inset, Syndication International.*)

fellow Brazilians when he feels justified. It never deters him if others retaliate with such retorts as 'Well, Pele is like many stars of the past. Nothing today is as good as yesterday.' No Brazilian would have been happier than Pele if the 1974 team had let itself go and won the World Cup in Germany or at least been runners-up in a worthy final. Who knows how much more successful than fourth place they might have been playing to their full attacking potential? In Germany, Pele knew, the South American player could have been the equivalent of the European. That Rivelino and Jairzinho, certainly, could have emulated Cruyff and Beckenbauer in star value. If only they had been allowed. . . .

There, in a European soccer citadel, the highly professionalized West Germany were living answers of how good South American players *could* be, or could have been. 'Especially Rivelino', emphasizes Pele. 'Especially him. With his all-round skills, sharpness and powerful shooting, he was a weapon Brazil needed up front. Right up front.' By 'up front', of course, he was referring to what he also likes to call 'the jungle', the striker's beat, where he is on his own too often, where he's fighting to get the ball, retain possession, release it, score goals, avoid the predators intent on shortening his effectiveness. Yes, indeed, the 'jungle', which he inhabited for around twenty years with the most success of anybody in the game and over 1,200 goals to prove it!

As Pele watched that '74 World Cup, his heart was heavy, yes, saddened by the defending champions, his beloved Brazil, repositioning themselves as No. 4 in the world with a team he knew was much, much more capable of higher stature, a more worthy ending. The theory that South American teams could not win the World Cup in Europe because they lacked the team discipline and temperament, was deflated by Brazil themselves in 1958 when they gave the game a new meaning, a new poetry which enriched some established reputations and created at least one new one, that of a seventeen-year-old who conquered a man's world. His name was Edson Arantes do Nascimento, but even those people who sounded knowledgeable by being able to pronounce it still wanted to call him Pele.

To jump ahead to 1978, and all that happened, and didn't happen, in the Argentine, the Brazil team with a different coach (Claudio Coutinho) moved up one and claimed third place when there was nowhere near the individual ability of the '74 team.

The truth of it all is that the South American player of flexible artistry is as bound to team discipline when it comes to World Cup football as the most disciplined of players, and, indeed, in domestic football far more than those from other continents might imagine. The heavy anchorage in the crowded defences, of some South American sides engaged in World *Club* Cup finals against various champions of Europe remains vivid in the minds of those witness to, and victims of the ruthless styles, notably in Argentinian club teams. It is also no secret that Cesar Luis Menotti, coach-architect of Argentina's victory in 1978, was hardly encouraged to pursue his flamboyant style by domestic League preference for the more cautious.

OPPOSITE ABOVE Football on a gravel pitch in Argentina. (*Photo: Colorsport.*)

OPPOSITE BELOW Pele, Tostao (left) and Jairzinho celebrate Pele's goal against Italy in the 1970 World Cup final.

(*Photo: Syndication International.*)

Pele did not expect his Brazil to win in Argentina. As he says: 'I knew that the music of Brazilian soccer was being played to a tune unfamiliar to those still judging Brazil by their past reputation. I did not cloud my thoughts with unpatriotic pessimism just because I did not support the withdrawn tactics of the team. But if I had dismissed all caution and proposed Brazil as the winners I'd have deserted reason for unashamed nationalism and perhaps provoked questions of my sanity from even the blindest of my fellow countrymen. It may have surprised many people, Brazilians included, to know that I regarded the 1978 descendants of the '58, '62 and '70 winners stronger defensively than any of those exciting champions. Their backline was tactically better organized. However, when it came to the midfield ability and the armoury of strikers, my enthusiasm was rapidly diluted.'

It was interesting to see in Argentina that the most discussed new personality to emerge in Brazil since the previous World Cup, Zico, found himself too obviously a lightweight in many situations in Argentina and had almost an indifferent tournament.

In effect, the Brazilian team mirrored a lean period in their domestic game. Outstanding players were at a high premium. Before his arrival in Argentina, Zico was billed by some 'as another Pele' and by others as 'another Tostao', the greatest player-off-the-ball Pele says he ever saw. Pele labelled this kind of comparison as a case of false identification, as he did the labelling of Johan Cruyff as 'the white Pele'.

'Cruyff is Cruyff,' says Pele, 'a world-class player in his own right. I certainly did not think Zico was another Pele, either, or another Tostao. Nor, unless I'm mistaken, does Zico.'

Always reluctant to make direct comparisons between players of any era, Pele still doesn't hesitate to liken Mario Kempes to Alfredo di Stefano. Their similarity did not start and end on the field. Both played for Argentina, their native country, and both ended up in Spanish League club football. Kempes has not yet gone as far as di Stefano by becoming a naturalized Spaniard, but in achievement he has climbed to a World Cup-winning final which Alfredo the Great never did manage.

Pele on the '78 tournament's most exciting star: 'Kempes was not only fortunate to play under a coach who invited him to be himself and express his talents fully; he also rose to that opportunity brilliantly in several departments. I'm not saying he's as great as di Stefano. Not yet. He might never be. Greatness demands, as well as other talents, consistency over a career. It's too early to vote Kempes into the Hall of Greatness, although he's already peeped into the Hall of Fame. He has the ingredients to get there. Like di Stefano, he is not shy of work. His first platform is the mid-field where can conduct the flow of the team. He has the confidence and ability to take on defenders. He has the stamina, and sharpness to transform into a striker, a dangerous goalscorer.'

Pele went on: 'I have seen plenty of England's Kevin Keegan on TV, and I guess that if you wanted to analyse the typical European and South American you would use Keegan and Kempes. Keegan is probably the quickest forward in

OPPOSITE ABOVE The World Cup of 1978. Brazil (dark shorts) in action against Italy whom they defeated 2–1 to finish in third place.

OPPOSITE BELOW Buenos Aires, 1978. It's Argentina's World Cup, held aloft by captain Passarella, after they had beaten Holland 3–1 in the final.

(*Both photos: Syndication International*.)

the game, the most athletic and a successful product of the frill-less English League programme who took his economic, get-there-in-the-shortest-route style and conquered West Germany at Hamburg. As a prototype of what is loosely called "the modern game," applicable to predictable League football in South America these days as well as Europe, Keegan has done great things for himself and his country, considering he has never had the chance of playing in the final stages of a World Cup.

'I have expressed my views of South American players using World Cup tournaments as a natural measure but Keegan represents an important minority of superstars who can boast little World Cup mileage. In any case, it should not decide whether a player is great or not. What should decide is *truth* at any high professional level of the game, and the truth is that Keegan, though never being a Stanley Matthews (I respected his name when I was a teenager and have done ever since); a Tom Finney (my English friend Steve Richards, of Pepsi-Cola, has told me he was the equal of Matthews); a Bobby Charlton (whom I admired, as so many other South Americans did); a Jimmy Greaves (another reputed "great" of whom I didn't see too much); though never being the equivalent of many English players of the past (discounting Scots, Welsh and Irish), was and is the revered name. My belief is that you could have put Keegan into any current South American team, at club or international level, and he would not lose a centimetre of stature. But, if you were to stretch my loyalty, give me a lie-detector, and threaten me with all kinds of recriminations, I'd still believe that a South American like Kempes has the edge in improvisation. I do not know whether either continent, Europe or South America, or any continent for that matter, has produced the perfect player, but it sounds like an interesting exercise for a television quiz game in Rio de Janeiro or Frankfurt-on-Main.'

There were few pre-tournament indications that Argentina would perform so positively in 1978. The fact that they won it in the end and won it in such style was a rejuvenation for South American football, which had long since become disillusioned with Brazil's decision to cross the line to adopt the more European defence-oriented game. The justification for being so withdrawn in the '74 World Cup was said to be the fact that the finals were being held in Europe. To take the natural attacking Brazil game to the European teams in one of their own home fortresses (Germany) was considered a reckless notion. To look even more defensive and unappealing in South America itself (meaning Argentina '78) could be interpreted only as a public confession that, this time, there weren't enough outstanding players around to be anything but defensive.

What now for South American football? Pele is optimistic. He says: 'There have been signs of a more open approach in the Brazil national team. I don't know how that will be carried over into the next World Cup in Spain in 1982 because strategy for a four-week tournament can be so different from that for individual games during the four years between tournaments. We'll have to see about Brazil.' And Argentina? Pele notes that his old friend Cesar Menotti did not join Pele's own club, New York Cosmos, despite all the rumours. Instead he stayed on as a much better-rewarded national coach of Argentina. 'Keeping

Menotti is good for Argentina and for the image of South American football,' says Pele.

The only player in history to collect three World Cup winners' medals, Pele took up Menotti's cause: 'Argentina were not by any measure the greatest team to win the World Cup, but they were fit to wear the crown in their own country, and if they go on under Menotti rebuilding towards a more complete squad by the time Spain is upon us, they will again be challenging strongly for the Cup and quite capable of winning it, even in Europe. After all, as many of us remember so vividly, Brazil did win it for South America in Europe in 1958. In returning to Europe to defend the crown they had retained in Chile, the Brazilians, as I know only too well, having been a member of that ill-fated squad in England, were woefully unprepared. Although the physical aggression shown against us on the field by the Bulgarians and the Portuguese was a decisive factor in our failure to reach the quarter finals—it made me threaten never to play in another World Cup—our real weakness was in planning. We put things right in Mexico. Menotti will, I expect, be well prepared for Spain. He has established himself and, because of the triumph in Buenos Aires in the final against Holland, he should have less outside pressures pushed at him than before the tournament in Argentina.'

Pele says South Americans are looking forward to Spain for various reasons. 'First, to see if Menotti, Kempes, Ardiles and others pursue their refreshing approach to football. Second, to see if it can take Argentina to a second successive victory which has been achieved only twice since the World Cup was launched in 1930, by Italy before the Second World War, and postwar by Brazil. Third, to see if Brazil's great football is going to carry a smile again and, finally, to see if another Peru emerges because, remember, despite the criticism and accusations made by Brazilians and others after their heavy defeat by Argentina, Peru did entertain as well as win important games in the '78 tournament.'

The last word of Pele on the variable subject of South American football: 'I called my autobiography *My Life and the Beautiful Game*. And it is still a beautiful game as the Argentinians reminded us in 1978. If only all countries would have the courage—yes, it needs courage to be ready to accept defeat sometimes in pursuing your own ideals—to give players free expression from boyhood onwards then the adjective "beautiful" would be applied internationally more often than it is today. I don't mean forsake team discipline on or off the field. I don't mean send players out there to do just their own thing. You have to have complete unselfishness. The team principle has to be foremost in a club or a national squad. What I mean is the kind of team unity and individual sacrifice for the team which we achieved for Brazil in Mexico in 1970 and the free expression that creamed the cake.

'Now somebody will tell me there aren't the same players around today, to which I can only respond: is there enough coaching freedom to encourage the development of that kind of player?'

Chapter 15

Soccer in the USA

By the turn of the century the whole power structure of world soccer may have changed, with the United States becoming a trendsetter both on and off the field. That's the American dream of one Britisher, Phil Woosnam, who has masterminded the emergence of American soccer. The country's only previous noteworthy appearance on the world football front until recent years was their shock win over England in the World Cup in 1950.

It is a little-known fact that the US Federation was affiliated to FIFA as long ago as 1913. Yet until the 1970s their football was, to us, just a joke and a minor rival to their national sports of grid-iron football and baseball. No one now, whether or not they completely share Woosnam's optimism, doubts that America has the potential to revolutionize the game and become equal partners with its giants in Europe and South America. America's advantages are obvious: finance, population and business knowhow.

Until now soccer in the States—you never call it football—has relied on overseas players and thus has been disregarded as an international force. But, as Bob Dylan would say, 'times they are a-changing' and there is no bigger advocate of that theory than Phil Woosnam. Americans say that 'soccer is a kick in the grass', yet according to Woosnam it could be a kick in a rather tender part of the anatomy for Brazil, West Germany and others in the next few years.

Woosnam, the one-time West Ham, Aston Villa and Welsh international player, stands on the threshold of converting one of the world's largest countries to football in a matter of fifteen years. He is the commissioner of the North American Soccer League (NASL) and a virtual dictator in their growing soccer empire. He has realized from the start that for soccer to catch the public imagination and compete with the traditional sports it had to make an impact at grass roots level: the schools and colleges.

The ethnic groups in the States (European and South American) helped give the sport the initial lift-off. Imported stars such as Pele, Beckenbauer and a batch of other big names were pioneers in the early days. But soccer was never going to gain countrywide recognition and acclaim until the appearance of the home-bred player. And, without that 'all-American boy', soccer had no chance on the international scene. Woosnam knew that. And he believes that long, painful process, covering a generation, is close to maturity. If evidence was needed to back up his claims you only have to look at the number of Americans now playing in the NASL.

Phil Woosnam, mastermind of American soccer. (*Photo: Colorsport.*)

The Americans, with no deep-rooted loyalty to the game, have also taught us how to sell it to the public and treat them to the same kind of facilities and courtesy we all expect when patronizing other forms of entertainment.

Woosnam shrugs off the cynicism towards the US razzmatazz style of soccer and seriously hopes that the country will stage the 1990 World Cup. He says: 'I want home-grown American players to combine the ball control and flair of the Brazilians with the technical perfection of the Dutch and Germans and the work rate of the English. I hope to see our stadia jam-packed, with whole families being excited by the skills of our teams. And I can foresee the day when an American side can compete and hold its own against the best teams in the world.

'America can become the world capital of soccer. Spain has been chosen as World Cup hosts in 1982, then it goes to Colombia four years later. But 1990. That will be ours, make no mistake. This country has a reputation for succeeding once it sets its mind to it. The World Cup is our goal and we do not intend to miss out.

'The game has taken root in the schools and colleges and there are 25,000 young players in Seattle alone and 40 per cent of NASL players are Americans.'

Woosnam's confidence cannot be disregarded when you consider that New York Cosmos were pulling in average crowds of 45,000 last season, and even beating the famed New York Yankees baseball team in attendances. Down in Florida Tampa Bay Rowdies were getting gates of 30,000 to 40,000. What English club other than the Liverpools and Manchester Uniteds would not like that kind of support?

Trevor Francis, scoring for Detroit. (*Photo: Colorsport.*)

It is significant that soccer has just obtained nationwide coverage on television—a big asset in the conversion of Americans to soccer. The appeal of the game is obvious compared with their football and baseball. In soccer a youngster does not have to be six foot with muscles to match, nor does he need expensive equipment to play the sport. There is also the hidden element of America's urge to compete and win against the rest of the world. Men in high political posts realize the possible advantage of playing the world's most popular game. Indeed, when Henry Kissinger was Secretary of State, he interceded with the Brazilian government to help get Pele to play for New York Cosmos.

Pele was the pioneer needed by Woosnam in those early days when American soccer was no more than a joke. For Pele to come to the States aroused interest even among the indifferent. His enthusiasm, instinctive command of public relations and, needless to say, his brilliant skill, acted as the springboard to the present soccer explosion. Not only that, his appearances in the States prompted others to follow. He gave American soccer respectability. The appearance of Beckenbauer and Carlos Alberto, two men who had led their countries to World Cup victories, added to their image. Three of the biggest names in the game appeared for New York Cosmos in 1977. The North American Soccer League had gained credibility.

But soccer needed more than actual players to entice the public, to preach the gospel and woo big-money backers. Woosnam had to sell soccer to industry, to businessmen. He had to convince them that there was money to be made in this previously unsupported and strange game that brought such fanatical followings from the rest of the world. It was no good relying, as we do in Britain, on local businessmen who take on the role of director of a local club as a hobby and expect no financial return. Soccer had to be run as a business, with rewards for those who invested in it. That was the American way. And it continues to teach our own administrators a lesson.

The average soccer fan in the States would laugh at the idea of being squeezed into our often outdated stadia, being asked to stand in the open in all kinds of weather, contend with hooliganism and with just the bare unglossed ninety minutes of entertainment which could end up as a goal-less draw. Woosnam and his American pathfinders considered soccer as part of the entertainment scene, not just a sport, as many consider it here. It was to be treated as such. The public came first, their needs had to be met. They had some advantages in virtually starting from scratch. Many clubs in England would like to start again without the handicap of outmoded grounds but lack the financial resources to make the change.

Woosnam courted millionaires who, at the very least, could offset their financial backing against taxes. But they were also shrewd enough to realize that the franchises could be worth millions in a decade. The giant Warner Communications took over New York Cosmos, and it is estimated that their initial 100,000 dollars outlay could now be worth five million dollars.

Woosnam gives three good reasons why soccer has made such a dramatic

OPPOSITE Georgio Chinaglia (right) of New York Cosmos in action against Chelsea during one of Cosmos' financially successful tours of Europe. The Chelsea player is Ron Harris. (*Photo: Bob Thomas.*)

impact in such a short time. He says: 'First, this country is blessed with magnificent facilities. All our stadia were built in the last ten years, filled with seats, with parking for up to 25,000 cars and situated near expressways. Then the climate. We play between April to September, most of the time in sunshine. Our players' creative talent is never curbed by mud-bound pitches. Lastly, the form of our competition drives away all fears and encourages players and their teams to express their skill. What we have done is to cast away the overriding anxiety of relegation. No teams are demoted in our league structure. That was something I lived with for many of my eleven years as a player, particularly with West Ham and Aston Villa. It is agonizing, frustrating and humiliating. It breeds too much fear among good players.'

Soccer in the States became a day out for the whole family. Picnics and parties were held in the car parks, followed by pre-match entertainment with marching bands, various competitions, circus acts and games between either youngsters or women. Nothing was missed out in the presentation of the game itself. Glamorous girls played out the role of cheer-leaders as the players were introduced individually. Throughout the game there was a constant stream of DJ-type comment and information. Goals were greeted with flashing lights on electric scoreboards, followed, at Cosmos, by an action replay. Pure carnival. Soccer had arrived American-style.

The Americans have been criticized for tampering with the laws of the game. But some think that their innovations could well be used all over the world. It was decided that the American public would want a result from every match. And that was soon overcome by the 'sudden death' and 'shoot-outs'. If two teams were level at the end of ninety minutes an extra fifteen minutes would be played, with the first team to score winning the match. If that failed, then there would be an exciting shoot-out. Five players from each side would, in turn, try to beat the goalkeeper in five seconds after collecting the ball 35 yards out. That one-against-one confrontation thrilled the spectators. There was also a 35-yard line from the goals and a player could only be offside if he was on the goal side of the line.

About half the clubs had astro-turf, the all-weather surface. Not that this was welcomed by the imported players. They complained that it burnt the skin on contact and virtually made the sliding tackle obsolete. In its favour it made for even surfaces which put the emphasis on skill.

In the League extra points were awarded for goals, an idea which people over here have also suggested. Woosnam's opinion that it encourages attacking football was hard to argue against.

Recently, to keep football going during the winter, six-a-side indoor soccer was introduced. It has proved a massive success. To quote Woosnam again: 'Indoor soccer is a way of keeping players occupied and sustaining revenue in our closed season. But it is already enjoying such a boom that clubs are starting to sign up specialist players for the six-a-side game.' In places like Minnesota and Memphis, teams are playing to packed houses of 12,000. The popularity of basketball had already dwindled, but even ice hockey now looks on the six-a-side soccer as major threat. FIFA President Joao Havelange was so impressed with the sport that he wants to stage a six-a-side world cup in his native Brazil.

The Americans have changed the rules from our own traditional five-a-side match. In the States there are no protective areas for goalkeepers and no restrictions on playing the ball above shoulder height.

Perhaps the fact that as many women watch soccer in the States as men is the reason for another growing form of soccer: women's teams and competitions. Their standard is surprisingly high and their games draw large crowds.

The marketing and promotion of soccer has been astonishing. TV commercials and billboards all over town bang out the message. The manufacture and sale of souvenirs, soccer kits and clothes puts the rest of the soccer world in the shade. The players themselves become the property of the club and are used to the full in public relations. They are in duty bound to talk to the media whenever asked, and no autograph hunter may be turned away. They also spend some of their spare time coaching youngsters from schools and colleges in the area. But the stars are treated handsomely and the financial rewards compare with any country and exceed most. Their life-style, with plush apartments and cars, makes that of their English counterpart seem drab.

In the early days it was this financial element and not the pioneering spirit that lured players from all over the world. The attraction to Englishmen was obvious. With seasons hardly overlapping it was a highly paid summer vacation. It prompted some bitterness between the two countries with the Americans being accused of disrupting the Football League and making unethical approaches to players. It led to a charter being drawn up between them and the end of the loan system. American clubs can no longer get away without paying a transfer fee for many of their recruits. The moves must now be permanent. This inspires a greater loyalty and devotion from their foreign players. They can match even our inflated transfer prices. It seems certain that there will be a steady flow across the Atlantic for a few years to come.

As in our own game, money does not guarantee success. In 1979, for the first time, New York Cosmos did not make the North American championship final. It was the less fashionable Vancouver Whitecaps, skippered by former England captain Alan Ball, who won, beating Tampa Bay Rowdies.

It is at places like Tampa, and unlikely outposts such as Tulsa, that soccer has caught the imagination of the public; it has yet to become nationwide in popularity. For example, even the signing of world star Johan Cruyff failed to have a great impact in Los Angeles, where the Aztecs played to crowds of only around 10,000. Even Cosmos get the majority of support from New Jersey rather than New York itself.

The one missing ingredient for Woosnam's dream to come true is the emergence of American stars, but with the NASL continually raising the number of Americans who must be in each team more and more are coming into the league sides. Experts close to the scene believe it will be the entry of black players that will produce homegrown superstars. They have not yet become heavily involved.

Woosnam says, 'When the people of Harlem start playing they will rival anyone in the world, and it will happen. But to understand the reason it has not happened yet, you must realize that sport here is organized differently. The school system provides little opportunity up to the age of fifteen. In the suburbs parents provide facilities and leadership for local leagues. In the inner cities this management is lacking. The city kids will learn eventually by watching soccer on television and then going into the streets and playing as they do in England. Maybe that is a better way to learn than by organized coaching.'

An American Pele? Perhaps one will be discovered. It is on the field now that the final push must be made. It is doubtful whether any of their club sides would survive in our First Division. Many would not last in the Second, and an all-American team is a long way from matching the top national sides.

It is a possibility that the Americans will start looking for the younger foreign player who could, within a couple of years, become an American citizen and play for the country. It is more probable that they will intensify the coaching of their own youngsters with the help of the best football knowledge money can buy. 'Eventually we will have teams with just the occasional star from overseas', predicts Woosnam. 'Don't forget that Americans only took to the game in the later sixties. Before then it was totally immigrant. It was played at the high schools and in the slums—and the 200 million in America's suburbia knew nothing about it. Now it's the in-thing, the fastest-growing sport in the country. We have youngsters of fifteen and sixteen equal in skill to others of the same age elsewhere and they'll be the basis of World Cup sides.'

Woosnam and his American dream have come a long way. The images of a top soccer country are taking shape. The rest of the world take heed.

OPPOSITE Johan Cruyff, in the colours of Los Angeles Aztecs this time, but still wearing the no. 14 shirt, as he has done all through his career. (*Photo: Colorsport.*)

Would You Believe It?

Englishman Stan Mortensen, of Blackpool, made his international debut for Wales. In a wartime match at Wembley in September 1943, England reserve Mortensen went on as second-half substitute for injured Welsh half-back Ivor Powell.

Few players can match the playing career of left-winger Alan Daley. From 1945 to 1961 he appeared in the colours of: Derby County, Mansfield Town, Hull City, Bangor City, Worksop Town, Doncaster Rovers, Boston United, Scunthorpe United, Corby Town, Mansfield (for a second spell), Stockport County, Crewe Alexandra, Coventry City, Cambridge City, and Burton Albion.

At the start of the 1946–47 season, Harold Bell played as a centre-half for Tranmere Rovers. On 30 August, 1955 he was dropped from the home match with Gateshead. In between these two games he did not miss a match—a record of 401 consecutive League appearances.

Chapter 16

Tactical Formations

Liverpool developed into arguably the best club side Britain—or the world—has produced by adding to 'total football' the traditional British qualities of fitness and resolution. During the last eight seasons they won the Championship five times and had four triumphs in European competition because they insisted on all ten outfield players being involved in every facet of the game, and obtained men of the right calibre for the tactics.

Celtic won the European Cup in 1967 with total football, although West Germany and Holland, the opponents in the 1974 World Cup final, are usually credited with inventing it. Brilliant exponents Franz Beckenbauer and Johan Cruyff gave it a special twist, as, before them in British football, Alex James, Tommy Lawton, Jimmy Greaves and Bobby Moore did to other tactical systems. And because attention was focused on the unique talents of these great players their indebtedness to the teamwork as a whole was often overlooked.

What is the best position of Kevin Keegan, the European Footballer of the Year in 1978 and 1979? Midfield, striker, or midfield player going forward to support the front men? He is clearly suited to all-round play, and Liverpool have had other versatile players like Ian Callaghan, Ray Kennedy, Terry McDermott and Emlyn Hughes. Even during the 1960s Chris Lawler was getting goals regularly from right-back and was second highest scorer in one season. Lawler lived up to the requirement of Helmut Schoen, manager of the West Germany World Cup-winning side in 1974: 'We use footballers who can defend, rather than defenders who *might* be able to play a bit.'

Liverpool had to make a subtle change when Keegan was transferred to Hamburg. His successor, Kenny Dalglish, could not cover so effectively in midfield, although he was more dangerous near goal, and Liverpool often made up by packing the midfield with four men.

Liverpool realize that football cannot stand still. The struggle between defence and attack is continuous, and once one element has an advantage the other strives to counter it. Great managers and great players adjust continually, mould teams according to the talent available and do not force players into styles unsuitable to them.

Total football is in complete contrast to the rigid system which evolved between the wars. Under ace manager Herbert Chapman Arsenal dominated the 1930s—winning five Championships in eight years—with men who had a specific job to do and rarely moved away from it. The central figure was Alex

OPPOSITE Tense moment for Manchester United goalkeeper Gary Bailey as Liverpool battle it out with United in the FA Cup semi-final, 1979. (*Photo: Sporting Pictures (UK) Ltd*)

James, of the long pants and 'fluttering foot' body swerve. He came to Arsenal from Preston as a scoring forward and was ruthlessly changed by Chapman into a goal-maker supreme. He linked with the defence and plied passes to fast-raiding wingers Cliff Bastin and Joe Hulme, who between them scored 53 goals in one season, and to fearless, buccaneering centre-forward Ted Drake. In defence Chapman moved the backs from a central position out to the wings and the centre-half concentrated on blocking the middle.

The new role gave the centre-half the names of third-back, stopper and policeman, and his negative task encouraged fans to hurl insults at the red-haired head of Arsenal's Herbie Roberts. He was completely unruffled.

Arsenal carried all before them. The defence soaked up pressure and the smash-and-grab raids launched by James brought goals galore (they topped the century three times in the 1930s) and cries of 'Lucky Arsenal'. Many teams who copied failed to appreciate the way James knitted the eleven into a co-ordinated unit. They saw the value of a tall, powerful centre-half and of speedy forwards, and often football degenerated into the two sections being bridged by a hopeful long pass upfield.

In truth, finding a player with the strategic ability, positional sense and passing skill of James was intensely difficult. There was a mere handful: Raich Carter, the silver-haired genius of Sunderland and Derby, little Jackie Bestall of Grimsby, then a First Division club, Scot Bob McPhail and Bolton's George Eastham, whose son played for Newcastle and Arsenal. Outstanding was fair-haired Wilf Mannion of Middlesbrough, deft, artful, perceptive. He master-minded England's 10–0 win over Portugal in Lisbon in May 1947 and said, 'They changed the ball, they changed the goalkeeper, they changed the backs and, it didn't matter what they did, we were completely in charge.'

The maximum wage was in force and there was little incentive for a player to leave the provinces for the higher cost of living in London. Arsenal scoured the country with open cheque book for James's deputy and in August 1938 persuaded Wolves to part with Bryn Jones for a record £14,000. Jones, technically very sound, was too retiring to be an adequate replacement for the extrovert James.

As the new style concentrated on blocking the middle, wingers revelled in greater freedom until the advent of a back line of four men. The 'Wizard of the Dribble', Stanley Matthews, mesmerized backs by feinting to come inside before darting upfield, and could pinpoint centres. He joined Stoke as a fifteen-year-old, £1-a-week office boy and spanned thirty-five years of first-class football before having his last First Division game in February 1965, five days after his fiftieth birthday. His finest achievement was winning the FA Cup for Blackpool in 1953 after being 3–1 down to Bolton.

Tom Finney, the Preston plumber, was a better all-round footballer and switched to outside-left several times to play with Matthews in the England team. He was a scorer as well, while Matthews concentrated on making openings. No club exploited wingers better than Wolves, under manager Stan Cullis. Johnny Hancocks and Jimmy Mullen made devastating cross-field passes to each other, and in four successive seasons Wolves topped 100 goals.

The dominance of wingers encouraged centre-forwards to lurk at the far post for centres floated invitingly across. They had to be big, strong and good in the air to wage aerial warfare against defenders. The ideal was Tommy Lawton, who was coached at Everton by the incomparable Dixie Dean in the arts of jumping and timing. He scored 231 League goals and played twenty-three full internationals between 1938 and 1948.

Several vied with Lawton: Drake, Derek Dougan, Welshmen John Charles, Trevor Ford and Ron Davies, Tommy Taylor and Scots Ian St John and Dave McCulloch. Not far behind Lawton was Nat Lofthouse, who went to the same school in Bolton. He was as good in the air, but not so skilful on the ground, and once led England's scorers with thirty goals from thirty-three internationals.

The formation was neat and orderly, although restrictive for individuals. There were three front men with the inside-forwards behind them—a 'W' shape, the opposing wing-halves marked the inside-forwards and the three at the back were responsible for the wingers and centre-forward—an 'M' shape. So the line-up was named 'WM'.

It was turned upside down when the Hungarians came to Wembley in 1953. Nandor Hidegkuti led the attack from behind and the wingers stayed deep and level with him. England centre-half Harry Johnston did not know whether to follow Hidegkuti or pick up one of the inside-forwards who were the front men.

Even before 1953, Manchester United and Spurs led the revolt against the rigidity of 'WM'. Backs Johnny Carey and Alf Ramsey showed that attacks could be built up from the rear and wingers were encouraged to roam at will.

Nandor Hidekut comes from deep to score for Hungary against England at Wembley in 1953. (*Photo: Central Press.*)

Jimmy Greaves, white shirt, scoring for England in the 9–3 defeat of Scotland at Wembley, 1961.
(*Photo: Central Press.*)

With Manchester United, Duncan Edwards (one of the victims of the Munich air crash), Denis Law, Bobby Charlton and George Best were allowed to use their initiative fully. Best showed how hard he found it to stick to a formation when United met Benfica in the European Cup in 1966. They took a fragile 3–2 lead to Lisbon and decided to begin with a defensive 4.4.2 line-up. But Best ran amok, scored two brilliant goals and inspired a 5–1 rout. Manager Matt Busby commented: 'He must have had cottonwool in his ears at the tactical talk.'

Charlton started as a winger with a tremendous shot, and United—and England—moved him to midfield where he sprayed 30–40-yard passes with deadly accuracy. Spurs had two fine play-makers in Danny Blanchflower and Dave Mackay, who harnessed their colleagues so well that they obtained the Cup and League double in 1961 for the first time this century.

Spurs also exploited a new method of using the centre-forward. Because he was closely marked he could lure the stopper centre-half out of the way before playing the ball off to a team-mate. Burly Bobby Smith was adept at doing this and could not have had a better partner than Jimmy Greaves, whom Spurs brought back from Milan for £99,999. An eye for the opening, sharp acceleration and accurate shot brought Greaves goals with clinical ease. He scored 44 for England and 357—all in the First Division—for Chelsea, Spurs and West Ham.

He gave impetus to the fashion of feeding off a target man. Fruitful

partnerships developed elsewhere, such as those of Geoff Hurst and Johnny Byrne (West Ham), John Toshack and Kevin Keegan (Liverpool), Mick Jones and Allan Clarke (Leeds United), Alan Sunderland and Frank Stapleton (Arsenal). Defences had to take extra precaution by having two central defenders. Usually both concentrated on defence, but Bobby Moore brought a new dimension with West Ham and England. By holding the ball and drawing opponents to him he created space upfield. His most telling pass was a 30-yarder, usually to Hurst in the inside-left position. One of these led to Hurst completing his hat-trick in the 1966 World Cup final.

West Germany captain Franz Beckenbauer, an attacker by instinct, was able to enlarge Moore's conception, thanks to growing awareness of the need for all-round players. When he made a sortie, colleagues filled in behind him, while others found space for his perceptive passing. He was the outstanding player in the 1974 World Cup and led Bayern Munich to a hat-trick of European Cup victories.

The closing of the middle by two defenders made life more difficult for far-post centre-forwards. They were losing the aerial battle and the result was a switch from fielding an orthodox leader such as Bob Latchford, Joe Jordan or John Toshack to playing without one altogether. The Dutch led the way when Johan Cruyff was available, by having a gap in the middle into which any one of four or five players could go. When Holland beat England 2–0 at Wembley in 1977 both goals were obtained by midfield man Jan Peters slipping into the gap. Ron Greenwood followed the example and found that the England attack functioned well with nominal inside-forwards Tony Woodcock and Trevor Francis as the strikers.

During the years when football was breaking from the straitjacket of 'WM', various formations were tried, 4.2.4, 4.3.3, 4.4.2 and even 1.4.3.2. England were using 4.2.4 when Alf Ramsey became manager in 1962 and, even with a genius like Fulham captain Johnny Haynes, too much responsibility was put on two midfield players to hold the team together. The limitations were exposed in the Little World Cup in Brazil in 1964 by Brazil, Portugal and Argentina. It was increasingly difficult, too, to find wingers because the growing emphasis on defence enabled backs to move wide and mark closely.

Ramsey failed to find wingers of adequate quality and won the World Cup in 1966 at Wembley with the 'wingless wonders'. The key players were Martin Peters, whom Ramsey described as 'ten years before his time', and Alan Ball, for the way they went forward to give width and thrust to the attack. The backs were also encouraged to move into the space along the touchlines for overlapping raids.

To many 4.3.3 was the new revelation, the ultimate in tactical systems. And had not the great Brazil side adopted it in winning the World Cup in 1962, by switching Zagalo, who later became manager, from outside-left to left-half? Unfortunately a large proportion of the imitators employed the midfield trio to strengthen the defence rather than to bolster the attack.

Ramsey knew that a new development had to be made, although the Football

Association did not give him time to do so. He said, 'I want all-purpose players—those who can fill in wherever required. They will have to be skilful and intelligent—and prepared to work hard.' Schoen was thinking along the same lines: 'We must open up the game again. We must banish negative play by having defenders who are willing and able to go forward.'

And so it goes on, the eternal battle between defence and attack, with each endeavouring to wipe out any advantage obtained by the other. There was an ironic twist at the end of the 1979–80 season when one of the weapons West Ham had forged recoiled against them. Short centres to a forward running to meet them brought some memorable goals, notably Martin Peters to Geoff Hurst for England's first goal in the 1966 World Cup final, and Bobby Moore to Hurst for the goal against Argentina earlier in the competition.

They became so concerned at cancelling this ploy when used by opponents that they left the far post loosely guarded. As a result they conceded goals and dropped vital points to Fulham and Cambridge in their bid for promotion, in season 1979–80. Goalkeeper Phil Parkes said, 'I've always felt it better to mark a player than cover the far post. I suppose we'll have to sit down and think about it again.' Being a progressive club, West Ham came to grips with the problem and finished the season as FA Cup winners.

Would You Believe It?

Willie Foulke was the biggest man to have played in the Football League. Foulke, who kept goal for England, Sheffield United and Chelsea just after the turn of the century, weighed 22 st 3 lb (141 kg), and was 6 ft 3 in tall. When he played the final game of his career, for Bradford, he tipped the scales at 26 st (165 kg). He once stopped a game by holding on to the crossbar, and breaking it.

When Hungary lost 3–5 to Austria in May 1950 it was their last defeat for twenty-nine games until they lost the World Cup final 3–2 to West Germany in July 1954.

On 20 January 1923 a broad-shouldered barrel-chested youngster called Jimmy McGrory scored his first League goal for Celtic. On 16 October fourteen years later, McGrory scored his 410th goal, also for Celtic. His total of goals has been surpassed, but he scored them in just 408 League games. McGrory made seven appearances for Scotland and scored six goals to maintain his average of over a goal a game.

On 18 March 1973 Maglioni, of Argentina side Independiente, scored a hat-trick in a League game against Gimnesia Y Escrima de la Plata. The scoring of the three goals is not an exceptional feat in itself, but the time in which he did it is, just one minute and fifty seconds.

OPPOSITE Joe Jordan, no. 9, showing strength and skill playing for Scotland against Holland. (*Photo: Colorsport.*)

Chapter 17

Yes, Television is Good for Football

Since my playing career finished in 1974 I have earned my living from the media—words and pictures, especially televised pictures. That makes me the proverbial sitting duck for the most obvious question of the lot. I wish I had a pound for every time I have been asked, as often as not in tones of accusation almost, what I think television does for the game. Usually, the query follows a controversial incident, and I realize I am being put on the spot. There is no way I can win, because I believe that television does a lot for football. As that isn't the answer the majority want to hear, let me take the chance of justifying my belief.

The first point in this very commercial day and age is that football, like any other commodity, has to be sold to the public. There is no doubt, as we go deeper into the eighties, which is the best vehicle for selling anything. Television, of course. As both football and television are here to stay, the course for both should be one of complement, not collision. Trial by television was one of the most emotive phrases ever to be coined. Beware the television producer, director, or editor who has his hands on the action-replay button. He will make more enemies than friends. So we're told. But will he?

Every referees' society in the country will be penning letters of protest should the cameras prove an error by the man in the middle or on the line. We will all be reminded that his is an instant decision; that he hasn't the benefit of an action-replay machine on his wristwatch.

The player whose dubious action was caught by the camera, but unavoidably missed by the referee, will be up in arms. I remember well the furore when George Best, in his very young days, received a disciplinary sentence that seems out of all proportion to the offence, which happened to be knocking the ball out of the referee's hands. Television was accused of being responsible for the severity of the sentence, merely by being on the ground and drawing the attention of the nation to the misconduct.

Television was also blamed for the much more frequent use of the charge of bringing the game into disrepute. Incidents that would have been missed by people on the ground suddenly became matters of heated controversy because they had been perpetrated in front of the electronic eye. Television was alleged to engender double standards; one sentence if the offence was off the box, and another if it was committed on it.

Now all that is difficult to defend. But I am going to try. Despite their not infrequent enmity, television and referees have one thing in common. They do not commit the crimes. Having said that, I know only too well how difficult it is for a player to control his temper all the time.

We can't all have the sunny disposition that took Ian Callaghan, of England and Liverpool, through nearly a thousand games with no more than one booking. We can't all be like Bobby Charlton, whose expression when hurt was one of disgust rather than pain. But I have seen Bobby sharpened to anger when getting the 'treatment' from an opponent whose lack of football skills hardly permitted him to be on the same pitch as the England and Manchester United star.

John Charles, who carried principally Wales, Leeds and Juventus on his back like an Atlas of football, was 6 ft 1 in tall and reckoned 13 st 12 lb his best fighting weight. He never used it. Perhaps Big John might have been an even greater player, though that must be open to some doubt, had he thrown his weight around more. But the only occasion on which he lost his temper on the field was while playing for Wales at Wrexham in 1955 when some members of the Austria team made John's younger brother Mel their prime target.

A similar thing happened to me once. I was angry at the time, and I am not particularly proud of it. The victim was Sammy Morgan, a Northern Ireland striker of the traditional powerful school, then leading Aston Villa's attack and enjoying the most successful period of his career. We faced each other at Highbury in what developed into quite a physical FA Cup tie. Neither Sammy nor I was pulling out of anything and one 50–50 ball just inside the box ended with me out like a light and Sammy, when I recovered after a long blackout, being sent off.

That was my trial by television. It was a night replay, and it was on the small screen. Sammy had been giving me the verbals, as we say in the game, and was certainly not the only vocal striker I ever met. But, on this occasion, for some reason, the words were getting home. I went for that ball determined to get it. The Highbury stand could have fallen in, but it was still going to be my ball, and not Sammy's. I did not, of course, intend to do anything to get Sammy sent off, but I was knocked out for rather a long time and the impression got around that I had made the whole incident look a lot worse than it was. The point I am trying to make is that, if I had not been so angry, I might easily have challenged for that ball a different way, might not have been injured, and Sammy might not have had to go. The fact that I was pilloried was not television's fault, but mine. The incident was played back again and again, of course, and, because I vowed never to allow myself to be put in that position again and succeeded, I became a better player.

My claim is that even in situations like these, television does good in the long term. If it exposes lies and denials, is that not to the credit of television?

I am sure Phil Thompson, the Liverpool and England defender, will take my point, though this story concerns disagreements in the heat of the moment, and certainly not lies and denials. Liverpool were playing Nottingham Forest in the 1977–78 final of the Football League Cup. Liverpool, attempting to win the trophy for the first time, had thrown everything at Forest at Wembley, but had

been held to a 0–0 draw, despite having 80 per cent of the game. The pattern was continued in the replay at Old Trafford, broken only when Thompson tackled a Forest player and was judged by referee Pat Partridge, a much respected official who was on the FIFA list, to have conceded a penalty. Scottish international John Robertson scored the winner from the spot and Thompson, in a television interview, left everyone in no doubt that, in his opinion, if he had committed a foul it was outside the box. Though the film appeared to support him, he was disciplined for bringing the game into disrepute.

Did it harm his career? It was a rare blemish. Thompson learned, went on to succeed Emlyn Hughes as Liverpool skipper, and captained England, too.

As you will now realize, I think trial by television does more good than harm. In any case, surely the worst crime of which television can stand accused is that of picture distortion, due to unavoidable foreshortening caused by camera heights and angles. The men behind the lens may have opinions, but the cameras cannot alter sacred facts.

On a much broader theme, that of taking the game to the people, television must do good. All the prospective fans just cannot get to all the games. Travel, work, infirmity and old age: four good enough reasons, surely? The standard of accommodation, at most grounds, especially for wives and daughters, is not television's fault. Nor is the language problem, nor the hooliganism. Television persuades more people to go and watch a game than ever it keeps away.

The ideal situation, of course, is to watch a game live, and be able to see the highlights on television later. For, no matter how good the vantage point at the match itself, television sees some things that the naked eye cannot. Only on television, for instance, can you pick up the beauty of a pass that pierces the opposition defence with nothing to spare on either side. Only on television can the onlooker really appreciate the instinctive joy of achieving what the game is all about, the scoring of a goal. It is not all about kissing and cuddling. When players have been trying for fifty-odd minutes, or even eighty-nine, to put together the fragments that blend into perfection, and they at last succeed despite eleven other chaps deliberately getting in the way, they have something they want to shout about.

There is one area of a team to which television can never do full justice, and that is the midfield. The fetchers and carriers, like Terry McDermott of Liverpool and England, are not adequately appreciated for those reasons of camera angles and the foreshortening of distances I mentioned earlier.

Television is almost perfection in making an accurate assessment of a goalkeeper's ability. The camera will pick up the angles with which the best full-backs work, and their overlapping runs. Strikers and wingers are almost in the same enviable position as goalkeepers. But, when the likes of McDermott and Archie Gemmill of Scotland, Derby County, Nottingham Forest and Birmingham City fame start making one of their exciting surges from midfield, the cameras just cannot do them justice—unless the player scores.

Two of the most unforgettable pieces of television soccer each cast Gemmill in the role of hero. One was the goal he scored for Scotland against Holland in the

OPPOSITE A sequence of photographs showing one of the great goals scored by Archie Gemmill for Scotland against Holland in the 1978 World Cup finals. He starts in midfield and suddenly decides not to pass the ball. A drop of the shoulder puts no. 5 off balance, no. 2 is too late and is left grounded. Gemmill is through the gap, another Dutch defender sprawls helplessly and Gemmill has scored. (*Photos: Colorsport.*)

1978 World Cup finals in Argentina. The other was that superb effort when he netted for Forest, starting a move just outside his own penalty area and finishing it off just inside opposing Arsenal's penalty area, in the same year. The BBC were so impressed that they used it as part of the opening sequence to their Match of the Day programme for nearly a whole season. That goal of Gemmill's was so good that youngsters must have learned a great deal from it about the art of running and taking up position. They did not lack for opportunities to see it.

This brings me to the third value of television—its use in coaching. I do not think that aspect can be overstressed, or opposed, even by the most anti-television people. To be able to slow down movements, to stop and dissect skills and techniques, to explain the use and intricacies of one–twos, wall-passes etc . . . it must have been so much more difficult for coaches of yesterday. A coach must be able to keep firing a youngster's enthusiasm when he can show, again and again, the greatest players varying tactics at set pieces and, for instance, the banana-ball of Glenn Hoddle, the young Spurs player who made so dramatic a start to his England career with a glorious goal against Bulgaria.

There is the light relief, too, of seeing famous players trying something different. There is always something new, as the two Coventry City thinkers, Ernie Hunt and Willie Carr, proved a few years ago. This was yet another variation on how to beat the defensive wall. At a free kick, Hunt would face the wall, with the ball between his ankles. At the referee's whistle, he would jump and flick it, with both feet, behind him. There Carr would be waiting to hit the ball before it touched the ground. They scored with it once and that goal, too, became part of the Match of the Day introduction. Only for a short while, unfortunately. The Football Association, on the advice of their rules experts, decreed that the move was illegal. Nevertheless, it was fun, and television had supplied a talking point for weeks.

Not only the youngsters learn from the box: the professional players do too. For Trevor Francis, the Nottingham Forest and England striker, football is compulsory viewing when he is at home. This is why.

One night, watching Johan Cruyff, he saw one of the brilliant Dutchman's favourite tricks, the ploy with which he disposed of the defender playing right behind his back. Cruyff, facing his own goal, would dip his left shoulder, convincing the defender that he must go to his left. But, while the left shoulder was moving, so was the right foot, round the ball. With the ball safely controlled by the right instep, Cruyff would spin and burst past the groping defender's right shoulder and off into space. Francis has told me: 'I was amazed. But I tried it in training the following day and found I could do it.' If television can inspire a world-class player to improve his game, can that be so bad?

Would You Believe It?
Bjorn Nordqvist of Sweden played in 111 international matches in the 1930s.

Do You Know?

Q: May an injured player come back on to the field after receiving treatment whilst the game is in progress?

A: Provided the referee indicates that the injured player may return, he may do so whilst the game is in progress.

Q: A team starts short of three players. Two of the missing players arrive during the first half, and the third ten minutes before the end of the second half. Are they permitted to take part in the game?

A: Yes. A team short of players may make up the number any time during the period of the match.

Q: When extra time is necessary in a Cup Competition, which team kicks off at the start of such extra time?

A: The two captains should again toss for choice of ends or kick-off as they would at the start of the match (Law 8, Advice to Referees).

Q: May a goal be awarded if the goalkeeper throws the ball from his own penalty area direct into his opponent's goal? (This would appear to be an almost impossible feat.)

A: A goal would be awarded if this unlikely event occurred (Law 10).

Q: It is permissible under certain circumstances for a player to charge an opponent in the back?

A: No. A player may be charged from behind if he deliberately turns his back to his opponent when he is about to be tackled. Charging in the back can never be permitted.

Q: Are there any circumstances under which a referee may reverse a decision?

A: Yes. At any time before play recommences.

Q: If the ball rebounds off either the referee or a linesman, should play be allowed to continue?

A: Yes, provided the ball is within the field of play when it strikes them.

Q: The referee notices that the goalkeeper is wearing gloves with hard rubber protrusions on the outside, designed to assist him when punching the ball. Should the referee permit such equipment?

A: Law 4 states that a player shall not wear anything which is dangerous to another player. If, therefore, the referee considered that this type of glove was dangerous, he would be correct in asking the player to remove them.

Q: A goalkeeper is dribbling the ball in his own goal area. He is charged fairly by a forward, who obtains the ball and scores. Should a goal be awarded?

A: No. A goalkeeper may only be charged in his own goal area if he is holding the ball or is obstructing an opponent. The referee would award an indirect free kick to the defence which may be taken from any point in that half of the goal area in which the offence occurred.

Q: A goalkeeper is fouled on the goal-line in between the posts, and the referee awards a free kick. From where may the free kick be taken?

A: The Law states that the kick may be taken from any part of that half of the goal area in which the offence occurred.

Q: A free kick is awarded for a foul tackle four or five yards from the touchline. The offended player wishes to take a quick free kick. The referee signals his approval and the kick is taken. Unfortunately the player miskicks the ball over the touchline. He appeals for the kick to be retaken as an opponent was only two or three yards from the ball and the kicker alleges that he was 'put off' by the close proximity of the opponent. What should be the referee's decision?

A: If a team wish to take a quick free kick which subsequently is unsuccessful, they cannot expect a second attempt. The referee in the circumstances outlined should award a throw-in to the kicker's opponents.

Q: Law 3 contains instructions regarding the correct method for a player to be substituted. Please give details.

A: (a) The referee shall be informed of the proposed substitution, before it is made.
(b) The substitute shall not enter the field of play until the player he is replacing has left, and then only after having received a signal from the referee.
(c) He shall enter the field during a stoppage in the game, and at the halfway line.

Q: If, at the taking of a penalty-kick, the goalkeeper moves his feet after the whistle is blown but before the ball is kicked, and at the same time a player from each side enters the penalty area, what should the referee's decision be?

A: Even though the defence have committed two infringements and the attackers one infringement, the kick must be retaken.

Q: A player taking a corner kick slips and miskicks the ball so that it moves only a few inches. He picks it up to replace it for another kick. What action should the referee take?

A: None. Providing the ball did not travel the distance of its circumference (27 inches), the kick has not technically been taken and the ball should be replaced and kicked again.

Q: Define a fair charge from behind.

A: A fair charge from behind means a charge in the region of the shoulder and not in the back itself. Any kind of charge near the spine is obviously very dangerous.

Would You Believe It?

A dog named Pickles became a hero overnight when, just four months before the beginning of the 1966 World Cup finals in England, the Jules Rimet trophy was stolen. Pickles discovered it, unharmed and wrapped in a newspaper, in the garden of his owner's home.

The highest official attendance at a football match is 200,000, who paid £125,000 to see Uruguay defeat Brazil 2–1 in the 1950 World Cup final decided in Rio de Janeiro.

When Santos of Brazil began their game against Penarol of Montevideo, Uruguay in the Copa Libertadores at 9.30 p.m. on 2 August 1962, nobody could have foreseen how long they would remain at the match. Because of crowd interruptions and disturbances, the game did not finish until 1 a.m. on 3 August: three-and-a-half hours taken to complete the game set a duration record for a first-class football match. The result: a 3–3 draw.

Four days before the 1970 World Cup qualifying match play-off between Honduras and El Salvador, in Mexico City, diplomatic relations between the two countries were severed. The result of the game, a 3–2 victory to El Salvador in extra time, preceded a war with 3,500 casualties.

Soccer Statistics

World Cup Winners

1930 (Uruguay)	Uruguay
1934 (Italy)	Italy
1938 (France)	Italy
1950 (Brazil)	Uruguay
1954 (Switzerland)	West Germany
1958 (Sweden)	Brazil
1962 (Chile)	Brazil
1966 (England)	England
1970 (Mexico)	Brazil
1974 (West Germany)	West Germany
1978 (Argentina)	Argentina

European Championship Winners

1960	USSR	1972	West Germany
1964	Spain	1976	Czechoslovakia
1968	Italy	1980	West Germany

European Cup Winners' Cup Winners

1961 AC Fiorentina
1962 Atletico Madrid
1963 Tottenham Hotspur
1964 Sporting Club Lisbon
1965 West Ham United
1966 Borussia Dortmund
1967 Bayern Munich
1968 AC Milan
1969 Slovan Bratislava
1970 Manchester City
1971 Chelsea
1972 Rangers
1973 AC Milan
1974 FC Magdeburg
1975 Dynamo Kiev
1976 Anderlecht
1977 SV Hamburg
1978 Anderlecht
1979 Barcelona
1980 Valencia

European Champions Cup Winners

1956 Real Madrid	1969 AC Milan
1957 Real Madrid	1970 Feyenoord
1958 Real Madrid	1971 Ajax Amsterdam
1959 Real Madrid	1972 Ajax Amsterdam
1960 Real Madrid	1973 Ajax Amsterdam
1961 Benfica	1974 Bayern Munich
1962 Benfica	1975 Bayern Munich
1963 AC Milan	1976 Bayern Munich
1964 Inter-Milan	1977 Liverpool
1965 Inter-Milan	1978 Liverpool
1966 Real Madrid	1979 Nottingham Forest
1967 Celtic	
1968 Manchester United	1980 Nottingham Forest

European Fairs Cup Winners

1958 Barcelona	1965 Ferencvaros
1960 Barcelona	1966 Barcelona
1961 AS Roma	1967 Dynamo Zagreb
1962 Valencia	1968 Leeds United
1963 Valencia	1969 Newcastle United
1964 Real Zaragoza	1970 Arsenal
	1971 Leeds United

UEFA Cup Winners

1972 Tottenham Hotspur
1973 Liverpool
1974 Feyenoord
1975 Borussia Moenchengladbach
1976 Liverpool
1977 Juventus
1978 PSV Eindhoven
1979 Borussia Moenchengladbach
1980 Eintracht Frankfurt

Football League Champions
(since the Second World War)

1947 Liverpool
1948 Arsenal
1949 Portsmouth
1950 Portsmouth
1951 Tottenham Hotspur
1952 Manchester United
1953 Arsenal
1954 Wolverhampton Wanderers
1955 Chelsea
1956 Manchester United
1957 Manchester United
1958 Wolverhampton Wanderers
1959 Wolverhampton Wanderers
1960 Burnley
1961 Tottenham Hotspur
1962 Ipswich
1963 Everton
1964 Liverpool
1965 Manchester United
1966 Liverpool
1967 Manchester United
1968 Manchester City
1969 Leeds United
1970 Everton
1971 Arsenal
1972 Derby County
1973 Liverpool
1974 Leeds United
1975 Derby County
1976 Liverpool
1977 Liverpool
1978 Nottingham Forest
1979 Liverpool
1980 Liverpool

FA Cup Winners
(since the Second World War)

1946 Derby County
1947 Charlton Athletic
1948 Manchester United
1949 Wolverhampton Wanderers
1950 Arsenal
1951 Newcastle United
1952 Newcastle United
1953 Blackpool
1954 West Bromwich Albion
1955 Newcastle United

1956 Manchester City
1957 Aston Villa
1958 Bolton Wanderers
1959 Nottingham Forest
1960 Wolverhampton Wanderers
1961 Tottenham Hotspur
1962 Tottenham Hotspur
1963 Manchester United
1964 West Ham United
1965 Liverpool
1966 Everton
1967 Tottenham Hotspur
1968 West Bromwich Albion
1969 Manchester City
1970 Chelsea
1971 Arsenal
1972 Leeds United
1973 Sunderland
1974 Liverpool
1975 West Ham United
1976 Southampton
1977 Manchester United
1978 Ipswich
1979 Arsenal
1980 West Ham United

League Cup Winners
1961 Aston Villa
1962 Norwich City
1963 Birmingham City
1964 Leicester City
1965 Chelsea
1966 West Bromwich Albion
1967 Queen's Park Rangers
1968 Leeds United
1969 Swindon Town
1970 Manchester City
1971 Tottenham Hotspur
1972 Stoke City
1973 Tottenham Hotspur
1974 Wolverhampton Wanderers
1975 Aston Villa
1976 Manchester City
1977 Aston Villa
1978 Nottingham Forest
1979 Nottingham Forest
1980 Wolverhampton Wanderers

Scotland's Cup Winners
(since the Second World War)

1947	Aberdeen	1949	Rangers
1948	Rangers	1950	Rangers

1951	Celtic	1966	Rangers
1952	Motherwell	1967	Celtic
1953	Rangers	1968	Dunfermline
1954	Celtic		Athletic
1955	Clyde	1969	Celtic
1956	Hearts	1970	Aberdeen
1957	Falkirk	1971	Celtic
1958	Clyde	1972	Celtic
1959	St Mirren	1973	Rangers
1960	Rangers	1974	Celtic
1961	Dunfermline	1975	Celtic
	Athletic	1976	Rangers
1962	Rangers	1977	Celtic
1963	Rangers	1978	Rangers
1964	Rangers	1979	Rangers
1965	Celtic	1980	Celtic

Scotland's League Champions
(since the Second World War)

1947	Rangers	1964	Rangers
1948	Hibernian	1965	Kilmarnock
1949	Rangers	1966	Celtic
1950	Rangers	1967	Celtic
1951	Hibernian	1968	Celtic
1952	Hibernian	1969	Celtic
1953	Rangers	1970	Celtic
1954	Celtic	1971	Celtic
1955	Aberdeen	1972	Celtic
1956	Rangers	1973	Celtic
1957	Rangers	1974	Celtic
1958	Hearts	1975	Rangers
1959	Rangers	1976	Rangers
1960	Hearts	1977	Celtic
1961	Rangers	1978	Rangers
1962	Dundee	1979	Celtic
1963	Rangers	1980	Aberdeen

Scotland's League Cup Winners
(since the Second World War)

1946	Aberdeen	1956	Aberdeen
1947	Rangers	1957	Celtic
1948	East Fife	1958	Celtic
1949	Rangers	1959	Hearts
1950	East Fife	1960	Hearts
1951	Motherwell	1961	Rangers
1952	Dundee	1962	Rangers
1953	Dundee	1963	Hearts
1954	East Fife	1964	Rangers
1955	Hearts	1965	Rangers

1966	Celtic	1973	Hibernian
1967	Celtic	1974	Dundee
1968	Celtic	1975	Celtic
1969	Celtic	1976	Rangers
1970	Celtic	1977	Aberdeen
1971	Rangers	1978	Rangers
1972	Partick	1979	Rangers
	Thistle	1980	Dundee United

Welsh Cup Winners
(since the Second World War)

1947	Chester	1963	Borough
1948	Lovell's		United
	Athletic	1964	Cardiff City
1949	Merthyr	1965	Cardiff City
	Tydfil	1966	Swansea
1950	Swansea	1967	Cardiff
1951	Merthyr	1968	Cardiff
	Tydfil	1969	Cardiff
1952	Rhyl	1970	Cardiff
1953	Rhyl	1971	Cardiff
1954	Flint	1972	Wrexham
1955	Bury	1973	Cardiff
1956	Cardiff City	1974	Cardiff
1957	Wrexham	1975	Wrexham
1958	Wrexham	1976	Cardiff
1959	Cardiff City	1977	Shrewsbury
1960	Wrexham	1978	Wrexham
1961	Swansea	1979	Shrewsbury
1962	Bangor	1980	Newport County

**Northern Ireland's
League Champions**
(since the Second World War)

1948	Belfast Celtic	1965	Derry City
1949	Linfield	1966	Linfield
1950	Linfield	1967	Glentoran
1951	Glentoran	1968	Glentoran
1952	Glenavon	1969	Linfield
1953	Glentoran	1970	Glentoran
1954	Linfield	1971	Linfield
1955	Linfield	1972	Glentoran
1956	Linfield	1973	Crusaders
1957	Glentoran	1974	Crusaders
1958	Ards	1975	Linfield
1959	Linfield	1976	Crusaders
1960	Glenavon	1977	Glentoran
1961	Linfield	1978	Linfield
1962	Linfield	1979	Linfield
1963	Distillery	1980	Linfield
1964	Glentoran		

Northern Ireland's Cup Winners
(since the Second World War)

1946	Linfield	1964	Derry City
1947	Belfast Celtic	1965	Coleraine
1948	Linfield	1966	Glentoran
1949	Derry City	1967	Crusaders
1950	Linfield	1968	Crusaders
1951	Glentoran	1969	Ards
1952	Ards	1970	Linfield
1953	Linfield	1971	Distillery
1954	Derry City	1972	Coleraine
1955	Dundela	1973	Glentoran
1956	Distillery	1974	Ards
1957	Glenavon	1975	Coleraine
1958	Ballymena United	1976	Carrick Rangers
1959	Glenavon	1977	Coleraine
1960	Linfield	1978	Linfield
1961	Glenavon	1979	Cliftonville
1962	Linfield	1980	Linfield
1963	Linfield		

European Nations

Albania	Liechtenstein
Austria	Luxembourg
Belgium	Malta
Bulgaria	Netherlands
Cyprus	Northern Ireland
Czechoslovakia	Norway
Denmark	Poland
England	Portugal
Finland	Romania
France	Scotland
East Germany	Spain
West Germany	Sweden
Greece	Switzerland
Hungary	Turkey
Iceland	USSR
Republic of Ireland	Wales
Italy	Yugoslavia

Olympic Winners

1908	(London)	Great Britain
1912	(Stockholm)	Great Britain
1920	(Antwerp)	Belgium
1924	(Paris)	Uruguay
1928	(Amsterdam)	Uruguay
1936	(Berlin)	Italy
1948	(London)	Sweden
1952	(Helsinki)	Hungary
1956	(Melbourne)	USSR
1960	(Rome)	Yugoslavia
1964	(Tokyo)	Hungary
1968	(Mexico City)	Hungary
1972	(Munich)	Poland
1976	(Montreal)	East Germany
1980	(Moscow)	Czechoslovakia

Footballer of the Year

1948 Stanley Matthews (Blackpool)
1948 Johnny Carey (Manchester United)
1950 Joe Mercer (Arsenal)
1951 Harry Johnston (Blackpool)
1952 Billy Wright (Wolverhampton Wanderers)
1953 Nat Lofthouse (Bolton Wanderers)
1954 Tom Finney (Preston North End)
1955 Don Revie (Manchester City)
1956 Bert Trautmann (Manchester City)
1957 Tom Finney (Preston North End)
1958 Danny Blanchflower (Tottenham Hotspur)
1960 Bill Slater (Wolverhampton Wanderers)
1961 Danny Blanchflower (Tottenham Hotspur)
1962 Jimmy Adamson (Burnley)
1963 Stanley Matthews (Stoke City)
1964 Bobby Moore (West Ham United)
1965 Bobby Collins (Leeds United)
1966 Bobby Charlton (Manchester United)
1967 Jack Charlton (Leeds United)
1968 George Best (Manchester United)
1969 Dave Mackay (Derby County) shared with Tony Book (Manchester City)
1970 Billy Bremner (Leeds United)

1971 Frank McLintock (Arsenal)
1972 Gordon Banks (Stoke City)
1973 Pat Jennings (Tottenham Hotspur)
1974 Ian Callaghan (Liverpool)
1975 Alan Mullery (Fulham)
1976 Kevin Keegan (Liverpool)
1977 Emlyn Hughes (Liverpool)
1978 Kenny Burns (Nottingham Forest)
1979 Kenny Dalglish (Liverpool)
1980 Terry McDermott (Liverpool)

European Footballers of the Year

1956 Stanley Matthews (Blackpool)
1957 Alfredo di Stefano (Real Madrid)
1958 Raymond Kopa (Real Madrid)
1959 Alfredo di Stefano (Real Madrid)
1960 Luis Suarez (Barcelona)
1961 Omar Sivori (Juventus)
1962 Josef Masopust (Dukla Prague)
1963 Lev Yashin (Dynamo Moscow)
1964 Denis Law (Manchester United)
1965 Eusebio (Benfica)
1966 Bobby Charlton (Manchester United)
1967 Florian Albert (Ferencvaros)
1968 George Best (Manchester United)
1969 Gianni Rivera (Milan)
1970 Gerd Müller (Bayern Munich)
1971 Johan Cruyff (Ajax)
1972 Franz Beckenbauer (Bayern Munich)
1973 Johan Cruyff (Barcelona)
1974 Johan Cruyff (Barcelona)
1975 Oleg Blokhin (Dynamo Kiev)
1976 Franz Beckenbauer (Bayern Munich)
1977 Allan Simonsen (Borussia Moenchengladbach)
1978 Kevin Keegan (Hamburg SV)
1979 Kevin Keegan (Hamburg SV)

Appendix II

Laws of the Game

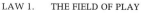

LAW 1.   THE FIELD OF PLAY
LAW 2.   THE BALL
LAW 3.   NUMBER OF PLAYERS
LAW 4.   PLAYERS' EQUIPMENT
LAW 5   REFEREES
LAW 6.   LINESMEN
LAW 7.   DURATION OF THE GAME
LAW 8.   THE START OF PLAY
LAW 9.   BALL IN AND OUT OF PLAY
LAW 10.   METHOD OF SCORING
LAW 11.   OFF-SIDE
LAW 12.   FOULS AND MISCONDUCT
LAW 13.   FREE-KICK (Direct and indirect)
LAW 14.   PENALTY-KICK
LAW 15.   THROW-IN
LAW 16.   GOAL-KICK
LAW 17.   CORNER-KICK

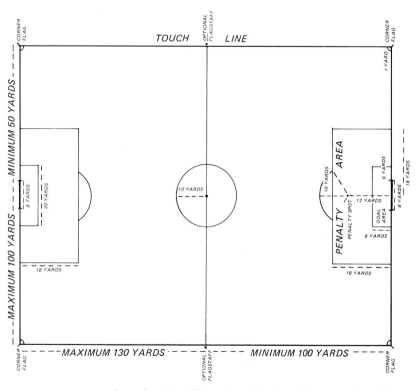

Provided the principles of these Laws be maintained they may be modified in their application:
1. To players of school age as follows:
(a) size of playing pitch;
(b) size, weight and material of ball;
(c) width between the goal-posts and height of the cross-bar from the ground;
(d) the duration of the periods of play.

2. For matches played by women as follows:
(a) size, weight and material of ball;
(b) duration of the periods of play;
(c) further modifications are only permissible with the consent of the International Board.

LAW 1.   THE FIELD OF PLAY
The field of play and appurtenances shall be as shown in the plan.

1. **Dimensions.**   The field of play shall be rectangular, its length being not more than 130 yards nor less than 100 yards and its breadth not more than 100 yards nor less than 50 yards. (In International matches the length shall be not more than 120 yards nor less than 110 yards and the breadth not more than 80 yards nor less than 70 yards.) The length shall in all cases exceed the breadth.

2. **Marking.**   The field of play shall be marked with distinctive lines, not more than 5 inches in width, not by a V-shaped rut, in accordance with the plan, the longer boundary lines being called the touch-lines and the shorter the goal-lines.

A flag on a post not less than 5 feet high and having a non-pointed top shall be placed at each corner; a similar flag-post may be placed opposite the half-way line on each side of the field of play, not less than one yard outside the touch-line. A half-way line shall be marked out across the field of play. The centre of the field of play shall be indicated by a suitable mark and a circle with a ten yards radius shall be marked round it.

3. **The Goal-Area.**   At each end of the field of play two lines

shall be drawn at right angles to the goal-line, 6 yards from each goal-post. These shall extend into the field of play for a distance of 6 yards and shall be joined by a line drawn parallel with the goal-line. Each of the spaces enclosed by these lines and the goal-line shall be called a goal-area.

4. The Penalty-Area.   At each end of the field of play two lines shall be drawn at right angles to the goal-line, 18 yards from each goal-post. These shall extend into the field of play for a distance of 18 yards and shall be joined by a line drawn parallel with the goal-line. Each of the spaces enclosed by these lines and the goal-line shall be called a penalty-area. A suitable mark shall be made within each penalty-area, 12 yards from the mid-point of the goal-line, measured along an undrawn line at right angles thereto. These shall be the penalty-kick marks. From each penalty-kick mark an arc of a circle, having a radius of 10 yards, shall be drawn outside the penalty-area.

5. Corner-Area.   From each corner-flag post a quarter circle, having a radius of 1 yard, shall be drawn inside the field of play.

6. The Goals.   The goals shall be placed on the centre of each goal-line and shall consist of two upright posts, equidistant from the corner-flags and 8 yards apart (inside measurement), joined by a horizontal cross-bar, the lower edge of which shall be 8 feet from the ground. The width and depth of the goal-posts and the width and depth of the cross-bars shall not exceed 5 inches (12 cm). The goal-posts and cross-bars shall have the same width.

Nets may be attached to the posts, cross-bars and ground behind the goals. They should be appropriately supported and be so placed as to allow the goalkeeper ample room.

International Board Decisions on Law 1

1. In International matches the dimensions of the field of play shall be: maximum 110 metres × 75 metres; minimum 100 × 64 metres.

2. National Associations must adhere strictly to these dimensions. Each National Association organising an International Match must advise the Visiting Association, before the match, of the place and the dimensions of the field of play.

3. The Board has approved this table of measurements for the Laws of the Game:

	METRES			METRES
130 yards	120		12 yards	11
120 yards	110		10 yards	9.15
110 yards	100		8 yards	7.32
100 yards	90		6 yards	5.50
80 yards	75		1 yard	1
70 yards	64		8 feet	2.44
50 yards	45		5 feet	1.50
18 yards	16.50		28 inches	0.71

	METRES		
27 inches	0.68	14 ozs.	396 grams
9 inches	0.22	16 ozs.	453 grams
5 inches	0.12	9 lb./sq. in.	600 gr/cm²
½ inch	12.7 millimetres	10.5 lb/sq. in.	700 gr/cm²
⅜ inch	10 millimetres		

4. The goal-line shall be marked the same width as the depth of the goal-posts and cross-bar so that the goal-line and goal-posts will conform to the same interior and exterior edges.

5. The 6 yards (for the outline of the goal-area) and the 18 yards (for the outline of the penalty-area) which have to be measured along the goal-line, must start from the inner sides of the goal-posts.

6. The space within the inside areas of the field of play includes the width of the lines marking these areas.

7. All Associations shall provide standard equipment, particularly in International matches, when the Laws of the Game must be complied with in every respect and especially with regard to the size of the ball and other equipment which must conform to the regulations. All cases of failure to provide standard equipment must be reported to FIFA.

8. In a match played under the rules of a competition if the cross-bar becomes displaced or broken play shall be stopped and the match abandoned unless the cross-bar has been repaired and replaced in position or a new one provided without such being a danger to the players. A rope is not considered to be a satisfactory substitute for a cross-bar.

In a friendly match, by mutual consent, play may be resumed without the cross-bar provided it has been removed and no longer constitutes a danger to the players. In these circumstances, a rope may be used as a substitute for a cross-bar. If a rope is not used and the ball crosses the goal-line at a point which in the opinion of the referee is below where the cross-bar should have been he shall award a goal.

The game shall be restarted by the referee dropping the ball at the place where it was when play was stopped.

9. National Associations may specify such maximum and minimum dimensions for the cross-bars and goal-posts, within the limits laid down in Law 1, as they consider appropriate.

10. Goal-posts and cross-bars must be made of wood, metal, or other approved material as decided from time to time by the International FA Board. They may be square, rectangular, round, half round, or elliptical in shape. Goal-posts and cross-bars made of other materials and in other shapes are not permitted.

11. 'Curtain-raisers' to International matches should only be played following agreement on the day of the match, and taking into account the condition of the field of play, between representatives of the two Associations and the referee (of the International match).

12. National Associations, particularly in International matches, should

restrict the number of photographers around the field of play, have a line ('photographers' line') marked behind the goal-lines at least two metres from the corner-flag going through a point situated at least 3.5 metres behind the intersection of a goal-line with the line marking the goal area to a point situated at least six metres behind the goal-posts, prohibit photographers from passing over these lines, forbid the use of artificial lighting in the form of 'flash-lights'.

LAW 2. THE BALL

The ball shall be spherical; the outer casing shall be of leather or other approved materials. No material shall be used in its construction which might prove dangerous to the players.

The circumference of the ball shall not be more than 28 in. and not less than 27 in. The weight of the ball at the start of the game shall not be more than 16 oz. nor less than 14 oz. The pressure shall be equal to 0.6–0.7 atmosphere, which equals 9.0–10.5 lb/sq. in. ($=600$–700 gr/cm^2) at sea level. The ball shall not be changed during the game unless authorized by the referee.

International Board Decisions on Law 2

1. The ball used in any match shall be considered the property of the Association or Club on whose ground the match is played, and at the close of play it must be returned to the referee.

2. The International Board, from time to time, shall decide what constitutes approved materials. Any approved material shall be certified as such by the International Board.

3. The Board has approved these equivalents of the weights specified in the law:

14 to 16 ounces = 396 to 453 grams.

4. If the ball bursts or becomes deflated during the course of a match, the game shall be stopped and restarted by dropping the new ball at the place where the first ball became defective.

5. If this happens during a stoppage of the game (place-kick, goal-kick, corner-kick, free-kick, penalty-kick, or throw-in) the game shall be restarted accordingly.

LAW 3. NUMBER OF PLAYERS

1. A match shall be played by two teams, each consisting of not more than eleven players, one of whom shall be the goalkeeper.

2. Substitutes may be used in any match played under the rules of an official competition at FIFA, Confederation or National Association level, subject to the following conditions:

(*a*) that the authority of the International Association(s) or National Association(s) concerned, has been obtained,
(*b*) that, subject to the restriction contained in the following paragraph (*c*) the rules of a competition shall state how many, if any, substitutes may be used, and
(*c*) that a team shall not be permitted to use more than two substitutes in any match.

3. Substitutes may be used in any other match, provided that the two teams concerned reach agreement on a maximum number, not exceeding five, and that the terms of such agreement are intimated to the referee, before the match. If the referee is not informed, or if the teams fail to reach agreement, no more than two substitutes shall be permitted.

4. Any of the other players may change places with the goalkeeper, provided that the referee is informed before the change is made, and provided also that the change is made during a stoppage in the game.

5. When a goalkeeper or any other player is to be replaced by a substitute, the following conditions shall be observed:
(*a*) the referee shall be informed of the proposed substitution, before it is made,
(*b*) the substitute shall not enter the field of play until the player he is replacing has left, and then only after having received a signal from the referee.
(*c*) he shall enter the field during a stoppage in the game, and at the half-way line.
Punishment:
(*a*) Play shall not be stopped for an infringement of paragraph 4. The players concerned shall be cautioned immediately the ball goes out of play.
(*b*) For any other infringement of this law, the player concerned shall be cautioned, and if the game is stopped by the referee, to administer the caution, it shall be restarted by an indirect free-kick, to be taken by a player of the opposing team, from the place where the ball was when play was stopped. If the free-kick is awarded to a side within its own goal area, it may be taken from any point within that half of the goal area in which the ball was when play stopped.

International Board Decisions on Law 3

1. The minimum number of players in a team is left to the discretion of National Associations.

2. The Board is of the opinion that a match should not be considered valid if there are fewer than seven players in either of the teams.

3. A competition may require that the referee shall be informed before the start of a match of the names of not more than 5 players from whom the substitutes (if any) must be chosen.

4. A player who has been ordered off before play begins, may only be replaced by one of the named substitutes. The kick-off must not be delayed to allow the substitute to join his team.

A player who has been ordered off after play has started, may not be replaced.

A named substitute who has been ordered off, either before or after play has started, may not be replaced. (This decision only relates to players who are ordered off under Law 12. It does not apply to players who have infringed Law 4.)

5. A player who has been replaced shall not take any further part in the game.

6. A substitute shall be deemed to be a player and shall be subject to the authority and jurisdiction of the referee whether called upon to play or not. For any offence committed on the field of play a substitute shall be subject to the same punishment as any other player whether called upon or not.

LAW 4. PLAYER'S EQUIPMENT
A player shall not wear anything which is dangerous to another player. Footwear (boots or shoes) must conform to the following standard:

(a) Bars shall be made of leather or rubber and shall be transverse and flat, not less than half an inch in width and shall extend the total width of the sole and be rounded at the corners.

(b) Studs which are independently mounted on the sole and are replaceable shall be made of leather, rubber, aluminium, plastic or similar material and shall be solid. With the exception of that part of the stud forming the base, which shall not protrude from the sole more than one quarter of an inch, studs shall be round in plan and not less than half an inch in diameter. Where studs are tapered, the minimum diameter of any section of the stud must not be less than half an inch. Where metal seating for the screw type is used, this seating must be embedded in the sole of the footwear and any attachment screw shall be part of the stud. Other than the metal seating for the screw type of stud, no metal plates even though covered with leather or rubber shall be worn, neither studs which are threaded to allow them to be screwed on to a base screw that is fixed by nails or otherwise to the soles of footwear, nor studs which, apart from the base, have any form of protruding edge rim, or relief marking or ornament, should be allowed.

(c) Studs which are moulded as an integral part of the sole and are not replaceable shall be made of rubber, plastic, polyurethane or similar soft materials. Provided that there are no fewer than ten studs on the sole, they shall have a minimum diameter of three-eighths of an inch (10 mm). Additional supporting material to stabilize studs of soft materials, and ridges which shall not protrude more than 5 mm from the sole and moulded to strengthen it, shall be permitted provided that they are in no way dangerous to other players. In all other respects they shall conform to the general requirements of this law.

(d) Combined bars and studs may be worn, provided the whole conforms to the general requirements of this law. Neither bars nor studs on the soles shall project more than three quarters of an inch. If nails are used they shall be driven in flush with the surface.

The goalkeeper shall wear colours which distinguish him from the other players and from the referee.

Punishment. For any infringement of this Law, the player at fault shall be sent off the field of play to adjust his equipment and he shall not return without first reporting to the referee, who shall satisfy himself that the player's equipment is in order; the player shall only re-enter the game at a moment when the ball has ceased to be in play.

International Board Decisions on Law 4
1. The usual equipment of a player is a jersey or shirt, shorts, stockings and footwear. In a match played under the rules of a competition, players need not wear boots or shoes, but shall wear jersey or shirt, shorts, or track suit or similar trousers, and stockings.

2. The Law does not insist that boots or shoes must be worn. However, in competition matches, referees should not allow one or a few players to play without footwear, when all the other players are so equipped.

3. In International Matches, International Competitions, International Club Competitions and friendly matches between clubs of different national associations, the referee, prior to the start of the game, shall inspect the players' footwear and prevent any player whose footwear does not conform to the requirements of this Law from playing until they comply with the Law. The rules of any Competition may include a similar provision.

4. If the referee finds that a player is wearing articles not permitted by the Laws and which may constitute a danger to other players, he shall order him to take them off. If he fails to carry out the referee's instruction, the player shall not take part in the match.

5. A player who has been prevented from taking part in the game or a player who has been sent off the field for infringing Law 4 must report to the referee during a stoppage of the game and may not enter or re-enter the field of play unless and until the referee has satisfied himself that the player is no longer infringing Law 4.

6. A player who has been prevented from taking part in a game or who has been sent off because of an infringement of Law 4, and who enters or re-enters the field of play to join or rejoin his team, in breach of the conditions of Law 12 shall be cautioned. If the referee stops the game to administer the caution, the game shall be restarted by an indirect free kick, taken by a player of the opposing side, from the place where the ball was when the referee stopped the game. If the free kick is awarded to a side

within its own goal area it may be taken from any point within that half of the goal area in which the ball was when play was stopped.

LAW 5.   REFEREES

A referee shall be appointed to officiate in each game. His authority and the exercise of the powers granted to him by the Laws of the Game commence as soon as he enters the field of play.

His power of penalizing shall extend to offences committed when play has been temporarily suspended, or when the ball is out of play. His decision on points of fact connected with the play shall be final, so far as the result of the game is concerned. He shall:

(a) Enforce the Laws.

(b) Refrain from penalizing in cases where he is satisfied that, by doing so, he would be giving an advantage to the offending team.

(c) Keep a record of the game; act as timekeeper and allow the full or agreed time, adding thereto all time lost through accident or other cause.

(d) Have discretionary power to stop the game for any infringement of the Laws and to suspend or terminate the game whenever, by reasons of the elements, interference by spectators, or other cause, he deems such stoppage necessary. In such a case he shall submit a detailed report to the competent authority, within the stipulated time, and in accordance with the provisions set up by the National Association under whose jurisdiction the match was played. Reports will be deemed to be made when received in the ordinary course of post.

(e) From the time he enters the field of play, caution any player guilty of misconduct or ungentlemanly behaviour and, if he persists, suspend him from further participation in the game. In such cases the referee shall send the name of the offender to the competent authority, within the stipulated time,* and in accordance with the provisions set up by the National Association under whose jurisdiction the match was played. Reports will be deemed to be made when received in the ordinary course of post.

(f) Allow no person other than the players and linesmen to enter the field of play without his permission.

(g) Stop the game if, in his opinion, a player has been seriously injured; have the player removed as soon as possible from the field of play, and immediately resume the game. If a player is slightly injured, the game shall not be stopped until the ball has ceased to be in play. A player who is able to go to the touch or goal-line for attention of any kind shall not be treated on the field of play.

(h) Send off the field of play any player who, in his opinion, is guilty of violent conduct, serious foul play, or the use of foul or abusive language.

(i) Signal for recommencement of the game after all stoppages.

(j) Decide that the ball provided for a match meets with the requirements of Law 2.

International Board Decisions on Law 5

1. Referees in International matches shall wear a blazer or blouse the colour of which is distinctive from the colours worn by the contesting teams.

2. Referees for International matches will be selected from a neutral country unless the countries concerned agree to appoint their own officials.

3. The referee must be chosen from the official list of International referees. This need not apply to amateur and Youth International matches.

4. The referee shall report to the appropriate authority misconduct or any misdemeanour on the part of spectators, officials, players, named substitutes or other persons which take place either on the field of play or in its vicinity at any time prior to, during, or after the match in question so that appropriate action can be taken by the Authority concerned.

5. Linesmen are assistants of the referee. In no case shall the referee consider the intervention of a linesman if he himself has seen the incident and, from his position on the field, is better able to judge. With this reserve, and the linesman neutral, the referee can consider the intervention and if the information of the linesman applies to that phase of the game immediately before the scoring of a goal, the referee may act thereon and cancel the goal.

6. The referee, however, can only reverse his first decision so long as the game has not been restarted.

7. If the referee has decided to apply the advantage clause and to let the game proceed, he cannot revoke his decision if the presumed advantage has not been realized, even though he has not, by any gesture, indicated his decision. This does not exempt the offending player from being dealt with by the referee.

8. The Laws of the Game are intended to provide that games should be played with as little interference as possible, and in this view it is the duty of referees to penalize only deliberate breaches of the Law. Constant whistling for trifling and doubtful breaches produces bad feeling and loss of temper on the part of the players and spoils the pleasure of spectators.

9. By para. (d) of Law 5 the referee is empowered to terminate a match in the event of grave disorder, but he has no power or right to decide, in such event, that either team is disqualified and thereby the loser of the match. He must send a detailed report to the proper authority who alone has power to deal further with this matter.

10. If a player commits two infringements of a different nature at the same time, the referee shall punish the more serious offence.

11. It is the duty of the referee to act upon the information of neutral linesmen with regard to incidents that do not come under the personal notice of the referee.

* In England within two days (Sundays not included).

12. The referee shall not allow any person to enter the field until play has stopped, and then only if he has given him a signal to do so, nor shall he allow coaching from the boundary lines.

LAW 6.   LINESMEN

Two linesmen shall be appointed whose duty (subject to the decision of the referee) shall be to indicate when the ball is out of play and which side is entitled to the corner kick, goal kick or throw-in. They shall also assist the referee to control the game in accordance with the Laws. In the event of undue interference or improper conduct by a linesman, the referee shall dispense with his services and arrange for a substitute to be appointed. (The matter shall be reported by the referee to the competent authority.) The linesmen should be equipped with flags by the club on whose ground the match is played.

International Board Decisions on Law 6

1. Linesmen, where neutral, shall draw the referee's attention to any breach of the Laws of the Game of which they become aware if they consider that the referee may not have seen it, but the referee shall always be the judge of the decision to be taken.

2. National Associations are advised to appoint official referees of neutral nationality to act as linesmen in International matches.

3. In International matches, linesmen's flags shall be of a vivid colour—bright reds and yellows. Such flags are recommended for use in all other matches.

4. A linesman may be subject to disciplinary action only upon a report of the referee for unjustified interference or insufficient assistance.

LAW 7.   DURATION OF THE GAME

The duration of the game shall be two equal periods of 45 minutes, unless otherwise mutually agreed upon, subject to the following: (a) Allowance shall be made in either period for all time lost through accident or other cause, the amount of which shall be a matter for the discretion of the referee; (b) Time shall be extended to permit of a penalty-kick being taken at or after the expiration of the normal period in either half.

At half-time the interval shall not exceed five minutes, except by the consent of the referee.

International Board Decisions on Law 7

1. If a match has been stopped by the referee, before the completion of the time specified in the rules, for any reason stated in Law 5, it must be replayed in full, unless the rules of the competition concerned provide for the result of the match at the time of such stoppage to stand.

2. Players have a right to an interval at half-time.

LAW 8.   THE START OF PLAY

(a) At the beginning of the game, choice of ends and the kick-off shall be decided by the toss of a coin. The team winning the toss shall have the option of choice of ends or the kick-off.

    The referee having given a signal, the game shall be started by a player taking a place-kick (*i.e.*, a kick at the ball while it is stationary on the ground in the centre of the field of play) into his opponents' half of the field of play. Every player shall be in his own half of the field and every player of the team opposing that of the kicker shall remain not less than 10 yards from the ball until it is kicked-off; it shall not be deemed in play until it has travelled the distance of its own circumference. The kicker shall not play the ball a second time until it has been played or touched by another player.

(b) After a goal has been scored, the game shall be restarted in like manner by a player of the team losing the goal.

(c) After half-time; when restarting after half-time, ends shall be changed and the kick-off shall be taken by a player of the opposite team to that of the player who started the game.

Punishment.   For any infringement of this Law, the kick-off shall be retaken, except in the case of the kicker playing the ball again before it has been touched or played by another player; for this offence, an indirect free-kick shall be taken by a player of the opposite team from the place where the infringement occurred, unless the offence is committed by a player in his opponents' goal area, in which case, the free-kick shall be taken from a point anywhere within that half of the goal area in which the offence occurred. A goal shall not be scored direct from a kick-off.

(d) After any other temporary suspension; when restarting the game after a temporary suspension of play from any cause not mentioned elsewhere in these Laws, provided that immediately prior to the suspension the ball has not passed over the touch or goal-lines, the referee shall drop the ball at the place where it was when play was suspended and it shall be deemed in play when it has touched the ground; if, however, it goes over the touch or goal-lines after it has been dropped by the referee, but before it is touched by a player, the referee shall again drop it. A player shall not play the ball until it has touched the ground. If this section of the Law is not complied with, the referee shall again drop the ball.

International Board Decisions on Law 8

1. If, when the referee drops the ball, a player infringes any of the Laws before the ball has touched the ground, the player concerned shall be cautioned or sent off the field according to the seriousness of the offence, but a free-kick cannot be awarded to the opposing team because the ball was not in play at the time of the offence. The ball shall therefore be again dropped by the referee.

2. Kicking-off by persons other than the players competing in a match is prohibited.

LAW 9. BALL IN AND OUT OF PLAY

The ball is out of play:

(a) When it has wholly crossed the goal-line or touch-line, whether on the ground or in the air.

(b) When the game has been stopped by the referee. The ball is in play at all other times from the start of the match to the finish, including:

(a) If it rebounds from a goal-post, cross-bar or corner-flag post into the field of play.

(b) If it rebounds off either the referee or linesmen when they are in the field of play.

(c) In the event of a supposed infringement of the Laws, until a decision is given.

International Board Decision on Law 9

1. The lines belong to the areas of which they are the boundaries. In consequence, the touch-lines and the goal-lines belong to the field of play.

LAW 10. METHOD OF SCORING

Except as otherwise provided by these Laws, a goal is scored when the whole of the ball has passed over the goal-line, between the goal-posts and under the cross-bar, provided it has not been thrown, carried or intentionally propelled by hand or arm, by a player of the attacking side, except in the case of a goalkeeper, who is within his own penalty area.

The team scoring the greater number of goals during the game shall be the winner; if no goals, or an equal number of goals, are scored the game shall be termed a 'draw'.

International Board Decisions on Law 10

1. Law 10 defines the only method according to which a match is won or drawn; no variation whatsoever can be authorized.

2. A goal cannot in any case be allowed if the ball has been prevented by some outside agency from passing over the goal-line. If this happens in the normal course of play, other than at the taking of a penalty kick, the game must be stopped and restarted by the referee dropping the ball at the place where the ball came into contact with the interference.

3. If, when the ball is going into goal, a spectator enters the field before it passes wholly over the goal-line, and tries to prevent a score a goal shall be allowed if the ball goes into goal, unless the spectator has made contact with the ball or has interfered with play, in which case the referee shall stop the game and restart it by dropping the ball at the place where contact or interference occurred.

LAW 11. OFF-SIDE

1. A player is in an off-side position if he is nearer to his opponents' goal-line than the ball, unless:

(a) he is in his own half of the field of play, or

(b) there are at least two of his opponents nearer their own goal-line than he is.

2. A player shall only be declared off-side and penalized for being in an off-side position, if, at the moment the ball touches, or is played by, one of his team, he is, in the opinion of the referee

(a) interfering with play or with an opponent, or

(b) seeking to gain an advantage by being in that position.

3. A player shall not be declared off-side by the referee

(a) merely because of his being in an off-side position, or

(b) if he receives the ball, direct, from a goal-kick, a corner-kick, a throw-in, or when it has been dropped by the referee.

4. If a player is declared off-side, the referee shall award an indirect free-kick, which shall be taken by a player of the opposing team from the place where the infringement occurred, unless the offence is committed by a player in his opponents' goal-area, in which case, the free-kick shall be taken from a point anywhere within that half of the goal-area in which the offence occurred.

International Board Decision on Law 11

1. Off-side shall not be judged at the moment the player in question receives the ball, but at the moment when the ball is passed to him by one of his own side. A player who is not in an off-side position when one of his colleagues passes the ball to him or takes a free-kick, does not therefore become off-side if he goes forward during the flight of the ball.

LAW 12. FOULS AND MISCONDUCT

A player who intentionally commits any of the following nine offences:

1. Kicks or attempts to kick an opponent;

2. Trips an opponent, i.e., throwing or attempting to throw him by the use of the legs or by stooping in front of or behind him;

3. Jumps at an opponent;

4. Charges an opponent in a violent or dangerous manner;

5. Charges an opponent from behind unless the latter be obstructing;

6. Strikes or attempts to strike an opponent;

7. Holds an opponent;

8. Pushes an opponent;

9. Handles the ball, i.e., carries, strikes or propels the ball with his hand or arm (this does not apply to the goalkeeper within his own penalty area);

shall be penalized by the award of a direct free-kick to be taken by the opposing side from the place where the offence occurred, unless the offence is committed by a player in his opponents' goal area, in which case the free-kick shall be taken from a point anywhere within that half of the goal area in which the offence occurred.

Should a player of the defending side intentionally commit one of the above nine offences within the penalty-area he shall be penalized by a penalty-kick.

A penalty-kick can be awarded irrespective of the position of the ball, if in play, at the time of offence within the penalty-area is committed.

A player committing any of the five following offences:

1. Playing in a manner considered by the referee to be dangerous, *e.g.*, attempting to kick the ball while held by the goalkeeper;

2. Charging fairly, *i.e.*, with the shoulder, when the ball is not within playing distance of the players concerned and they are definitely not trying to play it;

3. When not playing the ball, intentionally obstructing an opponent, *i.e.*, running between the opponent and the ball, or interposing the body so as to form an obstacle to an opponent;

4. Charging the goalkeeper except when he
(a) is holding the ball;
(b) is obstructing an opponent;
(c) has passed outside his goal-area.

5. When playing as goalkeeper
(a) takes more than 4 steps whilst holding, bouncing or throwing the ball into the air and catching it again without releasing it so that it is played by another player, or
(b) indulges in tactics which, in the opinion of the referee, are designed merely to hold up the game and thus waste time and so give an unfair advantage to his own team; shall be penalized by the award of an indirect free-kick to be taken by the opposing side from the place where the infringement occurred, unless the offence is committed by a player in his opponents' goal area, in which case, the free-kick shall be taken from a point anywhere in that half of the goal area in which the offence occurred.

A player shall be cautioned if:

(j) he enters or re-enters the field of play to join or rejoin his team after the game has commenced, or leaves the field of play during the progress of the game (except through accident) without, in either case, first having received a signal from the referee showing him that he may do so. If the referee stops the game to administer the caution the game shall be restarted by an indirect free-kick taken by a player of the opposing team from the place where the ball was when the referee stopped the game. If the free-kick is awarded to a side within its own goal area it may be taken from any point within the half of the goal area in which the ball was when play was stopped. If, however, the offending player has committed a more serious offence he shall be penalized according to that section of the law he infringed.

(k) he persistently infringes the Laws of the Game;

(l) he shows by word or action, dissent from any decision given by the referee;

(m) he is guilty of ungentlemanly conduct.

For any of these three last offences, in addition to the caution, an indirect free-kick shall also be awarded to the opposing side from the place where the offence occurred unless a more serious infringement of the Laws of the Game was committed. If the offence is committed by a player in his opponents' goal area, a free-kick shall be taken from a point anywhere within that half of the goal area in which the offence occurred.

A player shall be sent off the field of play, if:

(n) in the opinion of the referee he is guilty of violent conduct or serious foul play;

(o) he uses foul or abusive language;

(p) he persists in misconduct after having received a caution.

If play be stopped by reason of a player being ordered from the field for an offence without a separate breach of the Law having been committed, the game shall be resumed by an indirect free-kick awarded to the opposing side from the place where the infringement occurred, unless the offence is committed by a player in his opponents' goal area, in which case the free-kick shall be taken from a point anywhere within that half of the goal area in which the offence occurred.

International Board Decisions on Law 12

1. If the goalkeeper either intentionally strikes an opponent by throwing the ball vigorously at him, or pushes him with the ball while holding it, the referee shall award a penalty-kick, if the offence took place within the penalty-area.

2. If a player deliberately turns his back to an opponent when he is about to be tackled, he may be charged but not in a dangerous manner.

3. In case of body-contact in the goal-area between an attacking player and the opposing goalkeeper not in possession of the ball, the referee, as sole judge of intention, shall stop the game if, in his opinion, the action of the attacking player was intentional, and award an indirect free-kick.

4. If a player leans on the shoulders of another player of his own team in order to head the ball, the referee shall stop the game, caution the player for ungentlemanly conduct and award an indirect free-kick to the opposing side.

5. A player's obligation when joining or rejoining his team after the start of the match to 'report to the referee' must be interpreted as meaning 'to draw the attention of the referee from the touch-line'. The signal from the referee shall be made by a definite gesture which makes the player understand that he may come into the field of play; it is not necessary for the referee to wait until the game is stopped (this does not apply in respect of an infringement of Law 14), but the referee is the sole judge of the moment in which he gives his signal of acknowledgement.

6. The letter and spirit of Law 12 do not oblige the referee to stop a game to administer a caution. He may, if he chooses, apply the advantage. If he does apply the advantage, he shall caution the player when play stops.

7. If a player covers up the ball without touching it in an endeavour not to have it played by an opponent, he obstructs but does not infringe Law 12, para. 3, because he is already in possession of the ball and covers it for tactical reasons whilst the ball remains within playing distance. In fact, he is actually playing the ball and does not commit an infringement; in this case, the player may be charged because he is in fact playing the ball.

8. If a player intentionally stretches his arms to obstruct an opponent and steps from one side to the other, moving his arms up and down to delay his opponent, forcing him to change course, but does not make 'bodily contact' the referee shall caution the player for ungentlemanly conduct and award an indirect free kick.

9. If a player intentionally obstructs the opposing goalkeeper, in an attempt to prevent him from putting the ball into play in accordance with Law 12, 5(a) the referee shall award an indirect free-kick.

10. If after a referee has awarded a free kick a player protests violently by using abusive or foul language and is sent off the field, the free-kick should not be taken until the player has left the field.

11. Any player, whether he is within or outside the field of play, whose conduct is ungentlemanly or violent, whether or not it is directed towards an opponent, a colleague, the referee, a linesman or other person, or who uses foul or abusive language, is guilty of an offence, and shall be dealt with according to the nature of the offence committed.

12. If a goalkeeper intentionally lies on the ball longer than is necessary he shall be penalized for ungentlemanly conduct and;
(*a*) be cautioned, and an indirect free-kick awarded to the opposing team;
(*b*) in the case of repetition of the offence, be sent off the field.

13. The offence of spitting at opponents, officials or other persons, or similar unseemly behaviour, shall be considered as violent conduct within the meaning of Section (*n*).

14. If, when a referee is about to caution a player, and before he has done so, the player commits another offence which merits a caution, the player shall be sent off the field of play.

LAW 13.   FREE-KICK

Free-kicks shall be classified under two headings: 'Direct' (from which a goal can be scored direct against the offending side), and 'Indirect' (from which the goal cannot be scored unless the ball has been played or touched by a player other than the kicker before passing through the goal).

When a player is taking a direct or an indirect free-kick inside his own penalty area, all of the opposing players shall remain outside the area, and shall be at least ten yards from the ball whilst the kick is being taken. The ball shall be in play immediately it has travelled the distance of its own circumference and is beyond the penalty area. The goalkeeper shall not receive the ball into his hands, in order that he may thereafter kick it into play. If the ball is not kicked direct into play, beyond the penalty area, the kick shall be retaken.

When a player is taking a direct or an indirect free-kick outside his own penalty area, all of the opposing players shall be at least ten yards from the ball, until it is in play, unless they are standing on their own goal line, between the goalposts. The ball shall be in play when it has travelled the distance of its own circumference.

If a player of the opposing side encroaches into the penalty area, or within ten yards of the ball, as the case may be, before a free-kick is taken, the referee shall delay the taking of the kick, until the Law is complied with.

The ball must be stationary when a free-kick is taken, and the kicker shall not play the ball a second time, until it has been touched or played by another player.

Notwithstanding any other reference in these Laws to the point from which a free-kick is to be taken, any free-kick awarded to the defending side within its own goal area, may be taken from any point within that half of the goal area in which the free-kick has been awarded.

Punishment: If the kicker, after taking the free-kick, plays the ball a second time before it has been touched or played by another player an indirect free-kick shall be taken by a player of the opposing team from the spot where the infringement occurred, unless the offence is committed by a player in his opponents' goal area, in which case the free-kick shall be taken from a point anywhere within that half of the goal area in which the offence occurred.

International Board Decisions on Law 13

1. In order to distinguish between a direct and an indirect free-kick, the referee, when he awards an indirect free-kick, shall indicate accordingly by raising an arm above his head. He shall keep his arm in that position until the kick has been taken and retain the signal until the ball has been played or touched by another player or goes out of play.

2. Players who do not retire to the proper distance when a free-kick is taken must be cautioned and on any repetition be ordered off. It is particularly requested of referees that attempts to delay the taking of a free-kick by encroaching should be treated as serious misconduct.

3. If, when a free-kick is being taken, any of the players dance about or gesticulate in a way calculated to distract their opponents, it shall be deemed ungentlemanly conduct for which the offender(s) shall be cautioned.

LAW 14.   PENALTY-KICK

A penalty-kick shall be taken from the penalty-mark and when it is being taken, all players, with the exception of the player taking the kick, and the opposing goalkeeper, shall be within the field of play, but outside the penalty area, and at least ten yards from the penalty-mark. The opposing goalkeeper must stand (without moving his feet) on his own goal-line, between the goal-posts, until the ball is kicked. The player taking the kick must kick the ball forward; he shall not play the ball a second time until it has been touched or played by another player. The ball shall be deemed in play directly it is kicked, *i.e.*, travelled the distance of its circumference and a goal may be scored direct from such a penalty kick. If the ball touches the goalkeeper before passing between the posts when a penalty-kick is being taken at or after the expiration of half-time or full-time, it does not nullify a goal. If necessary, time of play shall be extended at half-time or full-time to allow a penalty-kick to be taken.

Punishment: For any infringement of this Law

(*a*) by the defending team, the kick shall be retaken, if a goal has not resulted.

(*b*) by the attacking team, other than by the player taking the kick, if a goal is scored, it shall be disallowed and the kick retaken.

(*c*) by the player taking the penalty-kick, committed after the ball is in play, a player of the opposing team shall take an indirect free-kick from the spot where the infringement occurred.

If, in the case of paragraph (*c*) the offence is committed by the player in his opponents' goal area, the free-kick shall be taken from a point anywhere within that half of the goal area in which the offence occurred.

International Board Decisions on Law 14

1. When the referee has awarded a penalty-kick, he shall not signal for it to be taken, until the players have taken up position in accordance with the Law.

2. (*a*) If, after the kick has been taken, the ball is stopped in its course towards goal, by an outside agent, the kick shall be retaken.

(*b*) If, after the kick has been taken, the ball rebounds into play, from the goalkeeper, the cross-bar or goal-post, and is then stopped in its course by an outside agent, the referee shall stop play and restart it by dropping the ball at the place where it came into contact with the outside agent.

3. (*a*) If, after having given the signal for a penalty-kick to be taken, the referee sees that the goalkeeper is not in his right place on the goal-line, he shall, nevertheless, allow the kick to proceed. It shall be retaken, if a goal is not scored.

(*b*) If, after the referee has given the signal for a penalty-kick to be taken, and before the ball has been kicked, the goalkeeper moves his feet, the referee shall, nevertheless, allow the kick to proceed. It shall be retaken, if a goal is not scored.

(*c*) If, after the referee has given the signal for a penalty-kick to be taken, and before the ball is in play, a player of the defending team encroaches into the penalty-area, or within ten yards of the penalty-mark, the referee shall, nevertheless, allow the kick to proceed. It shall be retaken, if a goal is not scored.

The player concerned shall be cautioned.

4. (*a*) If, when a penalty-kick is being taken, the player taking the kick is guilty of ungentlemanly conduct, the kick, if already taken, shall be retaken, if a goal is scored.

The player concerned shall be cautioned.

(*b*) If, after the referee has given the signal for a penalty kick to be taken, and before the ball is in play, a colleague of the player taking the kick encroaches into the penalty-area or within ten yards of the penalty-mark, the referee shall nevertheless allow the kick to proceed. If a goal is scored, it shall be disallowed, and the kick retaken. The player concerned shall be cautioned.

(*c*) If, in the circumstances described in the foregoing paragraph, the ball rebounds into play from the goalkeeper, the cross-bar or a goal-post, the referee shall stop the game, caution the player and award an indirect free-kick to the opposing team, from the place where the infringement occurred.

5. (*a*) If, after the referee has given the signal for a penalty-kick to be taken, and before the ball is in play, the goalkeeper moves from his position on the goal-line, or moves his feet, and a colleague of the kicker encroaches into the penalty-area or within 10 yards of the penalty-mark, the kick, if taken, shall be retaken.

The colleague of the kicker shall be cautioned.

(*b*) If, after the referee has given the signal for a penalty kick to be taken, and before the ball is in play, a player of each team encroaches into the penalty-area, or within 10 yards of the penalty-mark, the kick, if taken, shall be retaken.

The players concerned shall be cautioned.

6. When a match is extended, at half-time or full-time, to allow a penalty-kick to be taken or retaken, the extension shall last until the moment that the penalty-kick has been completed, *i.e.* until the referee has decided whether or not a goal is scored.

A goal is scored when the ball passes wholly over the goal-line:

(*a*) direct from a penalty-kick.

(*b*) having rebounded from either goal-post or the cross-bar, or

(*c*) having touched or been played by the goalkeeper.

The game shall terminate immediately the referee has made his decision.

7. When a penalty-kick is being taken in extended time:

(*a*) the provisions of all of the foregoing paragraphs, except paragraphs 2 (*b*) and 4 (*c*) shall apply in the usual way, and

(*b*) in the circumstances described in paragraphs 2 (*b*) and 4 (*c*) the game shall terminate immediately the ball rebounds from the goalkeeper, the cross-bar or the goal-post.

LAW 15.   THROW-IN

When the whole of the ball passes over a touchline either on the ground or in the air, it shall be thrown in from the point where it crossed the line, in any direction, by a player of the team opposite to that of the player who last touched it.

The thrower at the moment of delivering the ball must face the field of play and part of each foot shall be either on the touchline or on the ground outside the touchline.

The thrower shall use both hands and shall deliver the ball from behind and over his head. The ball shall be in play immediately it enters the field of play, but the thrower shall not again play the ball until it has been touched or played by another player.

A goal shall not be scored direct from a throw-in.

Punishment

(*a*) If the ball is improperly thrown in the throw-in shall be taken by a player of the opposing team.

(*b*) If the thrower plays the ball a second time, before it has been touched or played by another player, an indirect free-kick shall be taken by a player of the opposing team from the place where the infringement occurred, unless the offence is committed by a player in his opponents' goal area, in which case the free-kick shall be taken from a point anywhere within that half of the goal area in which the offence occurred.

International Board Decisions on Law 15

1. If a player taking a throw-in plays the ball a second time by handling it within the field of play before it has been touched or played by another player, the referee shall award a direct free-kick.

2. A player taking a throw-in must face the field of play with some part of his body.

3. If, when a throw-in is being taken, any of the opposing players dance about or gesticulate in a way calculated to distract or impede the thrower, it shall be deemed un-gentlemanly conduct, for which the offender(s) shall be cautioned.

LAW 16.   GOAL-KICK

When the whole of the ball passes over the goal-line, excluding that portion between the goal-posts, either in the air or on the ground, having last been played by one of the attacking team, it shall be kicked direct into play beyond the penalty-area, from a point within that half of the goal-area nearest to where it crossed the line, by a player of the defending team. A goalkeeper shall not receive the ball into his hands from a goal-kick in order that he may thereafter kick it into play. If the ball is not kicked beyond the penalty-area, *i.e.*, direct into play, the kick shall be retaken. The kicker shall not play the ball a second time until it has touched or been played by another player. A goal shall not be scored direct from such a kick. Players of the team opposing that of the player taking the goal-kick shall remain outside the penalty-area whilst the kick is being taken.

Punishment.   If a player taking a goal-kick plays the ball a second time after it has passed beyond the penalty-area, but before it has touched or been played by another player an indirect free-kick shall be awarded to the opposing team, to be taken from the place where the infringement occurred, unless the offence is committed by a player in his opponents' goal area, in which case the free-kick shall be taken from a point anywhere within that half of the goal area in which the offence occurred.

International Board Decision on Law 16

1. When a goal-kick has been taken and the player who has kicked the ball touches it again before it has left the penalty-area, the kick has not been taken in accordance with the Law and must be retaken.

LAW 17.   CORNER-KICK

When the whole of the ball passes over the goal-line, excluding that portion between the goal-posts, either in the air or on the ground, having last been played by one of the defending team, a member of the attacking team shall take a corner-kick, *i.e.* the whole of the ball shall be placed within the quarter circle at the nearest corner-flag post, which must not be moved, and it shall be kicked from that position. A goal may be scored direct from such a kick. Players of the team opposing that of the player taking the corner-kick shall not approach within ten yards of the ball until it is in play, *i.e.* it has travelled the distance of its own circumference, nor shall the kicker play the ball a second time until it has been touched or played by another player.

Punishment

(*a*) If a player who takes the kick plays the ball a second time before it has been touched or played by another player, the referee shall award an indirect free-kick to the opposing team, to be taken from the place where the infringement occurred, unless the offence is committed by a player in his opponents' goal area, in which case the free-kick shall be taken from a point anywhere within that half of the goal area in which the offence occurred.

(*b*) For any other infringement the kick shall be retaken.

Index

Page numbers in *italic* refer to the illustrations.

Aberdeen, 17, 133
AC Milan, 47, 88, 123–5
advertising, *see* sponsorship
Africa, World Cup, 102
Ajax Amsterdam, 5, 50, 86–8, 93–4, 130–2
Alberto, Carlos, 10, 155
Alliance Premier League, 9
Allison, Malcolm, 82; *8*
Anastasi, Pietro, 115; *117*
Anderson, Vivian, 102, 103; *104*
Ardiles, Osvaldo, 13, 67, 90–1; *12*
Argentina, World Cup: 1930, 21–2; 1934, 22;
    1938, 22; 1950, 23; 1966, 26; 1978, 13, 25,
    29–31, 65–7, 143–4, 148, 150; *30, 149*; 1982,
    32
Argentinian Metropolitan League, 90
Arsenal, 5, 9, 133; v. Blackpool (1955), 71;
    history of, 125–8; v. Liverpool (1971), 39;
    6; v. Manchester United (1948), 134; v.
    Manchester United (1979), 67–8; v. Mos-
    cow Dynamo (1945), 137; in 1930s, 160–2;
    v. West Ham United (1980), 68–70
Aston, Johnny, 58, 118
Aston Villa, 71
Atletico Madrid, 100
Auld, Bertie, 50
Australia, 19
Austria, 23, 25
Austria/WAC, 96–7

Balaidos stadium, 33
Ball, Alan, 65, 76, 157, 165
Bangor City, 158
Banks, Gordon, 28, 48, 62, 73, 80
Barcelona, 32, 33, 39
Barcelona football club, 5, 94–6, 113, 122,
    139
Batson, Brendon, 101, 102, 105; *104*
Bayern Munich, 50, 76, 119–20, 165
BBC, 42, 74, 172
Beckenbauer, Franz, 16, 26, 50, 75–6, 77, 78,
    93, 147; *72*; and football in America, 152,
    155; plays for Bayern Munich, 119, 120;
    total football, 160, 165; 1966 World Cup,
    76; 1970 World Cup, 28, 76; 1974 World
    Cup, 29, 75, 88
Belgium, 16, 21
Benfica, 58–9, 77, 113–14, 124, 132
Bernabeu, Santiago, 83
Bernabeu stadium, 33
Berry, George, 105; *104*
Best, George, 58–9, 74–5, 84, 118, 164, 168;
    59, 72
Bettega, Roberto, 91–2, 115
Birmingham City, 46, 67, 73
Bishop Auckland, 19
Blanchflower, Danny, 48, 82, 164
Blissitt, Luther, 105; *104*
Bonhof, Rainer, 50

Bonetti, Peter, 28
Boniperti, Giampiero, 91, 115
Book, Tony, *8*
Borussia Moenchengladbach, 40, 53, 61,
    98–100, 129; *11*
Boston United, 158
Bradford City, 31, 53, 141
Bradford Park Avenue, 141
Brady, Liam, 68, 70, 127; *69, 126*
Brazil, 10, 21; Feola and, 83–4; Pele on
    football in, 144–51; stadia, 17; World Cup,
    1938, 22; 1950, 22–3; 1954, 23, 24; 1958,
    24–5; 1962, 25–6, 139, 165; 1966, 26;
    1970, 26–8, 31; 1974, 28, 29; 1978, 29; *149*
Bremner, Billy, 28
Bristol Rovers, 141
Brooking, Trevor, 13, 70
Bruges, 53, 61, 92
Budapest, 45, 56
Bulgaria, 17, 26, 31, 138
Burnley, 100
Burton Albion, 158
Busby, Sir Matt, 45, 46–7, 58–9, 84, 116–18,
    164; *85*
Byrne, Roger, 24, 46, 84, 118

Callaghan, Ian, 48, 53, 160, 169
Cambridge City, 158
Cardiff City, 134, 137
Carey, Johnny, 46, 118, 163
Chalmers, Steve, 50, 133
Channon, Mike, *14*
Chapman, Herbert, 82, 125, 160–2
Charles, John, 80, 92, 114, 115, 163, 169; *79*
Charles, Mel, 127, 169
Charlton, Bobby, 24, 26, 48, 150, 164, 169;
    72; v. Benfica (1968), 58–9, 84, 118;
    Munich air crash, 46; popularity, 74; 1962
    World Cup, 25; 1966 World Cup, 76; 1970
    World Cup, 28
Charlton, Jack, 62–5
Charlton Athletic, 31, 34
Chelsea, 31, 34, 46, 58, 71, 111, 133, 137; *136*
Cherry, Trevor, *14*
Chesterfield, 89, 100
Chiedozie, John, 105–7; *106*
Chile, 25–6
Clarke, Allan, 50, 165
Clemence, Ray, 37, 71, 80–1, 107, 129; *79*
Clough, Brian, 53, 82, 103
Cologne, 10; *11*
coloured cards, 15
coloured players, 101–11
Connor, Terry, 107; *106*
Corby Town, 158
Corinthians, 81
Corunna, 33
Coventry City, 10, 111, 158

Craig, Jim, 133
Crewe Alexandra, 158
Crooks, Garth, 107; *106*
Cruyff, Johan, 16, 50, 74, 77–8, 94, 147; *79,
    131, 159*; 1976 European Championship,
    140; goes to America, 96, 157; joins
    Barcelona, 132; *131*; v. Liverpool (1967),
    88; Pele on, 148; tactics, 172; total
    football, 160, 165; 1974 World Cup, 28,
    29, 77; 1978 World Cup, 65
Cruz, 114
Crystal Palace, 108; *6*
Cullis, Stan, 82, 162
Cunningham, Laurie, 10, 102, 103, 105, 107;
    121
Curry, Tom, 118
Cyprus, 50
Czechoslovakia, 22, 23, 25, 26, 31, 138,
    139–41

Daley, Alan, 158
Daley, Steve, 53
Dalglish, Kenny, 28, 40, 53, 74, 92–3, 130,
    160; *93, 131*
Davies, Ron, 163
Dean, Dixie, 94, 134, 163
Del Sol, Luis, 57, 78, 83
Denmark, 10, 138, 141
Derby, 48
Derby County, 31, 158
Detroit, 16
Devine, John, 70
Devonshire, Alan, 70
Dickinson, Jimmy, 45
Didì, 24, 25, 46, 57, 78, 83
Dietz, *97*
di Stefano, Alfredo, 46, 57–8, 77, 78, 83, 122,
    148; *57*
Dobias, Karel, 140
Docherty, Tommy, 74, 108, 127
Doncaster Rovers, 10, 37, 89, 158
Dougan, Derek, 10, 163
Drake, Ted, 94, 134, 162, 163

East Germany, 28, 138
Eastham, George, 127, 162
Edwards, Duncan, 24, 46, 84, 118, 164
Eintracht Frankfurt, 46, 56–8, 122
England, 21, 31, 48; *30*; v. Bulgaria (1979),
    31; European Cup, 50; v. Hungary (1953),
    45–6, 48, 54–6, 83, 163; v. West Germany
    (1966), 62–5; World Cup, 1950, 23; 1954,
    24; 1958, 24, 25; 1962, 25, 26; 1966, 26,
    165; *27*; 1970, 28; 1974, 28, 50–2; 1978, 29
European Champions Cup, 24, 61
European Cup, 40, 46–50, 53, 113–34, 138,
    139, 140–1
European Cup Winners' Cup, 47–8, 62, 139

Eusebio, 26, 59, 77, 103, 113–14, 124; *79, 112*
Everton, 19, 133, 141

FA Cup, 34, 39, 40, 61, 62, 67–70, 116; *161*
FA Youth Cup, 118
Fairs Cup, 47–8, 115
Fashanu, Justin, 107–8; *106*
Feola, Vicente, 26, 83–4; *85*
Feyenoord, 5, 130–2
FIFA (Federation of International Football Associations), 15, 19, 21–31, 32–4, 138, 152
Finney, Tom, 16, 23, 150, 162
Football Association, 137, 165–7, 172
Football League, 5–8, 40, 46, 58, 61, 73
France, 21–6, 31
Francis, Trevor, 53, 165, 172; *153*

Garrincha, 25–6, 78, 83, 139
Gemmell, Tommy, 50, 133
Gemmill, Archie, 171–2; *170*
Gento, Francisco (Paco), 46, 57, 78, 83, 122, 123–4
George, Charlie, 39
Glasgow Celtic, 5, 50, 61, 84–6, 92, 133–4, 160, 167; *135*
Glasgow Rangers, 5, 57, 133, 137; *135*
Greaves, Jimmy, 48, 77, 82, 150, 160; *164*; goals, 134, 164; 1962 World Cup, 25; 1966 World Cup, 26
Greenwood, Ron, 45, 86, 101, 111, 165
Guttmann, Bela, 82, 123

Hamburg SV, 10, 40–2, 53
Hancocks, Johnny, 162–3
Hapgood, Eddie, 16–17
Havelange, Joao, 32, 157
Haynes, Johnny, 25, 165
Hazell, Bob, 108; *109*
Heart of Midlothian, 133
Herberger, Sepp, 24, 88, 144
Herd, David, 43, 127
Herrera, Helenio, 47, 50, 84, 86; *87*
Hibernian, 133
Hidegkuti, Nandor, 46, 54–6, 144, 163; *163*
Hilaire, Vince, 108; *109*
Hill, Ricky, 109; *110*
Hoddle, Glen, 13, 172; *12*
Hoeness, Uli, 119, 141; *121*
Holland, 77–8; 1976 European Cup, 140; football in, 5, 7; Rensenbrink plays for, 96; total football, 50, 78, 88, 160, 165; World Cup, 1974, 28–9; 1978, 29–31, 65–7; *30*
hooliganism, 15–16
Howe, Don, 70, 76
Huddersfield Town, 7–8, 13
Hughes, Emlyn, 53, 105, 160, 171
Hughton, Chris, 109–11; *110*
Hull City, 158
Hungary, 31, 48, 144, 167; coloured cards, 15; v. England (1953), 45–6, 48, 54–6, 83, 163; World Cup, 1938, 22; 1954, 23–4, 138; 1966, 26
Hurst, Geoff, 26, 48, 62–5, 94, 165, 167; *64*

Inter Milan, 47, 48, 50, 86, 100, 123, 133
Ipswich Town, 5, 7, 13, 67, 71; *4*
Irish League, 73
Italy, 21, 31; tactics, 47; World Cup, 1934,

22; 1938, 22; 1962, 25; 1966, 26; 1970, 28; 1978, 29; *30, 149*

Jairzinho, 26, 81, 146, 147; *145*
James, Alex, 160–2
Johnston, Harry, 46, 54–6, 163
Jordan, Joe, 68, 165; *126, 166*
Jules Rimet Cup, 21, 23, 28, 175
Juventus, 91–2, 97, 98, 114–16

Keegan, Kevin, 10–13, 35–43, 53, 61, 92, 148–50, 160, 165; *36, 38, 41, 60*
Kempes, Mario, 31, 67, 148, 150; *30*
Kennedy, Ray, 127, 130, 160
Khomich, Alexei, 137, 139
KNVB Cup, 132
Kocsis, Sandor, 24, 46, 54
Kopa, Raymond, 46, 122
Krankl, Hans, 94–6; *95*
Krol, Rudi, 50, 65–7, 77, 78, 93–4, 130, 132, 140; *64, 79*

Lanerossi, Vicenza, 97–8
Law, Denis, 59, 74, 81, 118, 164; *72*
laws of the game, 15, 179–89
Lawton, Tommy, 94, 141, 160, 163
Leeds United, 43, 48, 50, 70, 100, 107, 119
Leicester City, 71, 111, 134
Leyton Orient, 103, 105–7
Lincoln, 10
Liverpool, 5, 67, 71, 128–30; *6*; under Bill Shankly, 52–3, 86–8, 129; v. Borussia Moenchengladbach (1977), 40, 53, 61, 129; *11*; 1955 European Cup, 48; Keegan plays for, 10, 37–40, 43, 53; Kenny Dalglish plays for, 92–3; 1979 FA Cup, *161*; v. Nottingham Forest (1978), 169–71; total football, 160
Lofthouse, Nat, 94, 163
Los Angeles Aztecs, 157
Los Apaches, 71
Luton Town, 81, 109, 141

Macari, Lou, 68, 129; *117, 126*
McBain, Neil, 100
McCulloch, Dave, 163
McDermott, Terry, 61, 92, 129, 160, 171
Macdonald, Malcolm, 94
McGrory, Jimmy, 133, 167
McIlroy, Sammy, 68
McIlvenny, Eddie, 23
Mackay, Dave, 48, 82, 164
McLintock, Frank, 75; *72*
McMenemy, Lawrie, 42–3, 70; *43*
McNeill, Billy, 133
McNichol, Johnny, 111
McPhail, Bob, 162
McQueen, Gordon, 68
McStay, Jimmy, 133
Maier, Sepp, 29, 72, 76–7, 119, 120, 140–1
Maley, Willie, 133
managers, 16, 82–9
Manchester City, 19, 31, 53, 61, 73–4, 81; *8*
Manchester United, 5, 40, 61, 70, 128, 133, 163–4; *47*; v. Arsenal (1948), 134; v. Arsenal (1979), 67–8; *161*; v. Benfica (1968), 58–9; Denis Law and, 74; history of, 116–18; v. Liverpool (1977), 129; Munich air crash, 24, 46–7, 58, 84, 118, 122; tactics, 45, 46

Mannion, Wilf, 162
Mansfield Town, 158
Maracana stadium, 23
Marindin, Major, 141
Martin, Alvin, 70
Masopust, Josef, 139–40
Matthews, Stanley, 16–17, 45, 56, 150, 162
Mazzola, Sandro, 78, 133; *79*
Mazzola, Vittorio, 78
Mee, Bertie, 101, 127
Menotti, Cesar Luis, 82, 147, 150–1
Mercer, Joe, 39, 82, 125
Merrick, Gil, 55
Mexico, 25, 26–8, 31, 71, 141
Michels, Rinus, 88
Milburn, Stan, 111
Millwall, 31
Mitchell, J. F., 13
Mizzoli, Andrea, 123
Moore, Bobby, 10, 48, 52, 75–6, 78; *72, 142*; tactics, 160, 165, 167; 1962 World Cup, 25; 1966 World Cup, 62–5, 75, 167; 1970 World Cup, 28
Moran, Ronnie, 128
Morgan, Sammy, 169
Mortensen, Stan, 45, 56, 158
Moscow Dynamo, 137, 139; *136*
Müller, Gerd, 28, 29, 50, 76–7, 119, 120; *72*
Munich air crash, 24, 46–7, 58, 84, 118, 122
Munich 1860, 62
Munoz, Miguel, 83, 122

Neal, Phil, 61, 129
Neeskens, Johan, 29, 50, 65, 88, 94, 132, 140
Nelson, Sammy, 68, 70
New York Cosmos, 103, 150, 153, 155, 156, 157
Newcastle United, 13, 31, 133
Nicholl, Chris, 68, 71
Nicholson, Bill, 9, 82
Nordqvist, Bjorn, 172
North American Soccer League (NASL), 152–5, 157
Northern Alliance, 9
Northern Ireland, 24
Norwich City, 53, 107–8
Nottingham Forest, 5, 9, 10, 34, 53, 103, 169–71; *6, 11*
Notts County, 56
Nou Camp Stadium, 32, 33, 39

Oldham Athletic, 71, 89
O'Leary, David, 68, 70, 127

Paisley, Bob, 10, 43, 48, 52, 86, 90, 128–9; *18*
Panathanaikos, 88, 132
Pearson, Stuart, 70, 129
Pele, 16, 46, 56, 58, 77, 78, 81, 101, 102–3, 139; *79, 142*; on Bobby Moore, 75; in New York, 103, 143, 152, 155; on South American soccer, 143–51; 1958 World Cup, 24, 25, 83; 1966 World Cup, 26; 1970 World Cup, 26–8, 80; *20, 145*; and 1974 World Cup, 28
Peru, 29, 151
Peters, Martin, 48, 62, 165, 167
Pike, Geoff, 70; *69*
Plymouth Argyle, 7
Poland, 22, 28, 39, 50–2, 138
Port Vale, 31

Portsmouth, 7–8, 13, 34, 53
Portugal, 26, 77, 103
Pozzo, Vittorio, 22, 82
Prati, 124, 132
Preston, 53
Preston North End, 13, 141
Price, David, 68, 70
PSV Eindhoven, 130
punishments, 15
Puskas, Ferenc, 78, 113, 138, 144; ball control, 45; v. Eintracht Frankfurt (1960), 57–8, 122; v. England (1953), 45, 46, 54–6, 83; *44*; 1954 World Cup, 24

Queen's Park Rangers, 34, 108

Ramsey, Sir Alf, 39; v. Hungary (1953), 48, 56; tactics, 48, 88–9, 163, 165–7; 1950 World Cup, 23; 1966 World Cup, 23, 25, 26, 62–5, 88, 165; *63*; 1970 World Cup, 28, 88; *89*
Rapid Vienna, 94
Real Madrid, 5, 10, 24, 33, 100; under Bernabeu, 83; v. Eintracht Frankfurt (1960), 56–8, 83; European Cup, 46, 83, 120–3, 132; Laurie Cunningham plays for, 103
Red Star Belgrade, 46, 96
Reeves, Kevin, 53; *8*
referees, 15, 17
Regis, Cyrille, 101–2, 105, 111; *110*
Rensenbrink, Robbie, 67, 96–7, 140; *97*
Rep, Johnny, 67, 132
Revie, Don, 39, 46, 50, 82, 119
Rial, Hector, 83, 122
Riazor stadium, 33
Rice, Pat, 68, 70; *66*
Richards, Steve, 150
Rimet, Jules, 21
Rivelino, 26, 81, 146, 147
Rivera, Gianni, 78, 124
Rix, Graham, 68, 70, 127
Roberts, Herbie, 162
Robertson, John, 171; *51*
Robinson, Peter, 43
Robson, Bobby, 16
Romania, 21, 138
Romareda stadium, 33
Rosaleda stadium, 33
Ross, Steve, 146
Rossi, Paolo, 97–8; *97*
Roth, Franz, 119, 120
Rous, Sir Stanley, 15–19, 45
Rowe, Arthur, 45, 82
Rowley, Jack, 118
Russia, 23, 24, 137, 138–9

St Etienne, 50, 119–20
St John, Ian, 163
Sainty, John, 108
Santos, Djalma, 24, 25
Santos, Nilton, 24, 25
Santos club, 81, 175
Saporta, Raimundo, 32, 33
Schiaffino, Juan, 23, 123
Schoen, Helmut, 88, 160, 167; *89*
Schroiff, Viliem, 48, 139
Scotland, 5, 7, 23, 24, 28, 29
Scottish League Championship, 133
Scunthorpe United, 37, 53, 158

Sewell, Jackie, 56
Sexton, Dave, 16, 86
Shackleton, Len, 141
Shankly, Bill, 10, 38–9, 48, 52–3, 86–8, 128–9; *38, 87*
Sheffield Wednesday, 37, 56
Shilton, Peter, 80; *79*
Simonsen, Allan, 61, 98–100, 129; *99*
Simpson, Peter, 130
Sims, Nigel, 116
Sivori, Enrico, 114, 115
six-a-side football, 156–7
Slovan Bratislava, 48, 139
Smith, Billy, 13
Smith, Bobby, 48, 164
Smith, John, 43
Smith, Tommy, 53, 61, 128, 129
Solitch, Fleitas, 84
Souness, Graeme, 53
South America, 17, 143–51
Southampton, 5, 7, 13, 42–3, 67, 70; *4*
Southern League, 9
Spain, 5, 7, 23, 25, 32–4
Spanish League, 120
Sporting Lisbon, 113
Stapleton, Frank, 68, 70, 127, 165
Stein, Jock, 50, 58, 84–6, 133; *85*
Stepney, Alex, 59, 77
Stevenson, Alan, 100
Stewart, Ray, 70
Stiles, Nobby, 62, 74, 114
Stockport County, 43, 134, 158
Stoke City, 71, 107
Stranraer, 34
Sunderland, 70, 133
Sunderland, Alan, 68, 70, 91, 127, 165
supporters, hooliganism, 16
Sweden, 23, 24–5
Swift, Frank, 73, 118
Switzerland, 23–4

tactics, 160–7
Talbot, Brian, 68, 70; *49, 69*
Tampa Bay Rowdies, 153, 157
Tapscott, Derek, 127
Tarantini, Alberto, 67
Taylor, Jack, 29
Taylor, Peter, 53, 82, 103
Taylor, Tommy, 24, 46, 84, 118, 163
television, 17–19, 168–72
Thijssen, Frans, 13
Thomas, Mick, 68; *18*
Thompson, Garry, 111; *110*
Thompson, Phil, 53, 169–71
Toshack, John, 165
Tostao, 26, 81; *145*
total football, 50, 88, 160
Tottenham Hotspur (Spurs), 128, 133; Ardiles plays for, 13, 67, 90–1; Chris Hughton plays for, 109–11; European Cup Winners' Cup, 47–8; successes, 100; tactics, 45, 82, 164
Tranmere Rovers, 71, 141, 158
Trautmann, Bert, 73–4; *72*
Turner, Bert, 31
Twentyman, Geoff, 128

UEFA, 15, 16
UEFA Cup, 47, 115, 139

United Nations, 23
United States of America, 9–10, 16, 19, 22, 23, 103, 152–8
Uruguay, 21–2, 23, 24, 26, 34, 175

Van Binst, Gilbert, 42
Van de Kerkhoff, Rene, 65, 67, 78
Van de Kerkhoff, Willy, *30*
Van Hanegem, Wim, 50
Van Hege, Louis, 123
Vancouver White Caps, 157
Viktor, Ivo, 140
Villa, Ricardo, 90, 134
violence, spectators, 16
Viollet, Dennis, 118
Vogts, Berti, 40, 50, 61

Wales, 24–5
Walford, Steve, 68
Walter, Fritz, 144
Warren, Arnie, 108
Watford, 105
Watson, Dave, *49*
Weber, Wolfgang, 62
Wembley, 17, 31, 34
West Bromwich Albion, 10, 103, 105, 111, 141
West Germany, 21, 31; 1976 European Cup, 140–1; Keegan plays for Hamburg, 40–2; total football, 50, 160; 1954 World Cup, 24; 1966 World Cup, 26, 62–5; *27*; 1970 World Cup, 28; 1974 World Cup, 28–9, 39, 88
West Ham United, 13, 62, 68–70, 167
Whalley, Bert, 116, 118
Whelan, Liam, 118
White, John, 48, 82
Whittaker, Tom, 125
Williams, Steve, *14*
Wilson, Ray, 25
Winterbottom, Walter, 24, 45
Wolverhampton (Wolves), 5, 53, 105, 162–3
Women's World Cup, 141
Woodcock, Tony, 10, 165; *11*
Woosnam, Phil, 152–6, 158; *152*
Worksop Town, 158
World Cup, 17; Eastern European countries in, 138–40; 1930, 21–2; 1934, 22; 1938, 22; 1950, 22–3, 175; 1954, 23–4, 138; 1958, 24–5; 1962, 25–6, 139–40, 165; 1966, 26, 48, 62–5, 139, 165; 1970, 26–8, 31, 102, 175; 1974, 28–9, 39, 50–2; 1978, 29–31, 65–7; *149*; 1982, 21, 32–4, 151; 1990, 153
World War II, 34
Wrexham, 23
Wright, Billy, 23, 45, 56, 125, 127; *44*

Xisto, Roberto, 143

Yashin, Lev, 139
Young, Willie, 68, 70
Yugoslavia, 21, 28, 31, 137, 138, 139

Zagalo, 25, 26, 146, 165
Zaïre, 28, 102
Zakarias, Josef, 138
Zarraga, Jose Maria, 122
Zoff, Dino, 80; *79*
Zompa, Carlos, 71
El Zorilla stadium, 33